LYING FOR THE ADMIRALTY

Captain Cook's *Endeavour* Voyage

Daniel Solander, Joseph Banks, Captain Cook, Dr Hawkesworth and Lord Sandwich in 1771. This painting by J.H. Mortimer is the earliest portrait of Cook yet discovered, and one of the most important paintings relating to the British exploration of the Pacific undertaken by him. National Library of Australia.

LYING FOR THE ADMIRALTY

Captain Cook's *Endeavour* Voyage

Margaret Cameron-Ash

ROSENBERG

For Peter

First published in Australia in 2018
by Rosenberg Publishing Pty Ltd
PO Box 6125, Dural Delivery Centre NSW 2158
Phone: 61 2 9654 1502 Fax: 61 2 9654 1338
Email: sales@rosenbergpub.com.au
Web: www.rosenbergpub.com.au

Copyright © Margaret Cameron-Ash 2018

All rights reserved. No part of this publication may be reproduced, stored in a retrieval system, or transmitted, in any form or by any means, electronic, mechanical, photocopying, recording or otherwise, without the prior permission of the publisher in writing.

Every effort has been made to contact people and organisations in relation to copyright but in some cases copyright could not be traced. If inadvertently something has been overlooked by the author or publisher, this will be promptly responded to and acknowledged, if necessary, in future reprints

ISBN 9780648043966 (paperback)
ISBN 9780648043973 (edpf)
Printed in China through Colorcraft Ltd, Hong Kong

Contents

Foreword   The Hon. John Howard OM AC   7
Introduction   8
Acknowledgments   13

1   Clarion Call: Science, Imperialism and the Transit of Venus   14
2   Terra Incognita: The Race for Dominance in the Southern Seas   18
3   The French Steal a March: Bougainville Takes the Falklands   24
4   The Man at the Admiralty: Philip Stephens and Anglo–French Rivalry   29
5   Byron and the *Dolphin*: Secret Orders, Lost Opportunity and Censorship   36
6   Chasing Clouds in the Pacific: Samuel Wallis Discovers Tahiti   44
7   Bougainville's Voyage to New Holland and Lost Opportunity   50
8   Wooing the Royal Society: Dalrymple Wins Command of the *Endeavour*   56
9   Dalrymple Sacked: The East India Company and the General Election   63
10   An Ambitious Young Gentleman: Joseph Banks Builds his Credentials   69
11   James Cook: Luck, Patronage and Mercantile Beginnings   76
12   Battles and Cartography: Cook Surveys the St Lawrence Under Fire   80
13   Cold-War Cartography: Cook Charts Newfoundland and Impresses the Admiralty   85
14   'Greater objects': The Admiralty's Instructions to Cook   94
15   'Close and secret in his intentions': Cook, the Admiralty, and Cartographic Secrecy   98
16   Cook Does his Homework: Abel Tasman, Joan Blaeu and the VOC   103
17   The Odd Couple: The Relationship Between Cook and Banks   110
18   Ghostly Presence: Cook Disproves Dalrymple's Theory of a Temperate Continent   113
19   Venus and a Tahitian Holiday   120
20   Farther South: The Wild Goose Chase for the Southern Continent   125
21   North Island: Synchronizing with Tasman and Possession Dilemmas   130
22   A Transformative Moment: Proving Cook Strait   136
23   Cook Covers his Tracks: Stewart Island Becomes a Peninsula   139

24	Choosing a Route Home	146
25	Inventing Promontories, Deleting Coastlines: Cook Lays a False Trail in Bass Strait	148
26	Interlude: Hiding Bass Strait for Thirty Years	155
27	Deception at Botany Bay	163
28	'A good Harbour and several islands': Cook Hides Port Jackson from his Crew	167
29	From Botany Bay to Cape York: The Map of New Holland Completed	176
30	Not Claiming New Holland: What Really Happened at Possession Island	180
31	Dutch Bureaucracy: Evasiveness and Delay at Batavia	185
32	Rewriting the Record: Cook's Phantom Possession Ceremony	190
33	Plague and Delay at Batavia	198
34	Homeward Bound through a Nest of Spies	201
35	The Authorized Version – Censorship	205

Appendix – An Analysis of Captain Cook's Possession Speech   215
Select Bibliography   216
Maps and Illustrations   221
Endnotes   223
Index   233

Foreword

As Margaret Cameron-Ash notes in her introduction, many books have been written about James Cook. What is different about this one is her assertion that some of Cook's errors canvassed in earlier publications were not errors at all. They were deliberate fabrications designed to serve the British national interest.

She argues, in effect, that Cook told lies to advance the British cause, through frustrating and denying, in particular, the French, as part of the simmering Anglo-French rivalry following the end of the Seven Years War.

The author mounts a strong circumstantial case that Cook both discovered Bass Strait and actually gazed upon Sydney Harbour. Her proposition is that Cook and some of his party walked overland from Botany Bay to the Harbour.

These are remarkable claims. Her case is based on documentary and circumstantial evidence gleaned after meticulous research. She argues that deliberate obfuscation and distortion were tools of trade for the British Admiralty, then effectively run by its long serving and very able Secretary Philip Stephens. Such was the colonial rivalry of the time that paranoia about Admiralty leaks was an incentive for deliberate inaccuracies to be included in formal reports of voyages and exploration.

I can't assert that the principal claims made by Margaret Cameron-Ash are correct. But I can say that she has cogently argued the case that strategic rivalry between Britain and other colonial powers so dominated Admiralty thinking and planning that previously accepted 'errors' on the part of Cook were deliberate fabrications designed to advance Britannia.

In the process she has authored a most readable book. Her painstaking research and analytical skills are evident throughout.

The Hon. John Howard OM AC

Introduction

Hundreds of books have been written about Captain James Cook, but this is the first to answer the critical questions raised by his seeming 'errors'. Perhaps they weren't errors at all, but deliberate fabrications for strategic reasons.

These fabrications are the main focus of this book, a book that I, a lawyer rather than a Cook scholar, might never have written but for two chance conversations with Australian yachtsmen who knew the waters Cook had sailed.

A few years ago, a veteran of the Sydney to Hobart Race – where the yachts are often severely tested while passing Bass Strait – told me he couldn't understand how Captain Cook had 'missed' the strait when he sailed several leagues into it in 1770. Soon after, another old salt wondered how a mariner as curious and diligent as Cook had resisted the temptation to sail though the majestic heads into Sydney Harbour, particularly after the dangerous shallows of Botany Bay. Both these sailors implied – but dared not say – that the great navigator was a bit of a fool who had failed to observe coastal features the dullest sailor would have noticed.

I was intrigued and started reading about Cook's voyages, especially the work of John Cawte Beaglehole, Cook's editor, biographer and champion.

Soon after, waiting for a film to start at the Moonlight Cinema in Sydney's Centennial Park, I gazed into the middle distance beyond the empty screen and saw the red tail of a Qantas plane dipping down towards Botany Bay, aiming for the airstrip. I suddenly realised how close those waters were – a mere five and a half miles away, as the crow flies. And just behind the amphitheatre rises the high ridge of Oxford Street, from where you can still glimpse Sydney Harbour, lying perhaps half an hour's walk down the hill.

If it seemed extraordinary that, after leaving the exposed anchorage at Botany Bay, Cook had sailed straight past Sydney Harbour, whose high headlands promised deep, safe water within, did the answer to this mystery lie in the proximity of the two waterways?

I began to make my own observations of the terrain between the two harbours. Even with detours to avoid shopping malls, churches, hospitals and apartments – not to mention Long Bay gaol – I walked along the ridge from Bellevue Hill to Botany Bay in under four hours. Following the original Aboriginal track, Cook – taller and younger than I am – could have done it in less. And he had time at Botany Bay – eight days where he 'went into the country' and, surely, would have tried to reach the highest nearby vantage point. But if Cook did make that walk and see the size of Sydney Harbour, why didn't his journals mention it?

With no specialized knowledge of Cook and no fixed opinions, but with considerable experience in the law of evidence, I looked afresh at the written records. Almost immediately, I found that my yachting friends were not alone. New Zealand historian Robert McNab said it was 'incredible' that Cook classified Stewart Island as a peninsula joined to the South Island.

Historical research has been transformed by the internet. Searchable documents make it so much easier to test hunches and turn up hidden gems. The digitization of original manuscripts reveals the author's changes of mind in erasures and alterations. Examining Cook's journals, charts and related commentaries, I soon noticed contradictions between his holograph originals and the 'authorized' versions published with Admiralty approval. I began to suspect that some of the 'errors' blemishing Cook's legacy might be deliberate attempts to obscure his discoveries, or that the Admiralty had altered details in the pursuit of its own agenda.

Extraordinarily, while Cook scholars have pointed to these anomalies, none has explained them, or even tried to. It seems that they cannot conceive that Cook – or the Admiralty – would deliberately misinform. Instead, they accept the excuse of a less cynical age: Cook made mistakes.

But the use of electronic resources isn't the only development in Cook scholarship. The zeitgeist has changed and with it the tendency to hagiography. James Cook was a talented, diligent marine surveyor and an ambitious, obedient naval officer, but he need no longer be treated as an infallible hero. And I have an instinct for when a witness is prevaricating.

I was puzzled by Cook's wavering about Bass Strait, where he claims to be:

> doubtfull whether [the mainland and Tasmania] are one land or no: however every one who compares this Journal with that of Tasmans will be as good a judge [as] I am, but it is necessary to observe that I do not take the situation of Vandiemens from the printed charts but from the extract of Tasmens Journal published by Dirk Rembrantse.

This sounded devious, so I returned to Beaglehole's edition of the journals and had my first great Eureka moment. There, on page 263, in relation to New Zealand, was another of Beaglehole's rigorous footnotes, the source of so many of my insights:

> We have come to the question of the insularity of Stewart Island. It is difficult to follow Cook's reasoning here without knowing all that was in his mind. On paper he is unconvincing.

Beaglehole and McNab might say Cook's account was 'unconvincing' and 'incredible' because they couldn't bring themselves to say 'lying', but that's when I did. It was a huge relief. If Cook could lie once, he could lie repeatedly.

Now I knew what I was looking for, it didn't take long to find more: botched charts of Foveaux Strait; journal entries showing that after landfall, Cook continued westing into Bass Strait for a whole two hours before turning around to proceed up the coast; alterations to charts and journals recording changes of name; the construction of events that never occurred along with the omission of some that did.

Many questions remained. If Cook was *uncertain* about Bass Strait, why didn't the Admiralty order him to resolve the issue on his next voyage? If he was *deliberately lying*, then why? This is the first book to tackle these questions.

As I searched for yet more documents – from Auckland to Berlin, in Newfoundland, Yale, Edinburgh, London and Greenwich, not to mention weeks of research in Sydney's libraries and many trips to Canberra to visit the National Library – I thrilled to the excitement of the chase. And the Admiralty's agenda became clear. At a time when maps and charts were an essential arm of warfare and commerce, Britain, like her neighbours, was pursuing the age-old practice of cartographic secrecy – which continued until made obsolete by aerial photography and satellite imagery.

Then I noticed that the Admiralty's written instructions to Cook effectively stopped at New Zealand, allowing him to choose whatever homeward route he wanted. Although these instructions were marked 'secret', they were largely reported in the London newspapers before Cook sailed. But evidently his instructions didn't stop at New Zealand, because Cook declared later that he hadn't explored Dusky Sound on the first voyage because he 'had other more greater objects in view, viz. the discovery of the whole Eastern Coast of New Holland'.

If he already had New Holland in view, Cook must have received even more secret – verbal – instructions: (1) to investigate the east coast; and (2) to keep strategic discoveries secret. Unwritten instructions leave no trace. Yet, while there may be no specific record of the Admiralty's secret agenda, many documents, facts and events point to it indirectly, adding to a growing body of circumstantial evidence – the faint traces of conversations, left for posterity.

In the course of uncovering Cook's secret agenda, the book places his discoveries firmly in their broader context: cartographical, geopolitical, and commercial.

The *Endeavour* voyage didn't occur in a vacuum: it was the fifth European voyage to the South Seas in as many years. These voyages occurred in the early years of the Anglo–French cold war between 1763 and 1776, between France's humiliating defeat in the Seven Years War and its first opportunity to revenge itself upon Britain by supporting the American colonists in their War of Independence.

Some Frenchmen couldn't wait that long. Deploring the loss of France's empire in the northern hemisphere, Louis de Bougainville hoped to build a new one in the southern hemisphere. He secretly led a group of Canadian refugees to build a French colony on the Falkland Islands, which guard the entrance to the Strait of Magellan and the Pacific. The South Seas became the new theatre of European rivalry.

This was the Yuri Gagarin moment in the Anglo–French race for new spheres of influence. As with the Russo–American space race in 1961, the French were out of the pits and rounding the first turn while British agents in Paris were asleep at the wheel. Intelligence didn't reach Whitehall for months, but when it did, it was Britain's great luck to have Philip Stephens as Secretary to the Admiralty. As soon as he learned that France had pre-empted Britain in the Falklands, he swung into action.

In the pursuit of strategic advantage, Stephens preferred to work in secrecy, and, perhaps for this reason, is little known today. But in sending out explorers like John Byron, Samuel Wallis, Cook, William Bligh and George Vancouver he won many gains for the British empire.

Setting Cook's voyage in its wider context enables a deeper understanding of the motivations of both Cook and the British Admiralty. And in broadening the angle, there's scope to discover or revisit lesser-known or even forgotten events, characters and conflicts – the birth of the first baby on the Falkland Islands, the circumnavigation of the world by 'Foul-weather Jack' Byron only four years before Cook, the fact that Cook wasn't the first person chosen to command the *Endeavour*, the fate of Banks's hunting dogs, a handwritten correction that Banks made on a little-known manuscript, that provides evidence for one of Cook's fabrications.

When the news of Cook's savage death in Hawaii reached London – via Russia – in January 1780, the American Revolutionary War was being lost. The war-weary people needed a hero, but instead, they learnt that Cook had been killed on the far side of the globe in circumstances that seemed confusing, even embarrassing, for imperial Britain. Within weeks, steps were taken to quash rumours of mistakes and bungling, while Cook's reputation was elevated to a mythical status. But the elevation went too far. By the mid-twentieth century, a backlash was underway which, in extreme form, portrayed Cook as someone who shot his way round the Pacific.

Today, some balance has been restored and Cook is seen as he surely would have wanted: as a plain man of considerable talent, courage and humanity.

In an age of crude Eurocentric assumptions, racism and unthinking cruelty, Cook – for the most part – showed care for the peoples of the Pacific. There were exceptions, of course, when he misjudged a situation or lost his temper, leading to violent episodes and tragic consequences. But in general, he demonstrated empathy, respect and fair-mindedness, and easily developed benevolent relationships with people he revisited in New Zealand and elsewhere.

Like many of his officers, Cook was concerned about the impact of European expansion and wondered whether civilization would prove destructive or beneficial for Native societies. During his second visit to New Zealand he wrote:

> We interduce among them wants and perhaps diseases which they never before knew and which serves only to disturb that happy tranquillity they and their fore Fathers had injoy'd.

If any one denies the truth of this assertion, let him tell me what the Natives of the whole extent of America have gained by the commerce they have had with Europeans. [3 June 1773]

His anguish reflected the contradictions thrown up by the Age of Discovery. If navigators were to venture into unknown seas and chart new coasts for the greater knowledge of the human race, they had to land on those coasts to replenish their supplies of wood and water and fresh food. They had to make first contact and, after that, there was no turning back for either party.

However, it isn't the purpose of this book to follow the swing of the pendulum of Cook's popularity. It is to answer the questions raised by his few, but rather startling, 'errors' by a forensic examination of altered charts, passages that Cook painstakingly wrote and rewrote, changed names and events omitted in a journal intended for publication, in line with the demands of national security. The book offers a new understanding of a complex man: an explorer and cartographer even greater than has been thought; and a patriot who was prepared to lie about his achievements when strategic imperatives demanded it, and tarnish his record for the sake of his country.

Acknowledgments

The writing of this book has been a hugely enjoyable process, and that is largely due to the generous help of many people and institutions.

A special expression of gratitude goes to the former Australian prime minister the Hon. John Howard OM AC for contributing the Foreword.

Particular thanks are due to the experts: Dr Charlotte Clutterbuck, structural editor of Sydney, who analysed the text and made valuable suggestions in shaping its progression; and Dr David Fraser, cartographer of Melbourne, who produced the elegant sketch maps to illustrate my arguments, proving indeed a picture is worth a thousand words.

I am also grateful to Dr Martin Woods, Curator of Maps, National Library of Australia, Canberra; Joanna Corden, Archivist, The Royal Society, London; Dr Andrew Cook, former Map Archivist, India Office Records, British Library; Professor Edmund S. Morgan of Yale University; Andrea Hart, Library Special Collections, Natural History Museum, London; Robert Harrison, Parliamentary Archives, House of Lords, London; John Murray of Canberra who did the French translations; Robert J. King, historian of Canberra; and Ian Boreham, editor for the international Captain Cook Society.

Thanks also to the staff at the Mitchell Library, State Library of New South Wales, Sydney; Geoscience Australia Library, Canberra; National Maritime Museum, Greenwich; Reference Library of the Library of Congress, Washington D.C.; Centre for Newfoundland Studies, St John's, Canada; Alexander Turnbull Library, Wellington, New Zealand; and The National Archives, Kew.

Then there is David Rosenberg for agreeing to publish the book and for working to make this the handsome volume it is.

The directors and trustees of the institutions listed have kindly given permission to reproduce the images from their collections.

Most importantly, I am grateful to my late husband, Peter, for his encouragement and support during the early years of my research.

For personal support, I offer warm thanks to our sons Sandy and Hugh and their families.

1 Clarion Call: Science, Imperialism and the Transit of Venus

The call came on 13 February 1766 when a carefully targeted paper was read before the Royal Society at its weekly meeting in London. Written by Professor Thomas Hornsby, Oxford University's leading astronomer, and titled 'On the Transit of Venus in 1769', it was an urgent call to the nation to seize this, their last chance for more than a century to witness the rare celestial event and calculate the size of the Solar System. Scientific rivals from Paris to St Petersburg all coveted these measurements, reflecting the quantifying spirit of the Enlightenment.[1]

The urgency arose because of the curious nature of the planet's orbit. Looking from Earth, Venus rarely crosses the face of the Sun, but when it does it does so in pairs. Two transits occur within a span of eight years, while the transit pairs are separated by more than a century. The first transit of the eighteenth century occurred on 6 June 1761 and many of Europe's learned academies mounted lavish campaigns to observe it. Because the measuring technique is triangulation, the observers were sent across the globe to widely separated locations. From Newfoundland to Siberia, from Cape Town to Jakarta, hundreds of skywatchers pointed their telescopes heavenward to watch Venus for the six hours it took to cross the face of the Sun. Their job was to record the times of the start and finish of the event and then, using a method devised by the late Edmond Halley, calculate the Astronomical Unit, that is, the distance from the Earth to the Sun.

The strategy seemed straightforward, but in 1761 the results were dismal. Those embarking on expensive expeditions had not reckoned on the Seven Years War being in full swing. Bold astronomers were thwarted as they tried to cross enemy lines, while others suffered bad weather or just bad luck. It was all very disappointing. The world had waited 122 years for this event and they had muffed it.

But all was not lost. The second of the pair of transits was due eight years later – on 3 June 1769 – and it would be the last in Hornsby's lifetime. As he declared in his paper, 'another transit of Venus will not again offer itself till the year 1874. It behoves us therefore to profit as much as possible by the favourable situation on Venus in 1769.'[2] He named various locations where the transit should be observed: several points in the northern hemisphere and one particular area in the southern hemisphere. Here, he calculated, the full transit could be best viewed in a small area of the Pacific Ocean lying to the north-east of New Zealand. But with the discovery of Tahiti still a couple of years away, Hornsby struggled to nominate a suitable island in that vast ocean that could serve as a viewing platform.

Contemporary charts of the Pacific were vague, if not fanciful, and coordinates of all discoveries were notoriously unreliable. Even so, Hornsby nominated a few islands discovered by the early Spanish and Dutch navigators as possible bases for the British expedition. One proposal was the Solomon Islands, but their position was unknown because, Hornsby alleged, the Spanish authorities had deliberately destroyed their charts 'for political reasons, by express orders from Old Spain, when Sir Francis Drake sailed into the South Seas'.[3]

Such accusations of cartographic censorship were common among Europe's rival states. Charts depicting new discoveries were hidden or deliberately distorted for military, political or commercial reasons. 'The map image itself was becoming increasingly subject to concealment, censorship, sometimes to abstraction or falsification,'[4] writes J.B. Harley, and continues, 'As much as guns and warships, maps have been the weapons of imperialism'.[5]

Without a certain viewing platform, Hornsby's Venus campaign was in jeopardy. Ships were needed not simply to transport the scientists and their equipment to the Pacific. They were also needed for the costly and dangerous preliminary task of searching its waters for a suitable island base.

Consequently, Hornsby's target audience was not his fellow astronomers, who had long been planning for the big event. Hornsby was appealing to the Royal Society's broader membership, and their guests. By night, these gentlemen indulged their scientific interests at the society's meeting in Crane Court, Fleet Street, but during the day they were often cabinet ministers and politicians, wealthy merchants and naval officers. They were, or they knew, the great and the good, the rich and powerful. If Hornsby was to win a government-funded expedition, he had to appeal beyond mere scientific curiosity to the national interest.

This was not difficult. The Seven Years War had recently ended with the Treaty of Paris in 1763, but nothing could end the perennial cold war of Anglo–French rivalry. Beneath the surface of mutual compliment and amicable cooperation, there thrived a fierce nationalism on both sides of the Channel. It ran deep and strong, spurring governments to hasty – often reckless – action and driving competition everywhere: in science and manufacture, commerce and trade, exploration and empire. National pride and prestige were at stake and Hornsby urged his audience to seize this opportunity for Britain to demonstrate her scientific supremacy:

> [W]e may be assured the several Powers of Europe will again contend which of them shall be most instrumental in contributing to the solution of this grand problem. Posterity must reflect with infinite regret upon their negligence or remissness; because the loss cannot be repaired by the united efforts of industry, genius or power.[6]

Hornsby knew he had to bring the Admiralty on board. The society's long-distance observers for the 1761 transit had been dispatched in East India Company ships, but the Company did not yet trade in the Pacific. Navy ships were needed and there was a precedent for naval involvement in such scientific ventures. An earlier Oxford scientist, Edmond Halley, had been given a temporary naval command and a ship, HMS *Paramour*, to make three voyages, including one that almost touched Antarctica when he measured and mapped magnetic variation in the North and South Atlantic. Knowing which of the government's buttons to press, Hornsby continued:

1. George III reigned from 1760 to 1820. A keen amateur astronomer, he encouraged the English campaigns to observe transits of Venus in 1761 and 1769.

> How far it may be an object of attention to a commercial nation to make a settlement in the great Pacific Ocean, or to send out some ships of force with the glorious and honourable view of discovering lands towards the South pole, is not my business to enquire. Such enterprises, if speedily undertaken, might fortunately give an advantageous position to the

2. Crane Court, off Fleet Street, was the Royal Society's home from 1710 to 1780.

astronomer, and add a lustre to this nation, already so eminently distinguished both in arts and arms.[7]

It may not have been Professor Hornsby's business to enquire into Whitehall's master plan, but he was certainly inviting his 'commercial nation … already so eminently distinguished … in arms' to 'make a settlement in the great Pacific Ocean' by using 'ships of force'. So much for the myth that the *Endeavour* voyage was principally a disinterested scientific one.

Hornsby was calling for nothing less than a scientific, strategic and commercial joint venture between the Royal Society and the Admiralty. His paper had the desired impact and a Pacific voyage was all but booked, to depart England in two years time. Word spread quickly and Hornsby's paper became a clarion call to anyone seeking fame and adventure in the South Seas.

Three keen young men started furbishing their skills in an effort to impress the selectors. None were astronomers, but all longed to embrace this unique opportunity to probe the South Pacific Ocean. The first was a Scot named Alexander Dalrymple. The second was Joseph Banks, a rich young Englishman who knew little about sailing and less about astronomy. And the third was a Yorkshireman named James Cook.

For all three men, the task of observing the transit of Venus was really just a means to an end. Like the Admiralty, their ulterior motive was the rare chance to explore the largely unknown Pacific Ocean.

2 Terra Incognita: The Race for Dominance in the Southern Seas

What discoveries did Professor Hornsby expect that Britain's 'ships of force' would make in the South Pacific, after completing the transit business? In the cold war years that followed Britain's victory in the Seven Years War, such voyages were crucial if Britain was to achieve, or to prevent France from achieving, commercial and strategic dominance in a largely unexplored ocean.

Almost 250 years had passed since Ferdinand Magellan became the first European to cross the Pacific Ocean. Since then, there had been twenty more circumnavigations, most of them by ships from Spain or England or the Netherlands. A few islands had been discovered in each of the three main island groups of Micronesia, Melanesia and Polynesia, but their coordinates were poorly recorded. The larger islands of New Guinea, New Holland and New Zealand had been discovered, but none of these had been fully surveyed.

The South Pacific remained a vast cartographic blank on the world map and geographers wanted to fill it with something. They turned to an ancient Greek hypothesis that the South Pole was surrounded by a landmass large enough to balance the planet. The imagined Southern Continent was originally called Terra Australis Incognita, because it was the most southerly continent. The Latin word 'Australis' comes from 'auster' meaning 'the south wind'. However, the tortuous phrase seemed vague and cumbersome to one German cartographer, so he decided to shorten it. In fact, German cartographers were becoming quite proactive in the continent-naming business. A few years earlier, in 1507, Martin Waldseemüller and his colleague, Matthias Ringmann, had coined the name America for the New World, immortalizing the Italian explorer Amerigo Vespucci. The German scholars thought the Latinized, feminine noun fitted well with the names of the known continents: Africa, Asia and Europa.

So it was not surprising when another harmonious name, Australia, was applied to the hypothetical Southern (Antarctic) Continent. The first known example of this appears on a small woodcut map titled 'Sphere of the Winds', published in Frankfurt in 1545 (Fig. 3). The map is thought to be based on the work of Johannes Honter, a Transylvanian Saxon. Although the term Terra Australis was more common, the shortened name – Australia – continued to be used in German-speaking Europe and in scholarly circles elsewhere. For example, Daniel Solander, the Swedish naturalist and alumnus of Uppsala University, used it when aboard the *Endeavour* in 1769.

Incidentally, the Antarctic or Southern Continent should not be confused with the fifth and smallest continent that used to be called New Holland. What we now know as Australia was discovered, and mostly mapped, by the Dutch during the seventeenth century. It was universally known as 'New Holland' for two centuries, up to and beyond its colonization by Britain in 1788. It is true that a mischievous map, published in 1663 by a Frenchman, Melchisédech Thévenot, suggested that the Dutch name – and claim – was limited to the western half of the continent,[1] an idea that was copied in 1744 by the English cartographer Emanuel Bowen.[2] In fact, both maps were works of national propaganda and were not taken seriously by geographers or navigators.[3] Captain Cook always referred to the whole of the fifth continent as New Holland.

However, in the nineteenth century, the colonial authorities gradually removed the Dutch name from the island continent, effectively expunging two centuries of foreign history. Instead of inventing a new name to replace New Holland, they snatched 'Australia' from the sixth continent and attached it to the fifth. Because of this confusion of names, it is essential to emphasize that all those navigators were searching for the Antarctic or Southern Continent – not the island of New Holland, which few were interested in – until they realized that the Southern Continent was not the rich market of their imagination, but was all too difficult, too distant, and too cold.

Meanwhile, the quest for the imagined – but still undiscovered – south-polar continent continued. Eventually, it was discovered in 1820, but no one knew what to call it. It had been stripped of its centuries-old name Australia, leaving a lacuna in continental nomenclature. During the following decades geographers had to make

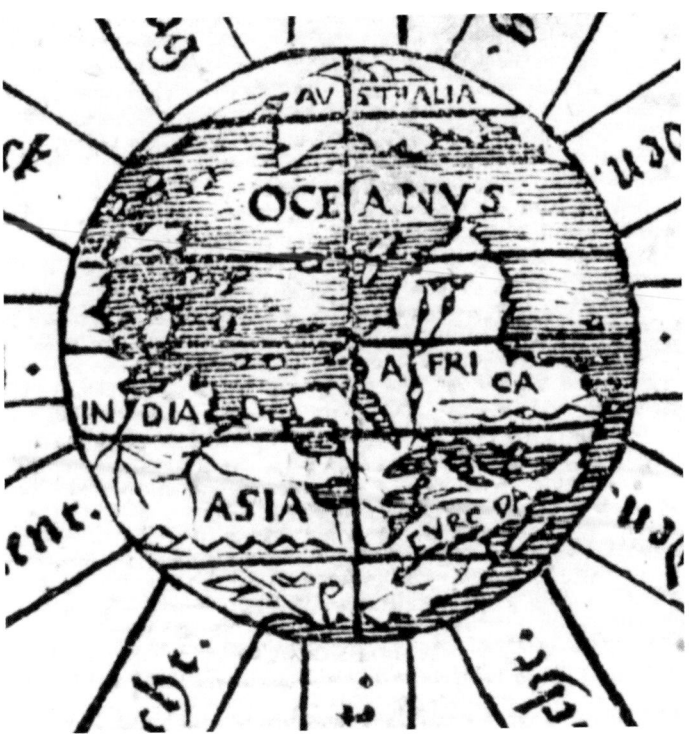

3. Australia at the South Pole in 1545. Detail from a woodcut map based on the work of Johannes Honter, showing the three known continents of the eastern hemisphere: Africa, Europa and Asia. Spread across its southern extremity, at the top of the map, is the imagined landmass named Australia. National Library of Australia nla.obj-230899009.

4. Australia at the South Pole in 1762. Redern's speculative map shows the South Pacific as Joseph Banks and Daniel Solander expected to find it when they sailed on the *Endeavour* voyage in 1768. The Southern Continent, named Australasie (later Antarctica), extends north from the Pole into the low latitudes of the South Pacific and incorporates New Zealand as its western limit. The island of New Holland (later Australia), with its conjectural east coast, is situated south of the Malay Archipelago. National Library of Australia nla.obj-232150652.

do with the clumsy phrase 'the Antarctic Continent' while they looked for a poetic replacement to harmonize with Europa, Asia, Africa, America and Australia. Various names such as Ultima[4] and Antipodea were suggested and, in the end, 'Antarctica' was adopted in the 1890s.[5] But this was all in the future.

In the Middle Ages, it was thought that Terra Australis Incognita filled much of the southern hemisphere, but it soon started to shrink. The voyages of Magellan, Le Maire and others cut great swaths from it as their ships ploughed across the southern oceans and down into ever-higher latitudes.

At the same time, another Dutch navigator readjusted the continent's boundaries in the Asian quarter of the globe. In October 1642, Captain Abel Tasman left Mauritius with three ships and, after searching for the continent in the southern Indian Ocean, he sailed through to the Pacific Ocean. On the way, he discovered two new coasts. The first was Van Diemen's Land (now Tasmania) and, after sailing south around it, Tasman thought it was just an island. He was hunting for a continent, so he hauled away and resumed his easterly course. Nine days later, the Dutchmen chanced upon New Zealand's South Island and decided to follow the coast northward. During the next three weeks they charted the coastline from their first landfall up to Cape Maria van Diemen at the northern tip of the North Island. From here, they departed New Zealand and visited Tonga and Fiji before returning to Batavia (now Jakarta) on the island of Java. Batavia was the headquarters of the Dutch East India Company or VOC (Vereenigde Oost-Indische Compagnie)

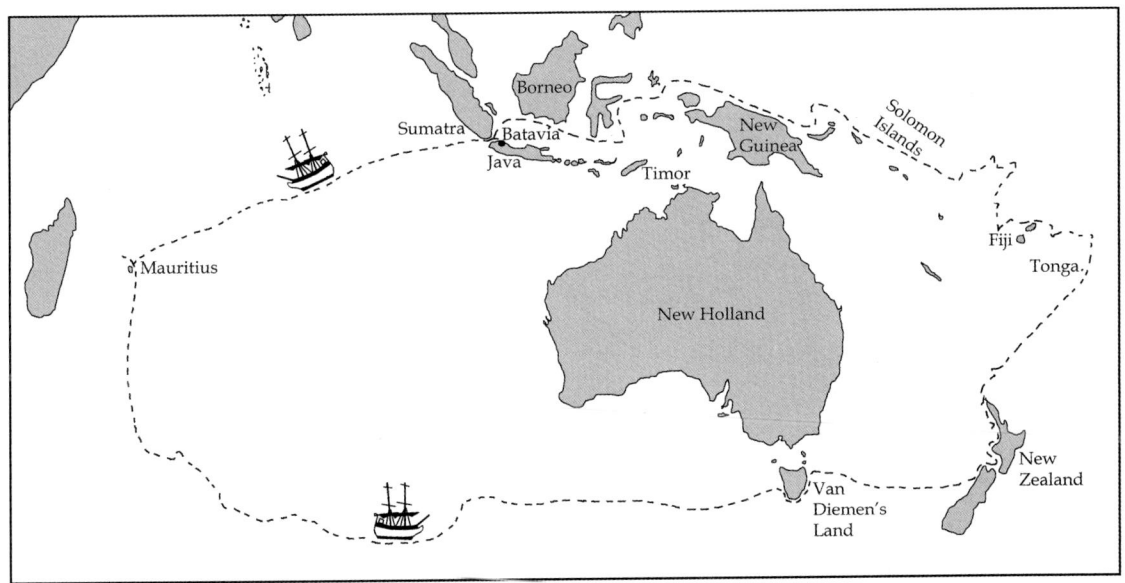

5. Sketch map of Abel Tasman's voyage in 1642-43 during which he completed the first circumnavigation of Australia, without seeing the mainland.

Tasman's ten-month expedition was, in the words of Cook's friend James Burney, 'one of the most importance to geography of any which had been undertaken since the first circumnavigation of the globe'.[6] It had three significant consequences. The first was that Tasman's unobstructed passage from Mauritius to New Zealand proved that New Holland, whatever its final size and shape, was not joined to the Antarctic Continent. The second consequence was Tasman's influential, though inaccurate hypothesis. On discovering New Zealand, Tasman thought he had found the western side of the elusive continent that stretched across the Pacific to the southern tip of South America. He wrote in his journal: 'We believe that this is the mainland coast of the unknown Southland'.[7] When this suggestion was reported back in Europe, it was seized upon by those armchair cartographers who still believed in a habitable southern continent. Many rushed to revise their atlases and published hundreds of maps depicting New Zealand as the west coast of a Terra Australis Incognita that rose gradually from the waters around Tierra del Fuego.

The third consequence was Tasman's intriguing conundrum. Having said that New Zealand was a single land mass, he later contradicted himself. On Christmas Eve 1642, while the Dutch ships were riding at anchor in Zeehaen's Bight – the gulf between the North and South Islands – Tasman detected a strong current. This was, of course, Cook Strait, but Tasman did not investigate it. Instead, he speculated in his journal: 'since the tide comes from the Southeast so that there might well be a passage'.[8] When this suggestion was reported back in Europe, it was seized upon by those geographers who did not believe there was a continent in the habitable latitudes of the South Pacific. For them, Tasman's observation was proof that New Zealand was not a continent but an archipelago, a small group of islands divided by at least one strait. Tasman's conundrum sparked a debate which lasted for 125 years, reaching its climax in the great cabin of HMB *Endeavour* in 1769.

Thirty years before Tasman's voyage, a Spanish expedition added another piece to the jigsaw puzzle of the southern land masses. In late 1605 a small squadron sailed west from the Peruvian port of Callao, on the last of the three exploratory voyages that Spain made to the south-west Pacific. Five months later the Portuguese commander, Pedro Fernández de Quiros, thought he had found the legendary Antarctic Continent when he saw the hills and valleys of a verdant land rising above the southern horizon. In fact, he was looking at the small archipelago of Vanuatu just west of Fiji, where the beautiful volcanic islands overlap each other to give the impression of a continuous and extensive coastline. Comparing himself to Columbus, Quiros claimed the land for King Philip of Spain and named it 'Australia del Espiritu Santo' (Southland of the Holy Spirit).

Ultimately of course, it was a red herring, but 'Quiros's Land' – of uncertain longitude – influenced cartographic thinking for more than a century. After Tasman's voyage, many geographers thought that the vast land which Quiros had found must be the eastern side of New Holland. So they joined 'Tierra del Espiritu Santo' to a hypothetical east coast, causing Queensland to bulge out like a pigeon's breast (Fig. 4 [Redern] and Fig. 26 [Vaugondy]). The error was eventually corrected in 1768 when the French navigator, Louis de Bougainville, sailed through the Coral Sea which separates Vanuatu from Queensland.

Meanwhile, many geographers still believed that an icy continent surrounded the

South Pole, with one or more giant promontories thrusting northward, like a camel's hump, into the lower latitudes of the Indian, Pacific or Atlantic Oceans. Instead of relying solely on hypothesis, cartographers started tracing the routes of the various navigators across the oceans and plotting their sightings, real or imagined, of the elusive continent. Eventually, the Prussian physicist Count von Redern wrote a paper in which he blended this hard data with the concept of 'le Continent Antarctique' and illustrated his idea with a remarkable map titled 'Hemisphere Meridional' (Fig. 4).[9] Redern's speculative chart was published in 1762 by the Prussian Academy of Sciences in Berlin, where learned papers were still being published in French. It shows the Pacific coast of the Antarctic Continent extending north from the south-polar circle up into tropical latitudes and, of course, it incorporates New Zealand in its west coast.

Redern has named the great land mass Australasie, a name which echoes Honter's long-established Australia and has little to do with today's Australasia. Redern's map also shows the separate island of New Holland, with its hypothetical east coast, situated over near the Dutch East Indies. Count von Redern was a foreign member of London's Royal Society and his map reflects the views of many of its members. These fellows expected that the forthcoming transit voyage to the Pacific would confirm Redern's general layout of land masses in the antipodes.

However, the British were not the only interested parties. As soon as the French lost their empire in the northern hemisphere they set themselves to build one in the southern hemisphere. Thus, when the Admiralty dispatched its transit of Venus expedition in August 1768 it was, in fact, Europe's fifth exploratory voyage to the South Seas in as many years.

First off the mark was the Frenchman Louis de Bougainville, who set out on his first voyage in 1763. Next was John Byron, who sailed from England in 1764, to be followed by Samuel Wallis in August 1766. Then in December 1766 Bougainville sailed again, making the fourth expedition to the South Seas before the *Endeavour*'s departure. The race for the southern hemisphere had already begun and Britain was being overtaken.

3 The French Steal a March: Bougainville Takes the Falklands

French possession of the Falkland Islands has been almost written out of history, but the first baby to be born in the Falkland Islands was French. He was François Benoit, the second son of the baker, Augustin Benoit, and his wife Françoise Thériot.[1] He arrived in early 1764 at the family home in the new French colony of Port St Louis on the shores of Berkeley Sound (as it was later named) in East Falkland. His family – Augustin, Françoise and two-year-old Nicolas-Jean-Sébastien – were Acadian refugees who had been expelled from Canada by the British and were now embarking on a new life in the South Atlantic. They had been recruited by an enterprising Frenchman whose goal was to establish French dominion over this uninhabited archipelago at the entrance to the Strait of Magellan, the gateway to the Pacific. The journey of these refugees was not as epic as the translocation of people to Botany Bay that occurred 24 years later, but it was no less political or audacious.

6. The French colony of Port St Louis established by Bougainville in 1764, situated at the head of Berkeley Sound in East Falkland.

The charming, spirited son of a patrician family, Louis-Antoine de Bougainville was given a sound education in mathematics, law and the classics. After enlisting in the royal military corps of Musketeers, he was seconded to the French embassy in London to serve as third secretary. He had just published a treatise on calculus, which gave him entré to elite and learned circles and, in due course, he was elected as a member of London's Royal Society. However, Bougainville's diplomatic career lasted barely five months. Disturbances in North America forced his recall to France and in early 1756 he sailed for Canada as captain of dragoons and aide-de-camp to the Marquis de Montcalm.

The Seven Years War had broken out and Bougainville fought valiantly and victoriously against the English, until one fateful day in 1759 when the English leader, General James Wolfe, landed his troops in a sandy cove hidden amongst the cliffs below the French city of Quebec. Before daybreak on 13 September, Wolfe's men scaled the rocks up to the Plains of Abraham that lay just outside the city walls. Here on the plateau above the St Lawrence River, they waited to confront the army of the French general, the Marquis de Montcalm.

At sunrise, the startled French hurriedly prepared for battle while a runner was sent upriver to alert Montcalm's aide, now Colonel Bougainville. He was monitoring the British ships at Cap-Rouge, but immediately turned around and led his 2000 exhausted men back along the riverbank to help defend the city. By the time they arrived, the Battle of the Plains of Abraham was all but over. General Wolfe was dead, General Montcalm mortally wounded, and the French city of Quebec fell to the enemy.

While the new French commander was signing the articles of capitulation, Bougainville strode across the abandoned battlefield to the cliff edge. In the river below, dozens of British ships lay at anchor, including the HMS *Pembroke* lying off Point Levis on the south shore.[2] Surveying the awful scene, Bougainville swore revenge on *la perfide Albion*, but the *Pembroke* was too far away for her

7. Louis Antione de Bougainville, 1729–1811, soldier, navigator, entrepreneur.

master, James Cook, to have heard. Although Cook and Bougainville never met, a decade later, first Bougainville and then Cook would cheat death at the same coral reef on the opposite side of the world.

Twelve months after Quebec, Montreal also capitulated, and Bougainville was taken prisoner. He had spent a total of four years with the army in Canada. He had been adopted into a tribe of the Iroquois nation and some said that he had fathered a son named Lorimier with the chief's daughter.[3] Now the proud Frenchman had to suffer the indignity of being transported back to France in a British prison ship. After 150 years, New France had collapsed and Canada was now a colony of the British Empire. The horror and humiliation of its loss convinced Bougainville that Britain's imperial aggression had to be curbed. Britain may have won dominion in the northern hemisphere, but France would build a second empire south of the equator.

His determination is captured in a letter written in 1765 by Fernando de Magallon, secretary at the Spanish embassy in Paris, to the Chief Minister in Madrid:

> It only remains for me to advise Your Excellency on the intellect and character of this officer. He is an extraordinarily courageous and passionate young man of 30 to 34 years, capable of embarking on the most difficult and boldest of ventures, imbued with a deadly hatred of the English against whom he'd declare war forthwith.
>
> He claims that he could devise a plan both offensive and defensive against them that would not be lacking in results. His hatred and natural zeal are no impediment to him acting rashly where others would fear to tread without first of all weighing up the pros and cons of their actions, particularly taking into account the strength and preparedness of their forces, aspects that require more time and a less fiery imagination.[4]

Back home in Paris, Bougainville drew up his plan for winning French dominion in the South Seas. In late 1762, even before the Seven Years War had officially ended, he delivered a preliminary draft to the formidable Duc de Choiseul.

Étienne-François, Comte de Stainville, Duc de Choiseul was France's 43-year-old Minister for War, Minister for the Navy and the most powerful person in the country after King Louis XV. Choiseul was determined that France's humiliation would be temporary and already he was preparing for the *guerre de revanche* against England. However, open warfare would have to wait until France's navy and dockyards were rebuilt.

In the meantime, Bougainville's plan offered the first opportunity for a resurgence of French power and prestige, plus the rebirth of her territorial empire in the South Seas. It also gave Choiseul a preliminary strike in his war of revenge against Britain – preceding France's collusion with the American rebels a decade later.

Bougainville's heroically ambitious plan was to win for France the three main prizes of his time. The first was to establish a base on the Falklands, while the second and third were the two holy grails which had driven navigation for centuries: the Great South Land and the Northwest Passage.

Choiseul was receptive to Bougainville's plan and studied it carefully. It was titled *Memoire relatif aux îles Malouines et aux Terres Australes*. The Falkland Islands had been given their French name of Îles Malouines by visiting sailors and fishermen from the Breton port of St Malo.

The plan had three components. The first addressed the strategic importance of the Falkland Islands, which guarded the entrance to the Strait of Magellan. In a world without the Suez or Panama Canals, the only exit for European vessels corralled in the Atlantic Ocean was through the Southern Ocean. Here Bougainville was taking a leaf out of a book written fifteen years earlier by the English commander, George Anson, after his return from a harrowing four-year voyage around the globe. In his book, Anson publicly urged the Admiralty to annexe the Falklands and build a refreshment station to service her ships venturing into the Pacific. Bougainville had read Anson's book and he intended to forestall the British.

So the first stage of his plan was to take three ships to the Falklands, claim possession of them and establish, in Bougainville's words, 'a settlement (so strongly recommended by Admiral Anson in the account of his voyage) which will serve as a supply store for all the following discoveries'.[5]

Next, he would sail south-east from this base to search for the Southern Continent which, according to most French cosmographers, lay near Cape Circumcision (Bouvet Island) in the South Atlantic Ocean. If Bougainville found the legendary continent he would build a colony there which would deliver great benefits to France's 'navy, her commerce and her glory'.

Finally, if no southern continent was discovered in the Atlantic, then Bougainville would abandon the search and return to the Falklands to reprovision his ships. Then, with the Northwest Passage in mind, he planned to sail round Cape Horn and follow the American coast northward in order to establish a French outpost 'to the north of California', where 'the Minister would establish lines of communication between this settlement and Louisiana'.[6]

The document is important because it was this first version of his plan that was eventually leaked to British agents in Versailles, who quickly dispatched it to London. As soon as it arrived in Whitehall, the Admiralty would hijack Bougainville's original plan in a frenzy of secrecy and speed.

However, Choiseul rejected the California section of Bougainville's proposal because he did not want to upset the king of Spain who still believed he owned the Pacific Ocean. Choiseul did not agree with him, particularly as Catholic France had been excluded from the Pope's largesse when he divided the unknown world between Portugal and Spain. However, this was not the right moment to challenge the fading superpower.

On the contrary, Choiseul was eager to humour the Spanish king. Just months before, he had organized the Bourbon Family Compact to bolster French and Spanish unity in their mutual hostility to Britain. Choiseul needed to consolidate this alliance if France was to regain the territory and prestige she had lost in the Seven Years War. So he asked Bougainville to submit a new plan, omitting the foray into the Pacific and the Californian outpost.

So Bougainville revised his plan. While he retained his first two goals, he removed the third one requiring the voyage around Cape Horn and north to the Californian coast. He resubmitted his plan and Choiseul gave it his approval on 10 May 1763.

The next four months were spent preparing the ships and recruiting volunteers. Bougainville found 29 colonists, most of whom were refugees from Acadia, a colony in French Canada. On 9 September, they sailed from France on a five-month voyage down the Atlantic, stopping briefly at the Portuguese colony on Santa Catarina Island and then at the Spanish port of Montevideo. At the end of January 1764, Bougainville rejoiced to see the Sebaldes or Jason Islands off the north-west point of the Malouines.

Looking for a safe anchorage, he inspected an inlet on the western island which he named Port de la Croisade (soon to be renamed Port Egmont). Unimpressed, he continued eastwards along the north shores of the two main islands and round to an inlet which he named Baie Accaron (now known as Berkeley Sound).[7] Here, at the inner cove of Port St Louis, he brought ashore the families, cattle, horses and tents and raised the French flag. Construction of a fort and community hall started immediately, and by the beginning of April the buildings were sufficiently advanced to perform an elaborate possession ceremony. On 5 April 1764, a 21-gun salute rang out, the *Te Deum* was sung and Bougainville claimed possession of the entire archipelago of the Îles Malouines in the name of King Louis XV of France.

Even if other nations claimed prior title as 'first discoverer', they were trumped by France's occupation, as John Milton had advised Oliver Cromwell in 1655 in relation to Spain's initial claim to America:

> Such an imaginary title founded on such a silly pretence, without being in possession, can't possibly create any true and lawful right. The best right of possession ... is that which is founded on one's having planted colonies there.[8]

A few weeks later, the thriving French colony celebrated the birth of its first baby, along with calves, foals and chickens while the corn seed sprang up on the outskirts of the settlement. France had won the first stage of the race for the southern hemisphere. As Louis Bougainville sailed back to Brittany to recruit more colonists, he had no idea that the English were hard on his heels.

4 The Man at the Admiralty: Philip Stephens and Anglo–French Rivalry

Extraordinarily, no hint of Bougainville's plan reached the Admiralty Office until March 1764, six months after he had sailed from France and two months after he had reached the Falklands. When Britain's agent at Versailles[1] finally obtained a copy of Bougainville's original plan in February 1764, he immediately sent it to London. It was addressed to Philip Stephens, Secretary to the Admiralty and de facto chief of the Secret Service.

When the blueprint appeared in the Admiralty Office at the beginning of March, Stephens was stunned. Back in 1749, the government had agreed to implement Admiral Anson's plan to occupy the Falklands, but Whitehall had been so busy securing Britain's newly won territory around the North Atlantic that the project had remained on the backburner for fifteen years.[2] Now the French had hijacked it.

At this crucial juncture, it was Britain's great luck to have Philip Stephens at the helm. As soon as he learned that France had stolen a march in the Falklands, he swung into action.

Stephens was one of the most powerful men in Britain. At the head of the Admiralty was the First Lord, usually a cabinet minister, presiding over the Admiralty Board of half a dozen Lords Commissioners who were all political appointments, likely to change with every change of ministry. The board met regularly but contributed little. By the mid-eighteenth century, the Secretary to the Admiralty was one of the few civil servants who enjoyed permanent tenure. Stephens' predecessor, John Clevland, had made the secretary's office his personal fiefdom, running the Admiralty as a chief executive officer under the chairmanship of the First Lord. As Secretary to the Admiralty, Stephens presided over the nerve centre of British maritime power.

Twenty years earlier, Stephens was an accounts clerk in the Navy Office when Commodore George Anson completed his epic voyage round the world in 1744.

8. Sir Philip Stephens, 1723–1809. Secretary to the Lords Commissioners of the Admiralty from 1763 until 1795.

The returning hero was quickly promoted to the rank of rear admiral and made a Lord Commissioner of the Admiralty. However, Anson soon became embroiled in a three-year legal battle over the prize shares of the silver looted from a Spanish galleon which he had captured off the Philippines. When Anson asked Stephens to sort the matter out, the young man demonstrated such skill and efficiency that Anson reassigned him to his personal staff for secretarial duties. In April 1751 Stephens was officially transferred to the Admiralty and appointed senior clerk, a few weeks before Anson became First Lord of the Admiralty.

At the same time, Stephens probably assisted Benjamin Robbins with the publication of Anson's 'official' account of the voyage, and learnt how a ghostwriter could turn a harrowing expedition into a triumphant legend, and a bestseller to boot – a lesson that would prove useful after the next Pacific voyages.[3] As he read the book and pored over the charts, the boy from a small village in Essex came to understand the immense commercial potential and military importance of the Pacific. In that book Anson laid out directions for ships bound for the Pacific via Cape Horn, urging the British government to build a base in the Falkland Islands to serve as a refreshment station and to secure the shipping lane for British ships.

Stephens was involved when the Admiralty decided to implement Anson's proposal in 1749. Two vessels were fitted out for the purpose of surveying the Falklands and then sailing round Cape Horn to make discoveries in the Pacific. However, the scheme was leaked to the Spanish ambassador in London, who fervently opposed it. So the government instructed the ambassador in Madrid, Benjamin Keene, to seek the approval of the Spanish court. But King Ferdinand's ministers insisted that the Pacific was their Spanish Lake and cited old treaties in support of what Keene called 'their whimsical notions of exclusive rights in those seas'.[4] In the end, the British

9. The Lords Commissioners of the Admiralty meeting in the Board Room at the Admiralty in Whitehall, c.1808.

government yielded and called off the expedition. Whitehall was more interested in winning concessions in the Anglo–Spanish commercial treaty which was then under negotiation.

Anson's scheme was aborted because it was leaked. The source of the leak was not discovered, but may have been the loose tongues of government ministers in a loosely knit cabinet.[5] The entire episode was a valuable lesson for Stephens. In his future career, he would take no chances, preferring to adopt the strategy famously expressed later by his contemporary, George Washington, during the American Revolution: 'keep the whole matter as secret as possible. For upon Secrecy, Success depends in most Enterprizes of the kind, and for want of it, they are generally defeated, however well planned.'[6] Secrecy, and the censorship necessary to maintain it, was a feature of Stephens's management of naval exploration.

Stephens had direct personal experience of naval life, going to sea with Anson at least twice. In 1752, the First Lord escorted the king across the channel from Harwich to Holland. Six years later, during the Seven Years War, Stephens spent four months aboard ship when Anson commanded the Channel Fleet during the blockade of France's naval bases.

In 1759, Stephens was promoted to second secretary and became a member of the House of Commons. At Anson's request, he was given pocket borough in Cornwall and, later, the Admiralty borough of Sandwich in Kent. At the time, it was the custom for Admiralty secretaries to be members of parliament, but they were generally unaffected by changes in the administration and enjoyed secure tenure in their job. Although Stephens was occasionally involved in politics, he was not attached to any political faction and preferred to remain in the background. A member of the House of Commons from 1759 to 1806, he never made a speech in the House.[7]

When First Secretary John Clevland became ill during Christmas 1762, Stephens took on his workload and on Clevland's death in June 1763 became Secretary to the Admiralty, a position he held for 32 years.

With a staff of about ten clerks, Stephens coordinated, and often initiated, the Admiralty's communication with other government departments, such as the Navy Board and the Treasury – and the ships at sea. He sent out thousands of letters of instruction using the modest language of the day: 'their Lordships require me to inform you …' and signed 'Your humble servant, Ph. Stephens'. Yet most of these instructions were his alone, issued without reference to the commissioners.[8]

In practice, most Admiralty business was left to the secretary's discretion. He was free to implement his own plans, use his own initiative and bypass official channels when swift or secret action was required. In a chapter titled *La tête de l'Intelligence Service*, a French historian has described Stephens at work:

> In this modest Whitehall chamber, on tables littered with a constant flow of papers and documents, is determined the real fate of England. From there are despatched orders that direct, like pawns on a chessboard of the seas, the movement of the Caribbean, American, East Indies or North Sea fleets …
>
> It is in this room where war is prepared, where war is made. Within these four walls sits the man who holds in his hands responsibility for the Navy and, therefore, that of the Kingdom. This man is not the minister answerable to the king and to Parliament … He is not the First Lord of the Admiralty … No, this man who cheerfully bears the crushing weight of England's massive naval machine is none other than Mr. Philippe Stephens, secretary of the Admiralty …
>
> Nothing is hidden from him and nothing escapes his oversight …
>
> Intelligence agents communicated directly to the Secretary of the Admiralty himself and it was on the table of this senior bureaucrat that were accumulated all the secret warnings, reports and investigations gathered from the four corners of England and the four cardinal points of the world.[9]

Not surprisingly, Stephens's extraordinary power attracted criticism. In 1770, a contributor to the satirical *Oxford Magazine* bemoaned the influence of senior civil servants generally and of Stephens in particular:

> Who is the real first lord of the admiralty? Philip Stephens ... P.S. is lord high admiral of England ... this man plies his authority so dexterously through the whole circle of the naval government, that no corner is secret from his all-piercing eye. He, or his busy influence, is every where felt, every where seen. Not an appointment or a promotion from the *Royal George* to an armed schooner, is effectual, without receiving the sanction of his almighty fiat; and we are told that he had once the effrontry to attack the gallant first lord of the admiralty, for daring to prick down a peer of England on the promotion list, in preference to one of his favourite captains.[10]

But most sailors would have agreed with Vice-Admiral Augustus Hervey, 3rd Earl of Bristol, who declared that Philip Stephens was 'the most diligent, most intelligent, most indefatigable man in business I ever knew'.

Stephens was responsible for the cavalcade of British navigators – from John Byron to George Vancouver – who sailed the Pacific in the late eighteenth century. Throughout his long campaign to protect and expand Britain's naval–commercial supremacy, his vision and dependability were highly valued. In 1798, when the veteran commander James Colnett, who had sailed on Cook's second Pacific voyage, published an account of his survey of the South Pacific fishery for the English whaling industry, he dedicated the book to Stephens:

> Sir,
>
> ... The difficulties which navigators have experienced in traversing the South Seas and Pacific Ocean have evidently, from the commencement of your connection with the Admiralty, excited your particular consideration: and it is certain, in all the changes to which that Board has been subject, that the explorer of remote seas has found in you, a zealous advocate ...
>
> If any distinct praise can confer an honor on your name ... it is most due to your public, as well as private acts of friendship to those, who like me, have embarked for the purpose of enlarging the bounds of Navigation and Commerce; and I feel a decided conviction, that every follower of the able Captain Cook, will give a cordial assent to this tribute.[11]

When Stephens first joined Anson's staff in the 1740s, the admiral's focus had been to sweep aside Spain's ancient claim to exclusive rights in the Pacific. Twenty years later, priorities had changed. Spanish maritime dominance was, like that of the Dutch, finished and, while neither Holland nor Spain could be snubbed in tension-ridden Europe, they were no longer contenders in the race for the Pacific. In the aftermath of the Seven Years War there was a new threat in the southern seas. Moribund Spain was superseded by vengeful France. Philip Stephens believed it was vital that France should not get a foothold in the new emporium of the Pacific. Even more importantly, the British installations in India and the East Indies had to be protected from French encroachment.

But was Philip Stephens over-reacting when he fired off one navigator after another in a bid to forestall the French in the South Seas? Was France really an aggressive imperialist during the final years of the *ancien régime*?

Some historians say that France had no interest in building an empire when she sent her ships to distant seas. They argue that, unlike England, France was not a maritime nation dependant on seaborne trade. France was continental in outlook and imbued with the spirit of the European Enlightenment. French navigators were not driven by ambition for imperial expansion, but by their enthusiasm for discovery and a passion for knowledge. Their mission was to identify new peoples and new species and use their new knowledge to liberate and improve the human race.

It is true that the expeditions of Bougainville and Lapérouse carried many more astronomers and naturalists than did the British voyages of Byron, Wallis and Cook. However, the French naval vessels were much more than floating laboratories. They were reconnaissance ships, sent to gather information. In 1766, King Louis XV presented Bougainville with detailed instructions to note all the places that could serve as ports of call for ships, to examine the Pacific islands carefully and 'take possession of them should they offer items useful to her trade and navigation'.[12] These royal documents included carefully planned itineraries with commercial and political objectives. While the promise of scientific discoveries may have camouflaged the more pragmatic programs, it did not diminish their importance.

Stephens believed that France's ambitions to find new commodities and new markets while bolstering national prestige were no less energetic than Britain's. This much was clear from the ground-breaking book by the French scholar, Charles de Brosses. Published in 1756, it was the first collection of all known voyages to the southern hemisphere. In a long preface, he urged enterprising Frenchmen to explore the South Seas and forestall the English who were seizing 'the universal monarchy of the sea without regard or consideration for any other nation'.[13] De Brosses expressed his great hope that the Southern Continent would be discovered by French entrepreneurs who would build settlements there to promote French interests.

Other Frenchmen shared his ambition. Through the British embassy in Paris, Stephens learnt of the vehement objection voiced by the Duc de Choiseul when he learnt of Samuel Wallis's expedition to the Pacific. The French minister swore that France would

> spare no pains to gain a footing also, in whatever seas the English attempt to settle in, and

that she will never consent to the formation by England of new colonies in any part of the world unless she herself be free to form colonies in like manner.[14]

Choiseul's aggression sounded more like the old imperial rivalry rather than the new universal Enlightenment. Stephens too had little time for the so-called borderless Republic of Letters championed by scientific intellectuals. Britain's elite could exchange pretty French phrases in the gentlemen's clubs of London, but Stephens would remain at his desk in the Admiralty Office and deal with global reality. Bougainville had pre-empted Lord Anson's plan and hoisted the French flag over the Falklands. Stephens had good reason to fear that King Louis's golden fleurs-de-lis would soon be bleeding right across the Pacific Ocean.

Anglo–French rivalry would shape the world in the Pacific Ocean as it did in the Indian and Atlantic Oceans. Fear of French encroachment was the fundamental reason for planting British garrison colonies at Sydney and Norfolk Island[15] in 1788 and at Hobart, on the island of Van Diemen's Land, in 1803.[16] Concern about the threat of French settlements on Australia's long, exposed coastline continued well into the nineteenth century. In 1817, Governor Macquarie wrote to the Colonial Office in Whitehall saying:

> I am perfectly sensible of the great importance, both in respect to the Mother Country and the future prosperity of this Colony, of preventing the French or any other European Nation from forming any Settlement in any part of this Continent, and [I concur] with Lord Bathurst and yourself as to the expediency and necessity of using every possible means and precaution to frustrate the present intentions of the French Government in this instance.[17]

Perhaps no one was more 'sensible of the great importance of preventing the French' than Stephens. It was he who sent out expeditions to explore the south seas and claim new territories for Britain. As First Secretary, he played an important role in planning the colonies at Sydney and Norfolk Island, and he was still serving on the Admiralty Board when Van Diemen's Land was colonized. The first expedition initiated by Stephens was that of John Byron in the *Dolphin*.

5   Byron and the *Dolphin*: Secret Orders, Lost Opportunity and Censorship

When the leaked document from France landed on his desk early in March 1764, Stephens acted swiftly. Within days, the frigates *Dolphin* and *Tamar* were selected for the voyage and John Byron was chosen to command it.

The haste and secrecy surrounding Byron's voyage have long puzzled historians. The Admiralty archives contain no board minutes or memoranda discussing a revival of Anson's plan or any other proposal by the Sea Lords. As one scholar has observed:

> The stages by which the British decided to mount Commodore John Byron's 1764–66 exploring expedition to the southern Atlantic and Pacific Oceans remain exceptionally obscure … there are presently no clear answers to the questions of who precisely took the decision? in what forums? and why?[1]

It was Philip Stephens who took the decision; in his Whitehall office; for the purpose of giving chase and clawing back France's lead. He acted swiftly and secretly, leaving no paper trail. He didn't want the expedition to be derailed by Westminster gossip and rumour, as had happened to Anson's plan in 1749. Stephens also knew that any hint of French involvement would alert foreign agents. So he told no one about the intelligence he had received from France, not even his minister. A year later the First Lord of the Admiralty, Lord Egmont, confirmed this:

> It was many months after Capt Byron's Expedition was plann'd & 6 or 7 weeks after he sail'd that the first suspicion was entertain'd in England of any design on the Part of France to attempt this Island.[2]

However, Egmont's recollection is inaccurate.[3] Within a fortnight of Byron's camouflaged departure, the London newspapers were awash with reports about the new French colony in the Falklands.

We get some idea of the extraordinary haste of the operation from a letter Byron wrote to his friend, Lieutenant Philip Carteret, on 12 March:

> If you should chose to go to sea with me, make all the haste you can to Town as not a moments time must be lost.[4]

Urgency was also paramount at the docks:

> [T]he Admiralty was in such haste to ready the ship for sea that it immediately authorized the Navy Board to have the civilian employees at the Woolwich Yard work overtime on her. So great was the hurry that in order to expedite the repairs the yard used on one Sunday, for example, a foreman, a quartermaster, thirty-six shipwrights, and one team of horses from six in the morning until six at night.[5]

But speed was not the only hallmark of this operation. It was also shrouded in secrecy. A security cordon was placed around the dockyards, much as a nuclear weapons facility would implement today. The Admiralty ordered the Navy Board 'to direct ... that no Foreigner of any Rank or Character whatever be admitted, upon any pretence, to visit His Majesty's said Yards, Docks, or Magazines, as they will answer the Contrary at their peril'. Foreigners were not the only ones to be kept in the dark. The cabinet was not told. It seems that no one outside the Admiralty, except the king, knew the true purpose of the expedition.[6]

Great effort was made to conceal the destination. Initially, the Admiralty nominated the 'West Indies' then three months later changed it to the 'East Indies'. Byron himself was given the phantom appointment of Commander in Chief of His Majesty's Fleet in the East Indies, a position which remained on the books for the next eighteen months. The storeship *Florida*, which was sent to reprovision the frigates at Cape Horn, was fictionally consigned to the Gulf of Mexico where John Harrison's chronometer was being tested. None of Byron's crew was told where they were going because, apart from the risk that some might abscond, ships' crews were notorious for leaking like sieves as poorly paid sailors and marines could be easily bought by France or Spain.

Naming India as the decoy destination had some amusing consequences. When the Bengal governor designate, Robert Lord Clive, called at Rio de Janeiro on a sluggish East Indiaman, he met Byron briefly and envied his faster ship. After Byron left Rio – supposedly for India via the Cape – Clive wrote crossly to the prime minister, George Grenville:

> Upon my arrival at this place, to our great surprise, we found Commodore Byron in the *Dolphin*, and Captain Mouat in the *Tamar*, who left England a month after us, and anchored here nearly a month before us. Had the situation of affairs permitted you, Sir, to suggest to

me the Commodore's destination, it would certainly have saved me much time; however, I propose embarking upon the *Dolphin* at the Cape of Good Hope, which will shorten my passage six weeks or two months.[7]

However, Byron's destination was not India, so he was unable to give Clive a lift from the Cape. By the time Clive landed in Calcutta in May 1765, Byron was sailing across the Pacific.

Another body that might have asked difficult questions if the destination had been made public was the South Sea Company. In 1711, the South Sea Company (a somewhat misleading name) was promised a monopoly of all British trade to the Spanish colonies in South America. Its monopoly area extended down the east coast of the continent from the Orinoco River (in Venezuela), south to Tierra del Fuego (excepting Dutch-owned Surinam and Portuguese-owned Brazil), round the Horn and up the entire west coast of North and South America, plus a coastal margin of 300 leagues (900 mi. or 1400 km) out to sea. The promised 'South Seas' trade failed to materialize and, by the late eighteenth century, the Company was moribund. Nonetheless, the directors at South Sea House in Threadneedle Street insisted on their rights. Any British ship engaged in commercial navigation inside the Company's zone had to purchase a licence. Both of Byron's destinations, the Falkland Islands and California, lay inside the monopoly zone and, although voyages of exploration did not require a licence, the Admiralty did not want Byron's operation delayed by pesky questions from the directors.

The Honourable John Byron was born at his family's baronial seat, Newstead Abbey in Nottinghamshire, in 1723. He was the second surviving son of William, 4th Baron Byron of Rochdale and his third wife, Frances Berkeley. He joined the navy when he was fourteen, died a vice-admiral of the white half a century later and earned the nickname 'Foul-weather Jack' because of his tendency to sail into storms. He was, in turn, the father of Captain John Byron, a handsome profligate known as 'Mad Jack'; the grandfather of the poet Lord George Byron, 6th Baron of Rochdale, who died of a fever while liberating the Greeks from the Ottoman Empire; and the great-grandfather of Ada, Countess of Lovelace, a mathematician who predicted computer programming.

Byron's naval career was even bit as colourful as that of his progeny. As a young midshipman, he had sailed with George Anson's squadron on a mission to capture Spain's possessions in the Pacific. They hit terrible storms while rounding Cape Horn and Byron's ship, the *Wager*, was wrecked off Patagonia. Anson sailed on with his remaining ships to capture an Acapulco galleon and circumnavigate the globe, while the *Wager*'s few survivors clambered ashore in Chile. Byron spent several years as a castaway in South America, dividing his time between Spanish prisons and Creole beds.[8] Eventually he found a French vessel at Valparaiso which delivered him to Brest. Six months later, in April 1745, Byron arrived home in England after an absence of almost five years. He was rapidly promoted and during the Seven Years War he commanded ships in European waters and in North America. Now Commodore Byron was ready to embark on another adventure in the South Seas

While the *Dolphin* and the *Tamar* were being prepared, Stephens drafted Byron's 'Secret Orders and Instructions' for the Sea Lords to sign.[9] Importantly, Stephens did not repeat the itinerary of Anson's aborted 1749 expedition which was directed towards the South Pacific. Instead, he copied the itinerary contained in the French document smuggled from Versailles, which was directed to the Atlantic and the American hemisphere. Accordingly, Byron's orders contained the same three components as Bougainville's initial proposal. First, he would survey the Falkland Islands (and the nearby 'Pepys Island', which did not exist). Second, he was to search for the Southern Continent 'in the Atlantick Ocean between the Cape of Good Hope and the Magellanick Streight'. Third, he would double the Horn and sail north to California in the hope of discovering the Pacific entrance to the Northwest Passage and following it home to England. If no passage was found, he was to leave the American coast before he ran out of provisions and quickly cross the North Pacific to China or the East Indies and return home via the Cape of Good Hope.

There was a problem, however. Bougainville's head start meant that the French would claim possession of both the Falklands and California before the British arrived. Though it could never trump title by occupation, the artful Stephens hoped to thwart this by asserting title by discovery. When he sat down to draft the recitals to the document, Stephens exaggerated Britain's back-story in these regions, so that early coastal sightings by English sailors and privateers now became declarations of sovereignty. All the places Byron was to visit – except the unknown Southern Continent – were listed as being already 'Parts of the British Empire'. They were referred to as 'His Majesty's Island called Pepys Island, as likewise His Majesty's Islands called Falklands Islands' and 'New Albion in North America'. All had been 'first discovered and taken possession of' by earlier British seaman, such as John Davis, Richard Hawkins or Francis Drake. It was mostly propaganda but it nicely underpinned Byron's instructions and, after being signed and sealed by the First Lord, it became official.

Consequently, these written instructions did not ask Byron to take possession of these places. Englishmen had already staked their claims and to do so for a second time would negate Britain's priority. Instead, Byron was ordered to revisit these places, purely 'to make better surveys thereof than had yet been made'.

The one place where Byron was ordered to claim possession was the longed-for Southern Continent:

> In case you shall discover any Land or Islands in your passage from the Cape of Good Hope to Pepys's Island which have not already been discovered or taken notice of by former navigators ... You are to endeavour by all proper means to cultivate a Friendship with the Inhabitants, if you shall find any ... You are also to make purchases, with the consent of such Inhabitants, and to take possession of convenient situations in the Country in the name of the King of Great Britain: But if no Inhabitants shall be found on such Lands or Islands, You must then take possession of them for His Majesty by setting up Proper Marks and Inscriptions as first Discoverers and Possessors.[10]

At last, on 3 July 1764, HMS *Dolphin* and the frigate *Tamar*, with a combined complement of 250 men, sailed out of Plymouth Sound. Less than two weeks later, on 14 July, the Admiralty learnt all it needed to know about the French advantage in the Falklands when London newspapers published a story which had already appeared in the European press:

> By letters from Montevideo ... dated 2nd of January last, we learn that Mr de Bougainville ... having set sail from St. Malo last Autumn, in order to fulfill a secret commission, was preparing to form a Settlement in the Isles of Malouines in the Strait of Magellan, with so much the more Justice, as the Name of these Isles, which are absolutely desert, indicated that they belonged to France, and consequently that he could take Possession of them, as well by this title as that of first Occupant; and that he intended to land there some Persons of both Sexes, in order to form a Colony.[11]

Just days later, up-to-date reports of the colony's success were published because Bougainville himself was now back in France recruiting more settlers. He would deliver them to the Falklands the following January, a fortnight before Byron arrived there. Meanwhile, the Admiralty chose not to send a speedy vessel after Byron, who was refreshing at Madeira, with a note suggesting that he cancel his Falkland stopover now that the French had already won sovereignty of the archipelago.

It was only after leaving Rio de Janeiro, their last European port before entering the unknown world, that Byron told his crew their true destination, as he wrote in his journal on 22 October:

> Being now at Sea again, I called all Hands upon Deck & informed them I was not immediately bound to the East Indies as was imagined, but upon some certain Discoveries which was thought might be of great importance to our Country, and that the Lords Commissioners of the Admiralty were pleased to promise them double Pay with several other advantages if they behaved themselves to my satisfaction. They all expressed the greatest Joy imaginable upon the occasion & assured me there was no Difficulties they

would not go through with the greatest cheerfulness to serve their Country & Obey every Order I should give them.[12]

The obedience of his crew stood in stark contrast to the cavalier attitude to orders that Byron would soon display.

The Falkland Islands were sighted a fortnight after Christmas. Byron searched the coast around West Falkland for an anchorage and found a good harbour at nearby Saunders Island which he named Port Egmont after the First Lord. Although Byron had no written instructions to take possession here, it seems that the Admiralty's verbal instructions were more pragmatic. On 22 January 1765, Byron went on shore with his senior officers and conducted a possession ceremony:

> I took possession of this Harbour & all these Islands for His Majesty King George the Third of Great Britain & His Heirs, tho' they had been before taken Possession of by Sir Richard Hawkins in the Year 1593.[13]

Every man was served a half allowance of brandy to drink the King's health and then it was time for the British to depart. Byron did not leave any marks or inscriptions, though the surgeon from the *Tamar* planted some vegetables for future travellers – a common practice on long scurvy-prone sea routes.

From Port Egmont, Byron coasted westwards, applying English names to the bays and headlands. Rounding the far corner of East Falkland, he sailed past the entrance to Baie Accaron, but did not penetrate it. Had he done so, Byron could have joined Bougainville and his pioneers, now numbering 75, who were celebrating the first anniversary of the French colony at the back of the bay.[14] Instead, Byron renamed the inlet Berkeley's Sound after his mother's family and continued his coasting. Now, however, the coast became dangerous and, afraid of being caught on a lee shore, Byron abandoned his survey of the islands. He sailed over to Port Famine in the Strait of Magellan where he was to rendezvous with the British storeship, *Florida*.

Byron had not only finished with the Falklands, he had also finished with the Admiralty's program. He would not search the Atlantic for the Southern Continent, nor would he sail to California. While his vessels were being restocked, he wrote to Lord Egmont from Port Famine in the Strait of Magellan, casually informing him that 'I intend now to run over for India by a new Track which if I succeed in I hope Your Ldship will approve of. Our Ships are too much disabled for the California Voyage.'[15]

In fact, Byron's ships were in such good condition that they withstood the foul weather of the next six weeks as they battled their way through the strait. The real reason for his change of plan may have been the hope of rediscovering the riches of the

Solomon Islands which their Spanish discoverers had described 200 years earlier.[16] In any event, with his vessels reprovisioned by the *Florida*, Byron had sufficient supplies to make a quick run across the Pacific without having to search for a bounteous island.

After entering the Pacific, Byron tried to sail due west but the headwinds made that impossible and he turned north to the tropics. Here he tracked westward along the northern side of the Tuamotu Archipelago and refreshed at a group of atolls which he named King George's Islands (now Takaroa and Takapoto). A few days later, on 16 June 1756, he recorded the incident which would be the chief legacy of his voyage:

> We saw vast Flocks of Birds which we observed towards Evening always flew away to the So'ward. This is convincing proof to me that there is Land that way, & had not the Winds failed me in the higher Latitudes as mentioned before, I make no doubt but I should have fell in with it, & in all probability made the discovery of the So[uthern] Continent.[17]

It was a thrilling idea, but illness amongst the crew dissuaded Byron from following the birds on their homing flights – and possibly discovering the continent or even Tahiti, which lay just south of his track. Instead, he continued on a north-west course to Tinian in the Mariana Islands, east of the Philippines. They spent August and September here to recuperate, because 'not a single man [was] wholly free from the scurvy'. Amazingly, only three died on Tinian and now it was time to head home. After stopping at Batavia (which cost three more lives due to that city's endemic diseases) and Cape Town, the *Dolphin* returned to England on 7 May 1766.

Here the crew found that the secrecy that had shrouded their departure continued to shroud their return, as the *Gentleman's Magazine* reported:

> The object of this ship's voyage is variously reported, but as the officers' journals were all delivered up upon oath, no authentic account can be expected, unless published by authority.[18]

But the French and Spanish embassies in London had no intention of waiting for the censored version. They asked their web of informers to get the classified information. Within a few weeks, the Spanish ambassador, Prince Masserano, purchased a journal allegedly kept by one of Byron's officers, which he sent immediately to Madrid.[19] The equally resourceful French chargé d'affaires, Durand, used his agent at the Admiralty to obtain a map of Byron's route and a copy of the ship's log and sent them to the Duc de Choiseul in Paris.[20] He also reported to Choiseul that the *Dolphin*'s crew was taken before a judge of the Navy and sworn to secrecy, while her officers took a vow of secrecy before the Treasurer of the Admiralty.[21]

Even the British public could not wait for the authorized publication, which would not appear for seven years. Eleven months after the *Dolphin*'s return, an unauthorized account was published on 11 April 1767, written by 'an Officer on board the said Ship'. The slick, melodramatic style of the writing suggests that the author was probably a Grub Street hack hoping to cash in on the huge public interest in the voyage. However, the accuracy of the account confirms that it was based on the journal of someone on board, who is now thought to have been young Charles Clerke, one of Byron's midshipmen. The publishers tried to sidestep the Admiralty's injunction by patriotically leaving blank the coordinates of Byron's discoveries, explaining in a footnote:

> As the precise knowledge of the situation of these new discovered islands can be of service only to the navigator, we have, in obedience to the government, and that the enemies of our country may not avail themselves of our discoveries, omitted the degrees of latitude and longitude; but blanks are left for the figures, and as soon as we are assured that these islands are in the possession of our countrymen, the exact degrees of longitude and latitude shall be inserted in the news papers, that gentlemen who have purchased this book, may insert the figures with a pen.[22]

The illicit book was an instant bestseller in England and throughout Europe, where it was hurriedly translated into French, Italian, Spanish and German. One very keen reader was a young man about town named Joseph Banks.

Meanwhile, John Byron may have expected a cold reception when he arrived at the Admiralty to announce his return. His voyage of 22 months was the fastest circumnavigation to date, but the Admiralty had not asked him to set a speed record or even to complete a circumnavigation. Byron had made no attempt to find the Northwest Passage; he had not searched for the legendary continent in the South Atlantic; the six small islands he had discovered were insignificant; and he had not even found the Solomon Islands.

However, the voyage was not entirely uneventful. Byron had found 'convincing proof' that the Southern Continent lay to the south of the Tuamotu Archipelago. The Admiralty's wrath subsided and preparations for another operation began immediately. There was no time to lose.

6 Chasing Clouds in the Pacific: Samuel Wallis Discovers Tahiti

By the time Byron arrived home in May 1766, the Falklands business had erupted into an international crisis. France, Spain and Britain were all claiming title to the islands. Eight months earlier, in a bid to shore up Britain's claim, the Admiralty had dispatched Captain John McBride with three vessels, 25 marines and several tons of building supplies to construct a proper British base at Port Egmont near West Falkland. But the Falkland Islands were soon to lose their strategic value in Pacific exploration, thanks to the serendipitous discovery of Tahiti by Samuel Wallis. This bountiful island would become the new port of shelter and refreshment, so that the Falklands were no longer, in Lord Egmont's words, 'the Key to the whole Pacific Ocean'. As the cartographic historian, Dr Helen Wallis, wrote in 1983:

> the geopolitical significance of the Falkland Islands changed, and in the nineteenth century it was, of course, their relationship to Antarctica, all that remained of the great Southern Continent, which gave them the strategic value which they enjoy today.[1]

Meanwhile, the search area for the Southern Continent officially switched from the Atlantic to the Pacific Ocean when Byron told the Admiralty about the south-bound flock of birds he had seen in the Tuamotu Archipelago. This was, he said, 'convincing proof' of a Southern Continent and the Admiralty must send another expedition to find it.

When Lord Egmont rushed to Buckingham House to impress upon the King the need to act,

> before a war with France or Spain, or the jealousy of those two powers should ... interrupt the attempts of Great Britain in that part of the world, His Majesty was graciously pleased to authorize this second expedition to be undertaken, in hopes of finding a continent of great extent never yet explored or seen between the Streights of Magellan and New Zealand.[2]

So the *Dolphin* was brought into Deptford Dock to be repaired and reprovisioned as quickly as possible. She had to be ready to sail before summer's end if she was to double the Horn at Christmas. Her new consort was to be HMS *Swallow*, commanded by Captain Philip Carteret who had been a lieutenant on the first *Dolphin* voyage.

The *Dolphin*'s new commander was Captain Samuel Wallis. Born in 1728, the same year as James Cook, Wallis was the son of minor gentry who owned land in Cornwall. Unlike Cook, he joined the navy in his teens as a midshipman and received his first command 1756. During the Siege of Quebec in 1759, Wallis commanded the HMS *Prince of Orange* which (like HMS *Pembroke* where Cook was master) was one of the 22 ships of the line that comprised that victorious fleet.

The Admiralty's plan was simple. After exiting the Strait of Magellan, Wallis was to keep south and sail directly westwards across the Pacific for 120 degrees of longitude. This would bring him to the spot where Abel Tasman made landfall on the west coast of New Zealand in 1642, when the Dutchman had postulated that this coast was the west coast of the Southern Continent. As with Redern's map (Fig. 4) published four years earlier, the Admiralty imagined that, at some point during his long westerly traverse, Wallis would bump into the Antarctic Continent.

Once again, the Admiralty aimed for secrecy, as Dr Wallis notes: 'Records of the planning of Wallis's voyage at Cabinet level are very scanty, and the intelligence of spies has to be relied on as the main source of information'.[3] But this time the cat was out of the bag. Both France and Spain protested against Britain's imperial ambitions, but to no avail. However, the French managed to buy some spies. In July the chargé d'affaires at the French embassy in London, François-Michel Durand, wrote to the Duc de Choiseul informing him that:

> [T]wo Englishmen, one a volunteer and the other Byron's draughtsman or artist, who were to sail with Wallis, had agreed to give him information regarding where the English would establish bases. They wanted 150 guineas and a guarantee that if they fell into the hands of either the French or the Spanish they would be freed with all their effects.[4]

By early August the *Dolphin* and *Swallow* were ready to sail. Wallis was lucky in that he had all Byron's path-finding reports – charts, maps and log books. He had at least seven of Byron's men, with their first-hand knowledge of the Pacific. Three of them – Carteret, Gower and Simpson – went to the *Swallow*, while John Gore, Cragg, Crosby and Gray sailed with the *Dolphin*. Among the newcomers were Tobias Furneaux, Robert Molyneux, Richard Pickersgill and a goat, all of whom would circle the world again, at least once.[5]

The *Dolphin* and *Swallow* sailed from Plymouth on 22 August 1766, just three and a half months after Byron's return. With them went the store ship *Prince Frederick*, to resupply them at Magellan Strait. Unfortunately, it soon became apparent that the *Swallow* was a badly built slug of a ship, quite inadequate for the long voyage ahead. Inevitably, the two ships became separated in the strait and never found each other again.

Wallis spent four horrible months in the strait, beating against the winds funnelling though the high mountains that line its shores, before breaking out into the Pacific on 11 April 1767. Now the *Dolphin* was travelling solo, having lost sight of the *Swallow*. Carteret did not turn back, however, but struggled on into the Pacific, nursing his ship across the ocean, taking a more southerly route than earlier mariners and discovering more than twenty islands, including Pitcairn Island. Carteret returned heroically to England in March 1769, ten months after Wallis.

Meanwhile, after emerging from the strait, Wallis set a course for New Zealand as instructed. The conditions were appalling. He pressed into the westerly gales for almost three weeks, reaching 15° further west in those latitudes than any previous ship.[6] By the end of the month, however, too many men were falling sick and the loss of manpower put the ship in danger. Wallis was forced to turn northwards into better weather, so he never reached New Zealand.

A week later, they crossed the Tropic of Capricorn and wandered westward, south of the track Byron had taken two years earlier. Initially, their discoveries were low and uninspiring atolls, similar to those Byron had found on his parallel track. Then, in mid-June, their hopes soared with two momentous events – the fruits of the voyage.

The first occurred on 17 June when a man was gazing south and thought he saw some mountain tops on the horizon. The ship's master, George Robertson, recorded: 'we saw the Appearance of a very high Land to the Southward, but the weather being so thick and hazy we could not see it plain Enough to know it for certain'.[7]

Robertson caught this 'glimpse' of the Southern Continent close to the spot where Byron had seen his 'convincing proof' two years earlier. Curiously, Wallis decided not to investigate it, even though the discovery of the Southern Continent was the purpose of his voyage. Perhaps his reluctance was due to the bilious attack which hit him in early June and never left him. He continued to command from his sick bed, while the day-to-day running of the ship passed to his Second Lieutenant Tobias Furneaux, Gore and Robertson. Nonetheless, the report of this vision of the Southern Continent would galvanize the Admiralty when it launched its third exploratory voyage the following year.

The second event came two days later when they saw high volcanic mountains rising from the sea in front of them, clothed in rich green forests. It seemed like paradise and everyone cheered. Samuel Wallis and his men became the first recorded Europeans to see the bountiful, populated island of Tahiti.

Wallis anchored first on the south side at Taiarapu, but here the islanders were so hostile that he was forced to try and intimidate them by firing the ship's cannons. The next day the British sailed around the coast in search of a happier anchorage and, on 23 June, they landed at Matavai Bay on the north side of the island. Here, with careful diplomacy, Wallis established harmonious relations with the people. Now the crew could recuperate and savour the islanders' hospitalit

10. The Admiralty's engraver has titled this plate 'The surrender of the island of Otaheite to Captain Wallis by the supposed Queen Oberea'. In fact, the event took place in very different conditions and only after the British had survived an attack by a large number of people in their war canoes. At the time, Wallis was ill and remained in his cabin while Lieutenant Furneaux went ashore, hoisted the colours and claimed Tahiti for Britain.

Much has been written about the readiness of the Tahitian women to engage with the British sailors. However, one of the more interesting aspects of this 'old trade' was the currency they demanded. The Admiralty had, of course, anticipated the need to barter for food, water and wood, and the *Dolphin* was well supplied with mirrors and beads. However, it was iron the Polynesians favoured, most readily available in the threepenny iron nails which held the ship together. Wallis had to stop his men from pulling nails from the ship's planking, lest it fall apart.

Iron nails were also the currency for which the Tahitians traded fowls, fruit and hogs to reprovision the ship. Meanwhile, Gore led a party into the country and found an enchanting valley where he planted the seeds and stones of lemons, limes and oranges as well as peach, plum and cherry trees.[8]

Many of the crew were keen to experiment when they found that the ancient art of tattooing flourished on the island. Wallis was too ill to acquire one himself, but his journal contains the earliest description of Polynesian tattoos:

> I observed, that it was here a universal custom both for men and women to have the hinder part of their thighs and loins marked very thick with black lines in various forms … These marks were made by striking the teeth of an instrument, somewhat like a comb, just through the skin, and rubbing into the punctures a kind of paste made of soot and oil, which leaves an indelible stain. The boys and girls under twelve years of age, are not marked; but we observed a few of the men whose legs were marked in chequers by the same method, and they appeared to be persons of superior rank and authority.[9]

From his sick bed on the ship, Wallis ordered Furneaux to claim possession of the island. There is no specific reference to any attempt to seek or receive the consent of the inhabitants, although Furneaux did have a discussion with one of the leaders and 'Emblems of Peace' were exchanged. Robertson records the ceremony:

> 26th June … the Boats set out, and in a few minutes Landed and formed on the Beach, and took possession of the Island In His Majst name, and Honourd it with the name of our Most Gracious sovereign King George the third … he ordered some men to fix a long pole in the Ground, and hoisted a pendant on it in token of our having taken Possession of that place.[10]

The lusciousness of the island and its inhabitants could not divert Wallis from his habit of naming his discoveries after members of the Hanoverian Court or Britain's admirals. He named Tahiti King George III's Island, much like the name Byron had given to 'King George's Islands', or atolls, a few hundred miles away. Any confusion was quickly removed by Bougainville, who was at Rio de Janeiro when Wallis was in Tahiti. When Bougainville found Tahiti ten months later, the red-blooded Frenchman cut to the chase and named it La Nouvelle Cythère after Aphrodite's Island of Love. But this could not last. A year later, Cook arrived and asked the inhabitants what they called their home. They told him and thereafter he referred to the island as Otaheite.

Wallis's sensational discovery of Tahiti was a pivotal event in Pacific exploration. Now navigators could plan their voyage in advance. No longer would they have to race across the ocean in fear of running out of food, water and wood. Here they had a base, a reliable pantry where ships could fill their barrels with fresh water and load their holds with hogs, fowls, yams, breadfruit, and plantains. Matavai Bay (or 'Port Royal' as Wallis named it) was a safe, sheltered anchorage – a haven where men could recover their health and ships could be repaired and resupplied. Tahiti was the single most important factor that would guarantee success of the *Endeavour* voyage.[11]

Another advantage of Tahiti was its magnetism. Many visiting sailors signed up for another tour of duty and brought their brothers and friends on later expeditions. In time the island's reputation as a warm utopia came to characterize the whole South Pacific. These were pull factors for new settlers when the Pacific coast of Australia was colonized. Those who could not afford the voyage gleefully put a match to a haystack or picked a pocket to earn a free passage.[12]

After five blissful weeks, Wallis left the island at the end of July and, like Byron, turned north-west for Tinian. From there, the *Dolphin* sailed for Batavia and then stopped at the Cape of Good Hope. Here in this cosmopolitan community, Wallis found it impossible to keep the discovery of Tahiti secret. No disciplinary threat was dire enough to stop the crew from boasting about their sexual conquests on the island. Their pub gossip was overheard by French agents and relayed via Mauritius to Pondicherry, the French settlement in India. A few months later, the trader and navigator, Jean de Surville, sailed from India in the *St Jean Baptiste* bent on locating the island, now swelled by rumour to fabulous wealth and size.[13]

The Admiralty faced the same problem when the *Dolphin* arrived home on 20 May 1768. The solution was to allow the newspapers to announce the discovery of the fabulous tropical island, but the Admiralty vetoed the publication of its coordinates. No longitude was printed and the published latitude was inaccurate.

Wallis's appearance at the Admiralty Office in Whitehall was most opportune. A new expedition was about to depart for the Pacific to observe the transit of Venus, due to occur in twelve months time. The problem for the organizers was that they knew of no suitable place in the Pacific where the observation could be carried out. When Wallis announced his discovery of Tahiti, the scientists cheered. The island was perfectly positioned within the cone of visibility: it would make an ideal platform for an observatory. Over in Oxford, Professor Hornsby breathed a sigh of relief. Instead of wasting weeks searching the ocean for a suitable base, the astronomers would travel directly to this splendid new island.

Wallis's second piece of news – the alleged sighting of the Southern Continent south of Tahiti – was also useful as it provided a datum point. When the scientists had finished with the transit of Venus, the Admiralty would instruct the leader of the expedition to head directly south from Tahiti. Here he would search for the imagined prize of the South Pacific, before exploring elsewhere. But again, the French were ahead of them.

7 Bougainville's Voyage to New Holland and Lost Opportunity

The Franco–British race for the Pacific had been underway for four years, but where were the French? Capitaine de Vaisseau Louis Bougainville had been first out of the starting gates in September 1763, ten months before Commodore John Byron left England. Yet four years later, two British expeditions had crossed the Pacific while Bougainville had not even entered it.

The problem was the Falkland Islands. Whereas the British had removed the Falklands from their larger South Seas agenda, poor Bougainville was still embroiled with the French colony. After delivering a second cohort of settlers to Port St Louis, Bougainville returned to Paris in August 1765 to find himself caught up in a diplomatic stoush between France and Spain. For Spain, the Falklands were territorially part of its province of South America. The Spanish king was concerned that the French colony would encourage the English enemy into the region and insisted that Port St Louis be handed over to him. Bougainville resisted and the negotiations were long and tortuous, but eventually political expediency forced him to yield. Spain agreed to pay him £25,000 as compensation and Bougainville agreed to hand over the colony at an official ceremony in the Malouines in a few months time.

Now he returned to his vision of building a French empire in the South Seas. However, with the recent geopolitical changes – France's loss of her Falklands base and Britain's new aggressive thrust into the Pacific – Bougainville refined his plan. He drew up a new itinerary and sent it to Versailles for approval. This was granted, with minimal changes, and the formal instructions were signed by King Louis on 26 October 1766.

The document ordered Bougainville to sail from Cape Horn to China and continued:

> During his crossing to China, he will examine in the Pacific Ocean as many as possible and as best he can the lands lying between the Indies and the western shores of America of which several were sighted by navigators and called Diemen Land, New Holland, Carpentaria, Land of the Holy Spirit, New Guinea etc.

> Knowledge of these islands or continent being very slight, it is of interest to improve it. Furthermore, as no European nation has any establishment or claim over these lands, it can only be in France's interest to survey them and take possession of them should they offer items useful to her trade and her navigation.
>
> With this in mind, the area that Mr de Bougainville must concentrate on examining is especially the one stretching from the fortieth degrees of southern latitude towards the north, surveying what may lie between the two tropics.
>
> It is in those climates that one finds rich metals and spices. Mr de Bougainville will examine the soils, trees and main productions ... He will note as far as is possible all the places that could serve as ports of call for ships and everything relating to navigation ...
>
> As soon as Mr de Bougainville lands in unknown places, he will see to it that posts bearing the arms of France are erected and draw up Acts of Possession in the name of His Majesty, without however leaving anyone behind to establish a settlement.[1]

This remarkable document sets an entirely new agenda in Pacific exploration. For the first time, there is no reference to either the Northwest Passage or the Southern Continent. The focus is the long-known continent of New Holland and its outliers. Suddenly, the focus shifted from the elusive Southern (Antarctic) Continent to the small, identified continent with its commodities and resources. The French strategists had turned their attention to the real prize in that hemisphere – New Holland and its Pacific frontage.

The Pacific leg of the voyage was artfully concealed. Bougainville's trip to transfer his Malouines to Spain was widely reported in the French and British press, providing the perfect cover for the long weeks of fitting out two ships for the circumnavigation. The port authorities explained to curious bystanders – and foreign agents – that two ships were needed to deliver harpoons and supplies to the Falklands whale fishery and to bring back any French colonists who wanted to return after the handover. This satisfied the British ambassador in Paris, Lord Rochford, who wrote to Lord Shelburne with the news that Bougainville was sailing down the Atlantic to hand over the Falklands. Yet, in the following months, Bougainville's failure to return to France seemed to go unnoticed.

Bougainville departed Brest in the *Boudeuse* on 6 December 1766, three months after Wallis left England in the *Dolphin*. His second ship, the *Etoile*, would join him later in South America. The civilian members of the expedition included Dr Philibert Commerson, a medical graduate from Montpellier University, who was appointed Royal Botanist and Naturalist for the voyage; and his mistress, Jeanne Baret, whom he smuggled aboard disguised as his valet and who became the first woman to circumnavigate the globe.

After signing the final agreement in Buenos Aires, Bougainville and several Spanish ships sailed across to Port St Louis, on East Falkland, for the official hand-over ceremony. Here, on 1 April 1767, the French royal ensign was lowered and France's title was ceded to Spain. The French Malouines became the Spanish Malvinas and Louis Bougainville recorded that Spain's claim 'was thus rendered stronger by that which we certainly acquired by the first occupation'.[2]

Leaving the islands for the last time, Bougainville backtracked to Rio de Janeiro to rendezvous with the *Etoile*. While they waited here, Commerson and Baret made many successful botanizing expeditions around the city gardens and into the countryside. Here they famously found a sprawling, colourful vine which they named bougainvillea, after their commander. When the Portuguese governor proved uncooperative, Bougainville returned to Buenos Aires where they wintered and replenished their stores.

In mid-November, the *Boudeuse* and *Etoile* set out round the Horn suffering a stormy two-month passage through the Strait of Magellan. Eventually, the exhausted Frenchmen broke through into the Pacific on 26 January 1768, almost six years after Bougainville had drafted his first plan for southern discoveries.

11. An English illustrator lampoons Bougainville's pre-Cook circumnavigation: 'Mons. Bougainville and his party landed on a small rock in the Streights of Magellan.... hoisted the colours ... and repeatedly shouted *Vive le Roi* ... A striking instance of the vanity by which the French nation is distinguished!'

Like all who had gone before him, Bougainville was pushed northward by the westerly winds. Eventually, he crossed the Tropic of Capricorn and on 2 April he found Tahiti – not knowing that the Englishman, Samuel Wallis, had discovered the island ten months earlier.

Unfortunately, Bougainville missed Wallis's protected Matavai Bay and anchored instead in Hitiaa Lagoon on the exposed east coast. Here the French ships lost six anchors in nine days, due to bad weather and some sabotage by the natives. These iron relics would puzzle and mislead the next European visitors.

Tahiti offered the same Polynesian charms as it had to Wallis's men, as Bougainville records in his journal:

> A great deal of bartering with the Savages who do not seem to be surprised to see us, and are skilful traders but display good faith. A fine-looking young girl came in one of the canoes, almost naked, who showed her vulva in exchange for small nails.[3]

Remembering the classical studies of his youth, Bougainville called the island after Cythera, mythical birthplace of Aphrodite, the goddess of love:

> These people breathe only rest and sensual pleasures. Venus is the goddess they worship. The mildness of the climate, the beauty of the scenery, the fertility of the soil everywhere watered by rivers and cascades ... everything inspires sensual pleasure. And so I have named it *La Nouvelle Cythère*.[4]

Bougainville had no qualms about claiming possession of the island for France, even though the Tahitians had informed him of earlier European visitors.[5] The French celebrated with a display of fireworks and a concert on bass viol, flute and violin.

Bougainville was impressed with Tahiti's products: 'This country is finer and could be wealthier than any of our colonies'.[6] The ships' holds were restocked with bartered food – hens, cocks, pigeons, pigs, fruit, bananas, pumpkins and fish – while hundreds of casks and barrels were filled with fresh water; and trees were cut down to provide the ships' wood.

At the Tahitians' request, their guests limited their visit to just nine days. On their final day, a local chief asked if his brother, Ahutoru, could join the expedition as he wanted to visit the Frenchmen's homeland. Bougainville agreed – a Polynesian interpreter and guide would be useful in these waters – and promised to return the man to Tahiti eventually.

Now the French ships headed north to the latitude of 15°S and followed it westward for another month. They passed through the Samoan group and on to the islands discovered earlier by Quiros, who thought he had found the Southern Continent. Bougainville quickly proved that Quiros's Australia del Espiritu Santo was merely an archipelago situated a long way east of New Holland. Still in classical mode, he named it Des Grandes Cyclades after the mythical birthplace of Apollo and Artemis in the Aegean Sea, and claimed it for France. In due course, the archipelago was renamed New Hebrides by Cook, changed later still to Vanuatu.

Leaving Vanuatu, Bougainville continued westwards across the Coral Sea, specifically to reach New Holland: 'I persevered in keeping in the parallel of 15° … because I wanted to verify our conjectures by getting sight of the eastern coasts of New Holland'.[7] His perseverance paid off. Eight days later they saw waves breaking over a sunken atoll which Bougainville named Diane Reef. He steered around it only to be confronted by a more ominous line of rocks, now known as Bougainville Reef. It is an outlier of the treacherous Great Barrier Reef, the world's largest coral reef system that stretches along the entire length of Queensland's tropical coast. They were positioned almost due east of present-day Cooktown, and from the masthead the lookouts could see the Australian mainland. Bougainville marked his chart 'on a cru voir cette terre du haut des mâts' and recorded: 'This land is nothing else than the eastern coast of New Holland'.[8]

With the raging surf and submerged coral blocking his passage to the coast, Bougainville had to alter course. His instructions required him to head south down to latitude 40°S and to investigate Van Diemen's Land. The many scientists and seasoned sailors on board surely told him that the shallow tropical coral reef would peter out at the Tropic of Capricorn when it met the colder waters of the temperate zone. Then he would have a clear run to the coast and find a safe anchorage where the crew could rest and recover. There the ships could be repaired and reprovisioned with some of the delights from the land that Abel Tasman had described in 1642: good quality water and a variety of vegetables; enormous trees; footprints of animals; and abundant bird life, including gulls, wild duck and geese. More importantly, Bougainville could raise the golden fleurs-de-lis and claim possession of the east coast of New Holland for His Most Christian Majesty Louis XV of France.

But Bougainville withdrew. It was a momentous decision and he was in no doubt about the significance of his retreat from eastern New Holland. He tried to justify it by citing William Dampier's damning assessment of the opposite coast in the distant Indian Ocean, while clearly overlooking Abel Tasman's glowing description of the southern corner of this Pacific coast. Later, back in Paris, where Bougainville received a mixed reception on his homecoming from the scientists and politicians, he was even more defensive and imputed divine intervention:

> The sea broke with great violence on these shoals, and some summits of rocks appeared above water from space to space. This last discovery was the voice of God, and we were obedient to it ... I gave orders to steer N.E. by N. abandoning the scheme of proceeding further westward.[9]

After hearing *la voix de Dieu* in the crashing waves, the French turned away from Australia and circled round to the north side of New Guinea. The condition of the ships and crew was still good enough for Bougainville to spend the next three months weaving through archipelagos and rediscovering the Solomon Islands, two centuries after the Spanish had found them. There was no thought of going to China, as his instructions required, and instead they headed westwards to the Dutch settlements in the East Indies.

At last, in late September 1768, they reached Batavia and reveled in the delights of their first European city since leaving Rio de Janeiro 22 months earlier. However, Bougainville cut short their stay to just seventeen days as the endemic diseases took hold. Even Ahutoru, their most enthusiastic tourist, did not escape:

> Our man from Tahiti, who had doubtless been sheltered from the influence of the climate by the extasy into which everything that he saw threw him, fell sick during the last days.[10]

Fortunately, unlike some others, Ahutoru recovered and five months later this first Polynesian visitor to Europe was being paraded around Paris and Versailles.

The first French circumnavigation of the globe was completed on 16 March 1769 when Bougainville anchored in the port of St Malo. His great achievement was to install a French presence in the Pacific and he was feted as a hero. His narrative of the voyage, *Voyage autour du monde*, was published in May 1771 and created enormous interest about the Pacific, particularly Tahiti.

However, there were mumblings. Bougainville had fulfilled few of the expedition's goals. In particular, he had not explored the South Seas as intended and, although his men made the first recorded sighting of the east coast of New Holland, he had not claimed it. His critics in scientific and naval circles would have agreed with Louis Saint-Germain, the ship's clerk who fulminated: 'Of what use is this voyage to the nation?'[11] Some of these men sat down at their desks and began to plan the next French circumnavigation, although it would be delayed for more than a decade.

Meanwhile, as soon as the news of Bougainville's return reached the British Admiralty in March 1769, every effort was made to glean the details of his discoveries. But, for the moment, this was overshadowed by the anticipation of the transit of Venus, which was now just eleven weeks away.

8 Wooing the Royal Society: Dalrymple Wins Command of the *Endeavour*

After Professor Hornsby's paper was read to the Royal Society in February 1766, the first person to put up his hand to join the transit voyage was Alexander Dalrymple, a former captain in the East India Company Marine, who had recently returned to England after ten years in South-East Asia. On the face of it, Dalrymple was exceptionally well qualified for the job.

The eleventh child of a baronet, Dalrymple was born near Edinburgh on 24 July 1737. When his father died, his mother used her family connections to secure a position for her son with the East India Company. Although he was under age, the fifteen-year-old lad sailed for Madras in November 1752 to spend more than a decade in the East.

12. Fort St George at Madras (now Chennai) was the East India Company's second permanent trading post.

Dalrymple joined the Company as a 'writer', or junior clerk, but instead of climbing the corporate ladder to its dizzyingly lucrative heights, he turned his attention to finding ways to extend the Company's trade into those parts of the eastern archipelago that were not under Spanish or Dutch control. He spent hours poring over the old maps and charts in the governor's library, reading the accounts of the voyages made by the early Spanish and Dutch navigators and asking visiting mariners for scraps of new hydrographical information. Soon he was drawing his own updated nautical charts.

Between 1759 and 1764, he made three voyages through these eastern seas, visiting Canton, the Philippines, Borneo and Sulu. For months at a time, he sailed through dangerously shallow waters, dogged by the erratic weather and wind patterns of the tropics. He charted the coasts and islands, reefs and shoals, he negotiated with sultans and befriended the local people. After five years at sea, Dalrymple had become an expert navigator, an adept marine surveyor, a brilliant cartographer and a highly competent professional sailor.[1]

In the course of his travels, Dalrymple obtained a grant of Balambangan Island, north of Borneo, from the Sultan of Sulu, and soon after he took formal possession of the island on behalf of the Company. He planned to build a trading station, which would also service an alternative route to China should the Strait of Malacca be closed by war. Such an ambitious scheme needed the approval of head office, so Dalrymple sought the governor's permission to return to London. This was granted and he went through the formality of resigning from the Company, knowing that he would be reinstated on his return.[2]

Dalrymple arrived back in England in July 1765 and headed straight to East India House in Leadenhall Street to present his plan to the Court of Directors. In the lavish boardroom Dalrymple presented his vision along with his magnificent charts of the Malay Archipelago. Unfortunately, although acknowledging that the Balambangan trade might be lucrative in the future, the directors were not interested in incurring the expenses of settlement at the present time.[3]

Dalrymple was furious. He didn't want to return to India empty-handed, so now he must find some other venture that would advance the interests of the East India Company. Fortunately, his friends at the Royal Society told him about Hornsby's Pacific proposal. The members had voted to mount an expedition to the Pacific to observe the transit of Venus, provided they could win the Admiralty's support. Most excitingly, after the transit mission was completed, the ship would be perfectly situated to explore that largely unknown ocean.

This was just the opportunity that Dalrymple was looking for and he immediately launched a robust campaign to win the job of leading the expedition. First, he contacted one of his friends at the Royal Society, the Reverend William Hirst, an amateur astronomer whom Dalrymple had met in Madras when Hirst observed the previous transit of Venus from the roof of the governor's house. Hirst introduced Dalrymple at the society's next meeting on 20 March and the young Scot charmed the members with tales of his explorations and discoveries in the East Indies. Nor did it escape the fine fellows that their guest was the son of a baronet and the grandson of an earl.

Dalrymple's next step was to publicize his knowledge of the Pacific Ocean. He had long believed in the existence of a vast Southern Continent – a Terra Australis Incognita. Now he would assemble all his cartographical research and publish his conclusions in a book. One day, while he was browsing in a bookshop at Covent Garden, Dalrymple came across two small volumes written in Spanish.[4] He purchased them and found they contained important manuscripts and printed material from the State Archives in Madrid. One of these was the 'Arias Memorial', a document written around 1620 by a Chilean lawyer, Juan Luis Arias, for the king of Spain.[5] The memorial purported to summarize the accounts of some early southern voyages, but it exhibited a curious mixture of fact and fiction.

Dalrymple paid particular attention to two of Arias' stories. The first told how Juan Fernandez, a Spanish sailor, had discovered the east coast of the Southern Continent in 1574 when he was sailing from Peru to Chile. Dalrymple estimated the coordinates of Fernandez's sighting to be 40°S and 90°W, placing it about 700 miles south-west of the Juan Fernandez Islands.[6] The second story told how, in 1606, Luis Vaez de Torres had discovered a strait separating New Holland from New Guinea. The first story was pure fabrication; the second was true. Unfortunately, Dalrymple's excitement seems to have clouded his critical faculties. He gave equal credence to both stories and entered both discoveries on his chart.

Dalrymple believed that Fernandez's sighting, plus many other sightings of the early navigators, were indeed promontories of the Antarctic Continent. He recalculated their coordinates using the latest methods and meticulously plotted them on his chart, much as Count von Redern had done in Berlin some years earlier. This data formed the perimeter of a great land mass and if Dalrymple had connected his dots and shown them on a polar projection, then his continent would have looked remarkably similar to Redern's 'Australasie' (Fig. 4). Dalrymple's continent stretched further east than Redern's continent and not as far north, but both agreed that New Zealand formed its western limit.

In short, Alexander Dalrymple maintained that the Southern Continent stretched across the temperate zone of the South Pacific, from New Zealand in the west to Fernandez's sighting in the east. He imaged a habitable and fertile continent 'extending from about 30°S towards the Pole' which was 'swarming with people', all of them eager to trade with the East India Company. Now Britain needed her own Columbus or Magellan to set sail as soon as possible and confirm it.

After Wallis departed on the second *Dolphin* voyage in August 1766, Dalrymple

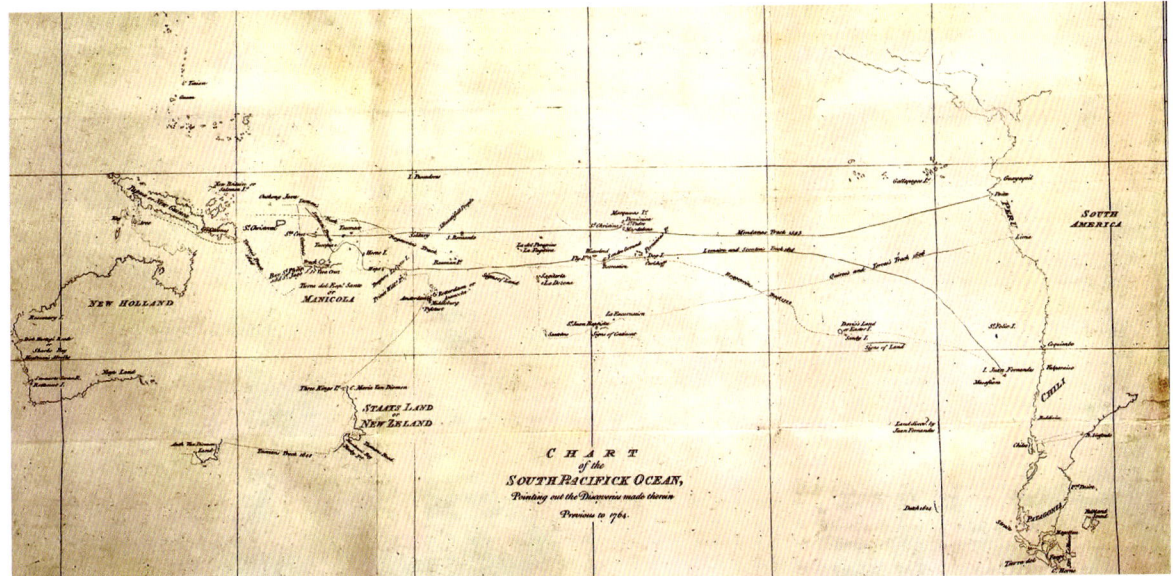

13. Dalrymple's chart of the South Pacific shows 'Land discovered by Juan Fernandaz' off the coast of Chile, and 'Torres's Track 1606' between New Holland and New Guinea. A copy of this chart was carried on the *Endeavour*.

lobbied even harder for the command of the next voyage. On 24 November, he wrote to the prime minister, the Earl of Chatham, enclosing a draft copy of the introduction to his forthcoming book. On the pretext of seeking official consent to its publication, Dalrymple promoted himself as leader of the next expedition:

> My Lord,
>
> … Having had five years experience in voyages of this kind, thro seas unknown and amongst people with whom we had before no intercourse, I presume to think myself qualified to be usefully employ'd in such an undertaking.

Then he addresses what he saw as the one weakness in his application – his lack of naval status:

> At the same time I am not insensible, notwithstanding the instances of Dampier, Halley etc. how foreign to rules of office it is … that a person may be employed in the publick Service by sea, who has no rank in the Navy.
>
> I must own in the words of Quiros 'that my impassioned desire towards this work hath grown up with me as it were from my Cradle, and that the magnanimity of the design wholly engages my attention.[7]

Next, Dalrymple asked his influential friend, Adam Smith, for support. On 12 February 1767, Smith sent extracts of Dalrymple's research to the Earl of Shelburne, the secretary of state for the Southern Department. Not surprisingly, this shrewd minister was very interested in Dalrymple's proposal. If a large and populous southern continent existed in the South Pacific, then trade and alliance with its inhabitants could affect the balance of power in Europe. Dalrymple later recalled that Shelburne 'expressed a strong desire to employ him on these discoveries, at the same time expressing his regret that he was not acquainted with Alexander Dalrymple when Captain Wallis was sent'.[8] Unfortunately for Dalrymple, this valuable support did not last long. Shelburne was already isolated in cabinet for his conciliatory policies towards the American colonies and resigned a year later.

In his accompanying letter to Shelburne, Adam Smith not only sung Dalrymple's praises, but also listed his friend's stipulations:

> Whether this continent exists or not may perhaps be uncertain; but supposing it does exist, I am very certain you never will find a man fitter for discovering it, or more determined to hazard everything in order to discover it. The terms that he would ask are first, the Absolute command of the Ship ... and ... He wishes to have but one ship with a good many boats. Most expeditions of this kind, he says, have miscarried from one ships being obliged to wait for the other, or losing time in looking out for the other.[9]

Dalrymple's terms of a single ship and sole command were not negotiable. As he later insisted in his book: 'A thousand motives recommend a single ship for discovery'.[10]

His next move was to speed up the publication of his research. His book would not be published until 1769, so he hastily assembled those sections relating to the Southern Continent into a pamphlet and printed a few copies under the title: 'An Account of the Discoveries Made in the South Pacifick Ocean previous to 1764'. These he circulated judiciously, with a view to influencing the council of the Royal Society as it mulled over the appointment of expedition leader. In his text he highlights the advantages that will flow to the East India Company from discoveries made in its monopoly zone:

> It is more than probable another Continent will be there found extending from about 30°S. towards the Pole. There can be no doubt that countries so well situated, so extensive, and so full of civilized inhabitants, must afford a very beneficial commerce: ... the examination of the countries situated in the South Pacifick Ocean, seemed to be an object of Great consequence to the [East India] Company.[11]

In March, he wrote a paper for the Royal Society highlighting his experience with the people and places of the eastern archipelago. Titled 'On the formation of Islands', the paper was read by the society's secretary to a meeting in July and later published in the journal.

Still his campaign continued. In June 1767 Dalrymple hoped the directors at East India House might help his campaign, writing to his old friend, Thomas Saunders, now the Company's deputy chairman, 'regarding some propositions for a voyage to the South Seas in order to make some discoveries which may tend to the Company's advantage'.[12] His request was unsuccessful, but he had no need to worry.

By November, the Royal Society's selection subcommittee was considering a short list of candidates. Dr Nevil Maskelyne recommended Dalrymple for 'having a particular turn for discoveries and being an able navigator, and well skilled in observation'. That seemed to clinch it. A week before Christmas 1767, James Douglas, Earl of Morton, president of the Royal Society, formally recommended Dalrymple for command of the transit voyage, on his own terms.[13] Dalrymple's twenty-month campaign had ended in triumph.

Over in Whitehall, the Lord Commissioners of the Admiralty accepted the appointment. On 29 February 1768, Lord Shelburne informed the Admiralty that the King, in response to a request by the Royal Society, had agreed to fund a suitable vessel. Now the Admiralty's preparations could begin and on 5 March, Philip Stephens wrote to the Navy Board asking it 'to propose a proper vessel to be fitted for this service'.[14] To celebrate this development, Lord Morton invited Dalrymple as his guest to the next Thursday dinner of the Royal Society Club at the Mitre Tavern on 10 March.

The Admiralty agreed to Dalrymple's precondition of a single vessel, even though it contravened naval practice for such long voyages and soon became an expensive problem for the Navy Board. All previous circumnavigations had been assigned at least two navy ships, for safety and for storage. Prior to the discovery of Tahiti, even the combined capacity of two navy ships was insufficient for a full circumnavigation, principally because English ships, unlike French ships, were not allowed to buy provisions or make repairs at the Spanish ports in Chile and Peru. Consequently, both Byron and Wallis had been accompanied by a third store ship, which restocked their frigates before they entered the Strait of Magellan.[15]

To dispatch Dalrymple in a single, sleek-hulled warship was out of the question, especially with the extra load of astronomers and their equipment, plus the additional food required while searching the Pacific for a suitable observation island. Finding nothing roomy enough among its own ships, the Navy Board was put to the expense of buying a cargo ship from a private merchant.

In the third week of March, a collier was suggested. These North Country cats were bulk carriers specially built in Whitby to haul coal up and down the North Sea coast. Unlike the naval man-of-war, these roomy, flat-bottomed colliers were designed for their cargo-carrying capacity rather than speed. They had the storage space needed for a long voyage, their shallow draught gave them the manoeuvrability required for coastal navigation and, in an emergency, they could be beached for repairs.

14. The collier *Earl of Pembroke*, built in 1764, leaving Whitby Harbour. In 1768 she was commissioned as HMB *Endeavour* and extensively refitted and strengthened at the naval dockyard at Deptford before sailing round the world.

A few colliers were now available on the Thames and Philip Stephens wrote to the Deptford Officers asking them to arrange a survey of the two most likely vessels: the *Valentine* and the *Earl of Pembroke*. This was a task for the Surveyor of the Navy, Sir Thomas Slade, who had already designed and launched the HMS *Victory*, best known as Nelson's flagship at the Battle of Trafalgar in 1805. Slade Point, a promontory in Queensland, would be named after him in 1770. Sir Thomas invited Dalrymple, as captain designate, to accompany him for the inspections, as Dalrymple later recorded in his memoir, written in the third-person:

> the Admiralty approving of his being employed for this service, as well as for prosecuting discoveries in that quarter, Alexander Dalrymple accompanied the Surveyor of the Navy to examine two vessels that were thought fit for the purpose. The one he approved was accordingly purchased.[16]

After examining both vessels, Slade and Dalrymple chose the *Earl of Pembroke* because she had the greater carrying capacity.[17] She was purchased on 27 March 1768 from Thomas Milner for £2800 and taken straight to the Royal Dockyards at Deptford. Here she was entered on the Navy List with the new name HMB *Endeavour*, before undergoing a major refit.

A week later, Alexander Dalrymple was sacked.

9 Dalrymple Sacked: The East India Company and the General Election

At Easter 1768, Alexander Dalrymple lost the command of the *Endeavour*, ostensibly because he was not in the navy.

On Good Friday 1 April, two days after being notified of the *Endeavour*'s purchase, Philip Stephens started drafting formal instructions which the Admiralty would give to her commander. He wrote to the Royal Society asking for the names of its official transit observers and for the approximate location of the place where the observation would be made. In response, the society's president, Lord Morton, arranged a meeting for Easter Saturday – with the First Lord, Sir Edward Hawke, hero of the Battle of Quiberon Bay.

At that meeting, Admiral Hawke informed Lord Morton that Alexander Dalrymple could not command the *Endeavour*. Morton immediately convened an extraordinary meeting of the council of the Royal Society and invited Dalrymple to attend, telling the gathering that the First Lord had said that 'such appointment [i.e., of a non-naval captain] was totally repugnant to the rules of the navy'.

Seeing Dalrymple's fury, Morton offered a compromise: Dalrymple could head the scientific party, while a compliant naval officer would run the ship. But Dalrymple had no interest in a divided command, which he believed unworkable and unsafe. From the start he had insisted on the sole command and, now that this was denied him, he withdrew from the voyage.

However, it is unlikely that absence of naval rank was the real reason for Dalrymple's loss of the command. If the navy had a blanket rule against non-navy captains, the Royal Society would surely have known, and Lord Morton would not have risked losing the Admiralty's support by ignoring it. On the contrary, the acceptance of Edmond Halley and William Dampier as commanders of navy vessels demonstrated that a non-navy sailor could be appointed for specific jobs. Dalrymple's experience in the merchant navy made him an exceptional candidate.

It is more likely that Dalrymple's civilian status was merely a pretext. Dalrymple always insisted that Hawke had wanted him to lead the expedition, writing in his memoir:

> the worthy Admiral Hawke, who then presided at the Admiralty, was wrought upon by insinuations that he would be exposed to a parliamentary impeachment if he employed any but a Navy Officer.[1]

Writing to Dr John Hawkesworth in 1773, Dalrymple declared:

> Notwithstanding the injury done me, in depriving me of the command of the Ship I had chosen for the Voyage, on pretense that I had not been bred up in the Royal Navy; so far was I from refusing my assistance to those who were going, that I gave Mr. Banks all the information I could …
>
> I am very far from intending the most distant insinuation of resentment to, or dissatisfaction with, the worthy and brave old Officer who was at the head of the Admiralty when the Endeavour was purchased; his ideas on the subject of discovery were clear and just in the only conference I ever had with him, and I have been told that afterward, 'He lamented I did not go'; but his open, honest, unsuspecting nature, I think, exposed him to the insinuations of cunning men.[2]

Dalrymple's testimony is important because, while he has been criticized for being irascible and pig-headed, he was known as a strictly truthful man and his claims have never been directly challenged.

Many historians agree that it was not Dalrymple's lack of naval experience that cost him the command and have suggested various alternative explanations. One is that there was a struggle for control of the voyage, in which the navy prevailed over the Royal Society. Another suggestion is that Cook's supporters bullied the Lords Commissioners of the Admiralty into appointing their man. An explanation that has been overlooked is the tension between the government and the East India Company.

The real reason for his dismissal was undoubtedly Dalrymple's fervent allegiance to his alma mater. He had made no secret of his intention to notify the East India Company of his discoveries, and this the Admiralty could never accept.

Dalrymple understood the need to keep valuable information secret from foreigners. When his colleague Charles de Brosses informed him in 1767 that Bougainville was about to depart on a great voyage of discovery, Dalrymple temporarily suspended their correspondence, fearing it 'might facilitate the enterprises of a rival state'.[3]

But the East India Company was not a rival state and Dalrymple was unlikely to accept that the Admiralty's suppression order applied to his communications with the Company. In his eyes, discoveries made inside the Company's monopoly zone, which included the Pacific, belonged to the Company.

15. A powerfully armed East Indiaman, painted from both the side and the stern, flying the Company's distinctive ensign of red and white stripes with the Cross of St George in the canton, c.1685.

From its standpoint, the Admiralty could not lose control of the results of its *Endeavour* voyage, whether they were the Southern Continent or other strategic discoveries. Only Admiralty staff could scrutinize the officers' charts and journals and decide what to publish and what to conceal. If the uncensored material was delivered directly to the Company, it could rely on its exclusive charter to stymie future government plans.

Since its creation in 1600, the Honourable East India Company had become the most privileged of Britain's trading houses. Various royal charters had granted to it a monopoly of all trade in the seas between the Cape of Good Hope and Cape Horn. All other independent British vessels and merchants (or 'interlopers') were forbidden to trade in the Indian and Pacific Oceans without a licence from the Company. Not surprisingly, this drew opposition from the independent merchants at the provincial ports of Bristol, Dublin, Aberdeen, Glasgow, Liverpool, Exeter and Hull. Denied access to the lucrative eastern markets, they pestered Whitehall with a steady stream of petitions for decades to come.

Their hostility was exacerbated by the Company's selfishness in preventing the interlopers from opening new markets in regions which it was unwilling or unable to exploit. The charter contained no 'use it or lose it' clause and, as early as 1695, economists were condemning charter companies 'who, like the dog in the fable, would neither supply those plantations themselves, nor suffer others to do it'.[4]

This obstructive behaviour was ridiculed again in 1744 when the Company brandished its charter to block enterprise in the new emporium of the Pacific. The famous commentator, Dr John Campbell, urged the East India Company to explore the east coast of New Holland with a view to colonization. The country's location is, he said, 'the happiest in the world' and its commodities must be 'extremely rich and valuable, because the richest and finest Countries in the known World lie all of them within the same Latitude'. It was the Company's duty to make such a voyage, he insisted, so that 'we might know as well, and as certainly, as the Dutch, how far a Colony settled there might answer our expectations'. Even so, Campbell fully expected his plea to fall on deaf ears, writing sarcastically:

> But if it should be thought too burdensome for a Company in so flourishing a condition, and consequently engaged in so extensive a Commerce as the East India Company is, to undertake such an Expedition, merely to serve the Public, promote the Exportation of our Manufactures, and increase the number of industrious Persons who are maintained by foreign Trade. If this, I say, should be thought too grievous for a Company that has purchased her Privileges from the Public by a large Loan at low Interest, there can certainly be no Objection to the putting this Project [with supporting legislation] into the hands of the Royal African Company, who are not quite in so flourishing a condition.[5]

But not even ridicule could prise open the closed shop and the Company continued to stifle proposals for the exploration and development of New Holland. Forty years later, Sir George Young blamed it for blocking his plans to develop Madagascar and New South Wales:

> Lord Sandwich very much approved [them], at the same time lamented the East India Company's charter, which precluded every attempt of this kind during its existence …

This jealousy of the India Company, I think, can be imputed to nothing but the principle of the old proverb, namely, the dog in the manger.⁶

Even Alexander Dalrymple blamed his alma mater's narrow-mindedness after it shelved his Balambangan scheme: 'the East India Company are too much engaged in territorial dominion to think of commerce and discovery'.⁷

Relations between the government and the Company deteriorated as their mutual dependence grew. The charter was not granted in perpetuity and so the Company depended on the government for its periodic renewal. At the same time, the government came to depend on the Company for large contributions to Treasury coffers. The crisis point came in 1765 when Robert Clive and the Company won the 'diwani' (i.e., the tax collecting rights) for Bengal, Bihar and Orissa. When the news arrived in Whitehall the prime minister, Lord Chatham, insisted that the territorial rights that accompanied the diwani belonged to the British Crown and not the Company. He instigated the first parliamentary inquiry into the Company's affairs, which paved the way for future government interference and, ultimately, the Company's nationalization.

16. General election 1768. The triumphant John Wilkes, having won the seat of Middlesex, being drawn into the city by the mob to the shouts of 'Wilkes and Liberty!'

Meanwhile, the London stock market erupted with the Bengal Bubble. Amongst the speculators were an embarrassing number of parliamentarians, prompting Horace Walpole to remark in 1767: 'in truth it is a very South Sea year – at least one third of the House of Commons is engaged in this traffic ... from the Alley to the House it is like a path of Ants'.⁸ Public rancour grew as they watched the returning nabobs of this millionaires' factory use their ill-gotten fortunes to set themselves up with a country estate, a town house and, too often, a seat in parliament. Rumours of the corruption and immorality of Company rule in India fuelled the hostility.

The free-traders and anti-monopolists joined the fray, arguing that the Company's commercial privileges damaged the national interest. Jealousy, morality and economic enlightenment had combined to ensure that the Honourable East India Company had become a thorn in the side of the government, when parliament was dissolved on 11 March to make way for the general election of 1768.

It was a difficult time for Chatham's ministry as it braced itself for the seven-week-long campaign. London was already seething with strikes and riots when the popular radical, John Wilkes, returned from his exile in France to stand for re-election to parliament. Benjamin Franklin, who had been sent to England as colonial agent for Pennsylvania, described London's chaotic streets in a letter home in May:

> Even this Capital, the Residence of the King, is now a daily Scene of lawless Riot and Confusion. Mobs are patrolling the Streets at Noon Day ... Sailors unrigging all the outward-bound Ships, and suffering none to sail till Merchants agree to raise their Pay; Watermen destroying private Boats and threatning Bridges ... Soldiers firing among the Mobs and killing Men, Women and Children, which seems only to have produc'd an universal Sullenness, that looks like a great black Cloud coming on, ready to burst in a general Tempest ... Meanwhile the Ministry ... worried by perpetual Oppositions ... intent on securing Popularity in case they should lose Favour, have ... little Time to attend to great National Interests.[9]

Voting began on 16 March and the *Endeavour* was purchased on 27 March, to sail five months later. Perhaps it was the acquisition of the vessel that now focused Whitehall's attention on who was to command the expedition. The Chatham ministry was not inclined to muddy its popularity by using taxpayers' funds to dispatch an intelligence-gathering ship for the benefit of the East India Company. It wanted a commander who would sail for the Crown, not the Company. When the government realized the implications of Dalrymple's appointment, they quashed it and, for a while, the question of the *Endeavour*'s commander hung in abeyance.[10]

Alexander Dalrymple would not sail with the *Endeavour* to the South Seas, but he and the Company were to remain ghostly presences on the ship.

10 An Ambitious Young Gentleman: Joseph Banks Builds his Credentials

While Dalrymple was lobbying for the appointment, another young man was hoping to join the Pacific voyage, not as commander but as a paying passenger. He was Joseph Banks, a young man whose driving enthusiasm vitalized every venture he touched.

Born in London in 1743, Banks was very rich. His people were landed gentry from Revesby Abbey in Lincolnshire and, although not a titled family, had some notable contacts. Perhaps the most significant was a Lincolnshire neighbour, John Montagu, the 4th Earl of Sandwich, who enjoyed three spells as First Lord of the Admiralty. Although he was 26 years older than Joseph, they became firm friends as Sandwich instructed the young man in the pursuits of fishing and wenching.

Banks also had powerful connections by marriage. In 1757, his aunt married the Honourable Henry (Harry) Grenville, one of the cosy cousinhood of Grenvilles, Pitts and Temples which dominated British politics for decades. Harry was the brother-in-law of the current prime minister (William Pitt the Elder, Earl of Chatham), the brother of a previous prime minister (George Grenville), the uncle of two future prime ministers (William Pitt the Younger and William Grenville) and the brother of the future Marquess of Buckingham.

Then, of course, there was the old school tie. William Banks was schooled at Westminster, but sent his son to Harrow, Eton and Christ Church, Oxford, whose alumni filled half the top positions in England. Friends and acquaintances made at these institutions would ease his projects – bold and discreet alike – through the corridors of Whitehall and Westminster throughout his long life.

Banks arrived at Eton a few months after England declared war on France in May 1756 and he quickly found a close friend in Constantine John Phipps (Lord Mulgrave). These were exciting times for thirteen-year-old boys. By late 1758 Europe had reached crisis point when British agents learnt that the newly appointed Duc de

17. Painted shortly after the return of the *Endeavour*, Benjamin West's portrait depicts Banks proudly displaying his treasures from the South Seas.

Choiseul was planning to knock Britain out of the fight by mounting a cross-channel invasion. The prime minister, the Duke of Newcastle, declared that 'flat-bottomed boats are preparing all along the French coasts'.[1]

Phipps left school and joined the navy as a cadet in the HMS *Monmouth*, taking part in Admiral Hawke's famous blockade of Brest though the summer of 1759. Banks remained at school but, during the holidays at Revesby Abbey, he and his father undoubtedly discussed the vulnerability of Lincolnshire's exposed coasts, just 25 miles away. In 1794, during the French Revolutionary Wars, Banks published a pamphlet, *Outlines of a Plan of Defence against a French Invasion; intended for the County of Lincoln*.[2]

Thus Banks's teenage years were coloured by the Anglo–French rivalry that had long become endemic on both sides on the Channel. Throughout his long life, in peace and war, Banks admired French scientists and fostered communication with them in the spirit of the Republic of Letters, transcending national boundaries. But Banks drew a clear distinction between international science and national loyalties. Science was neutral but, like most of his countrymen, Banks wasn't. He was a staunch imperialist and singularly interested in advancing England's commercial and strategic interests. Years later, he bluntly told a French geographer, 'I certainly wish that my Countrymen should make discoveries of all kinds in preference to the inhabitants of other Kingdoms'.[3]

Despite appearances, Banks was no dilettante. At Eton, he developed a lifelong

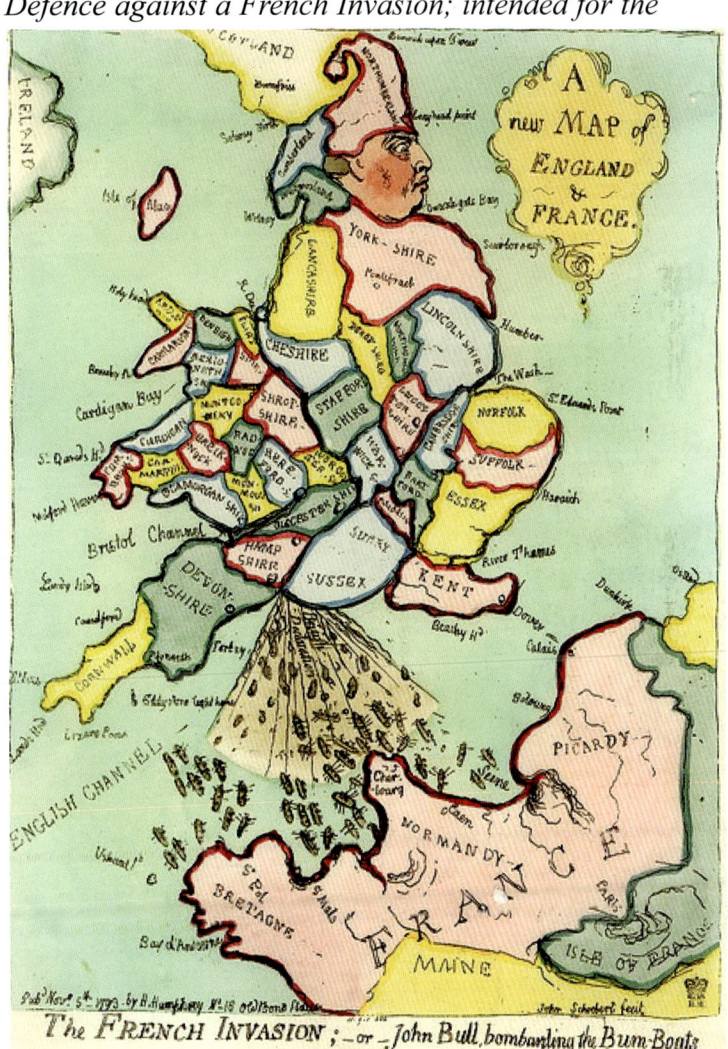

18. Gillray's crudely comic map was published in November 1793, when Britain was facing the threat of invasion by the French Republican Navy.

interest in botany and spent all his free time collecting plants and reading anything he could find on the subject. When he arrived at Oxford and heard that tuition in botany was unavailable, he paid a tutor from Cambridge to deliver a series of lectures at Oxford. Even so, Banks was not given to scholarship or scientific research and failed to acquire a degree. Rather, he became a collector and cataloguer in the fashion of the day.

Banks was only eighteen when his father died, so he had to wait another three years before he came into his enormous inheritance, largely derived from tenant farmers on his estates in Lincolnshire and elsewhere. Soon after, he left Oxford and could have joined his friends on the grand tour of Europe. One such friend was William Perrin, a contemporary at both Eton and Christ Church. Like Banks, Perrin was an only son who had already received his inheritance, including five plantations in Britain's sugar colony of Jamaica and a house in Bloomsbury. Perrin embarked on his Continental tour in early 1767 and spent two years abroad, but he maintained a warm and lively correspondence with Banks throughout his life – an invaluable source because much of it was written while Banks was still young enough to be unguarded about what he wrote.[4]

Meanwhile, Banks took up residence in London where he pursued his reading and botanizing during the day and enjoyed a rich social life at night. He was a member of the fashionable Society for the Encouragement of Arts, Manufactures and Commerce, as were Benjamin Franklin and many other fellows of the Royal Society. One of Banks's favourite haunts was the Reading Room of the British Museum, where he made several important friends including Philip Stephens, Secretary to the Admiralty, and Daniel Solander FRS, a Swedish botanist and one of the museum's librarians. He also met Lord Morton who was a trustee of the museum as well as presiding over the Royal Society.

It was probably late 1765 when Banks learnt that the Royal Society had received Hornsby's paper proposing an expedition to the Pacific in three years time. If he already nursed an ambition to join the expedition, he knew he was poorly qualified. He had no aptitude for mathematics or astronomy and he had never travelled abroad. However, in the New Year, Banks started adding to his list of achievements to bolster his chances.

First, he sought to join the Royal Society as a Fellow, as his grandfather, another Joseph Banks, had been. He was still 22 when he found five sponsors who signed a certificate assuring the membership that he was 'likely (if chosen) to be a valuable member'. After it had been read at ten of the society's meetings, no black ball was cast and on 1 May 1766 Joseph Banks was elected to the Royal Society, in absentia as he was in the mid-Atlantic.

Banks's Etonian friend Constantine Phipps, on half-pay during the peace, had accepted Captain Sir Thomas Adams's offer of a berth on the HMS *Niger*, a frigate which Adams was taking to Newfoundland to patrol its rich fishing grounds. Hearing of this, Banks asked if he could come too. Although a civilian was rarely allowed on a naval vessel, Banks was granted permission, perhaps by the intervention of his old friend the Earl of Sandwich, then between spells as First Lord of the Admiralty.

With his servant, Peter Briscoe, Banks travelled to Plymouth to meet the ship which set sail on 22 April. The rough Atlantic passage was a rude initiation for poor Banks. He suffered his first bout of seasickness, a malady that would always plague him at sea. He wrote to Perrin from Newfoundland describing the voyage as 'one continued puke', but struggled on valiantly.[5] After arriving at St John's, the *Niger* sailed north to Chateau Bay on the Labrador coast where the ship's company was charged with constructing a blockhouse. The building was completed in less than six weeks and a platoon of soldiers was left behind to overwinter in it. Always the data collector, Banks presented his thermometer to their commander, who promised to keep a daily record of the winter temperatures.[6] Their work done, the ship returned briefly to St John's and it was there that Banks happened to meet a navy surveyor named Master James Cook.

The voyage lasted for almost ten months, mostly in North American waters although six weeks were spent in Lisbon on the return journey. When he arrived back in London in late January 1767, Banks could rightly declare the voyage a grand adventure and a great success: he had coped with seasickness and the other discomforts of a long sea voyage; he had survived a month of serious illness; he had been an amiable sailing companion on a naval ship; and he had proved himself as a naturalist by bringing home an impressive collection of specimens, gathered under difficult field conditions.

Banks was thrilled to be back in the clubbable world of London. Before the Newfoundland trip, he had already joined the Society of Antiquaries and the Society for the Arts. Now he celebrated his 24th birthday by attending his first meeting of the Royal Society. Soon after, he joined the broadest secular club in eighteenth-century England, the Freemasons, where his brothers included members of parliament and admirals, savants and lawyers, noblemen and royalty.

Meanwhile, the illicit narrative of Byron's voyage was published in April 1767 and Banks purchased two copies, for himself and Perrin who was then in Paris.[7] The anonymous author – probably Charles Clerke – provided vivid descriptions of the exotic peoples and places in the South Seas, which whetted Banks's appetite, making him even more determined to join the transit expedition the following year.

After a long holiday spent hunting, fishing, botanizing and exploring in Wales, Banks arrived back in London at the end of January 1768 to learn that Alexander Dalrymple had been given the nod to lead the transit voyage. Now Banks escalated his own campaign to win over both joint-venturers. His difficulty was that he lacked the required skills. The Royal Society's purpose in promoting the voyage was primarily astronomical, for which Banks had no aptitude. The government's purpose was political, for which Banks had little interest. However, Banks's persistence, supported by wealth, usually enabled him to achieve his ends, and this was no exception.

First, Banks approached the Royal Society. Although its council was dominated by mathematicians, physicists and astronomers who found it difficult to take plant-collectors seriously, Lord Morton was amenable, possibly because Banks offered to travel as a paying passenger. He contributed a staggering sum, generally thought to be £10,000, although one newspaper reported a figure of £20,000, adding that the donor was to be admired for 'his public spiritedness, in risking his life, and dedicating so great a share of his property in the pursuit of new articles of commerce, or new countries, for the advantage of his own'.[8] Banks's subsidy only added to the public perception that he was the expedition's leader and that the ship's captain was merely his personal driver. The handsome young grandee did nothing to dissuade the press from this view because, in keeping with the social gradations of the eighteenth century, he vaguely believed it himself.

Winning over the Royal Society was the first step. The second was more formidable: Banks had to win over the Admiralty. He applied to Sir Edward Hawke, the First Lord, who gave permission for Mr Joseph Banks FRS to sail as an individual passenger, but insisted there was no room for his band of artists and servants. Not to be defeated, Banks turned to his friend, Philip Stephens, the all-powerful Secretary to the Admiralty and soon reported to Perrin that Stephens 'has done everything we wanted with as much alacrity & spirit as could be wished'.[9] When the *Endeavour* departed five months later, Banks went on board with a party of nine civilians. Only four of them would return.

Banks was delighted by the safe return of Wallis and the *Dolphin* in May. Among her crew was John Gore, the stalwart Virginian who had played a major role in bringing the *Dolphin* home. Now he was given just three months shore leave, and a promotion, before embarking on his third circumnavigation, as the *Endeavour*'s third lieutenant. When they met in London, Banks and Gore found an instant rapport despite the thirteen years separating them. It was undoubtedly Gore, the ship's hunter on both the *Dolphin* voyages, who advised Banks to include two hunting dogs – a spaniel and a greyhound – in his *Endeavour* party.

But it was Banks's friendship with Alexander Dalrymple that was to have the greatest impact on the voyage. The two men were eager to meet, of course, and did so early in the year through mutual friends at the Royal Society. Dalrymple was already popular with the fellows and would be elected a fellow himself before the *Endeavour* returned.

He seized the opportunity to tell Banks all about his research into the size and location of the Southern Continent, giving Banks a copy of the pamphlet he had printed privately relating to discoveries in the South Pacific. He explained that this unpublished version was incomplete as it only contained material relevant to the Southern Continent and therefore omitted everything westward of New Zealand. However, he also gave Banks his more expansive chart of the South Pacific which traced Torres's track passing between New Guinea and New Holland.

Having lost the chance to explore the Pacific himself, Dalrymple needed an agent on board the *Endeavour* to ensure that his theories were respected and properly tested. He hoped that Banks, as the Royal Society's representative and a civilian not bound by naval discipline, would take on that role. Joseph Banks was nobody's stooge, but his staunch and persistent belief in the continent – the antithesis of James Cook's opinion – would become one of Cook's predominant challenges on the *Endeavour*.

For his part, Banks had studied the charts and had no doubt that the voyage would achieve much more than the business of the transit. In the letter written Perrin shortly before embarking he wrote:

> Upon looking at the plan of the voyage, it might easily be seen that this would not be the extent of it. A ship in the midst of the South Seas would never attempt to return against the S[outh] E[ast] Trade. She must therefore necessarily go forwards & visit the Ladrones, some parts of the East Indies, & the Cape of Good Hope … This is the least of the plan. She may do much more, as if you look upon a chart you may see.[10]

Banks must have hoped that honours and praise that would be showered upon him when 'Mr. Banks's *Endeavour* voyage' returned home, having discovered the Southern Continent for England.

11 James Cook: Luck, Patronage and Mercantile Beginnings

Dalrymple's replacement was a 39-year-old warrant officer from Yorkshire named James Cook. Although neither a commissioned officer nor the son of a baronet, he had a prodigious talent for reading the land and navigating the sea. He was also fortunate in being able to align himself with the zeitgeist, riding the tide of imperial rivalry at a time when the remaining blank spaces on the map would be filled in. As a child Cook would run to the summit of Roseberry Topping, the thousand-foot-high crag near his home at Great Ayton. On this airy perch he spent hours surveying the panorama of mountains and valleys; scrutinizing the landscape of plains and woodlands; and, as he gazed across to the North Sea coast with the north-easterly breeze in his face, he would smell the approaching storms and study the wind. In his later explorations, Cook made some of his most significant discoveries from the tops of hills, displaying

19. Aireyholme Farm sits beneath the conical hill of Roseberry Topping, from where young Cook caught his first tantalizing glimpse of the North Sea. Aireyholme was owned by Thomas Skottowe, lord of the manor of Great Ayton, when Cook's father went to work there as the farm manager. The family lived in an estate cottage and Cook worked on the farm when he was not attending school.

d the interaction of sea and shore that he had

elligence, diligence and application. But he was
from a young age, he understood that intelligence
ious young man in eighteenth-century England.
ok was often lucky enough to attract the attention
ance his career.

een written about Cook and there's no need to
so well largely because the furniture in his head
f most of his naval colleagues and a brief account
ghlight those differences.

st future naval officers entered the King's navy as
ut not Cook: he didn't join the Royal Navy until

k, the second of eight children, was born to a poor family in North Yorkshire. His father, James Cook senior, was a day labourer but when young James was seven the family moved to Great Ayton, where Mr Thomas Skottowe of

20. J.M.W. Turner's watercolour depicts the prosperous port of Whitby in north Yorkshire, famous for its ship-building industry and maritime trade, where Cook began his life at sea.

Aireyholme Farm appointed Cook senior as his farm manager. Skottowe took a liking to young James and became his patron, paying for him to attend the Postgate School at Ayton where the lad became proficient at reading, writing and arithmetic. Skottowe also put him to work on the farm where the boy developed a good eye for the land and its products.

At the age of sixteen, Cook left the farm and travelled east to the coast where the village of Staithes fronted the fury of the North Sea. Here he spent a year as a shop-boy with William Sanderson, grocer and haberdasher. Cook's mathematical skills proved useful, but shop-keeping was not for him. So the kindly Sanderson took him over to Whitby, Britain's nursery for seamen.

Here Cook had his next great stroke of luck – and patronage. Whitby was a prosperous port town of some 5000 people and, in 1746, Cook signed a three-year apprenticeship with the 40-old John Walker, a wealthy shipping merchant who remained Cook's mentor and lifelong friend. After completing his apprenticeship, Cook remained with Walker's business for a further six years and, when he wasn't at sea, he lived in Walker's house where he became close friends with the Quaker family.

Walker was sophisticated, educated and humane. A man of integrity, he was also a shrewd businessman, networker, entrepreneur and opportunist. The Walker household was a stark contrast to the rural backwater of Cook's childhood.

While the Walkers' modest, disciplined Quaker way of life suited Cook, he did not adopt their religion. Far from being a pacifist, Cook was to become a military man, a patriot and an imperialist. When his patience was tried too far, he resorted to physical force. Nor was he a particularly religious man. Occasionally, when his ship survived a close shave in dangerous seas, he thanked providence – or luck – by naming the spot 'Providential Passage' (Great Barrier Reef) or 'Providence Island' (Unalaska). But he was certainly no missionary. In the years ahead, neither Cook nor his officers showed any desire to convert the Pacific Islanders.[1]

Those nine years in the merchant navy were the making of Cook. Walker Brothers owned and operated more than 200 ships across the North and Baltic Seas. Its principal business was the all-important coal trade, with its colliers continuously transporting coal from North Country mines down the east coast to London. The firm also had contracts for transporting Baltic timber and occasionally troops and horses. Thus young Cook sailed as far afield as Norway, Holland and Ireland. On the London trips, the colliers sailed up the Thames to Wapping, where the crew was billeted for a week while the coal was unloaded. It was here that he met Elizabeth Batts, the eleven-year-old daughter of the landlord of The Bell, whom he would marry years later. Cook also used this time to discover the city and its people and exchange stories with other seafarers from around the world.

Cook's nautical education with the Walkers combined shipboard training with book learning. For several weeks before he was allowed to go to sea, and later between voyages, Cook joined the other apprentices in John Walker's drawing room for tutorials designed to turn them into merchant mariners. Sometimes the students would walk up to the cliffs surrounding the town and practise using the sextant and other nautical instruments.

Cook's flair for mathematics served him well as he studied long into the night to master a curriculum that included navigation, astronomy, chart-making, geometry, logarithms, cargoes, accounting, note-keeping, ship's business and law.[2]

This experience of the commercial world had a lasting effect on Cook. Under Captain Walker's guidance he learnt about the market economy, about profits and costs, raw materials, local and foreign competition. He understood the importance of the sea and quickly learnt that Britain's prosperity depended on seaborne trade. He appreciated the importance of maritime infrastructure, of deep ports and sea lanes.

At sea, Cook learnt the practical and technical skills of his trade. Here, in the storms and tides and shifting sands of the dangerous North Sea, he became a seafarer. He learnt the three L's – lead, latitude and lookout; the rigging and repairing of his ship; and the care and safety of the crew. He also acquired the skills of leadership and decision-making. By the time of his 26th birthday, when the rumblings of war could be heard from across the Channel and across the Atlantic, James Cook had matured into a confident and driven seafarer. At this point, he resigned from Walker Brothers and volunteered for the Royal Navy.

Cook never said why he left a blossoming career in the merchant service to join the King's navy. But with war looming, the navy had the traditional attractions of pay, honour and loot (in the form of prize money for captured enemy vessels). Cook may also have looked beyond the war and seen the broader opportunities offered to him through employment in the Royal Navy.

12 Battles and Cartography: Cook Surveys the St Lawrence Under Fire

James Cook joined the Navy as an ordinary seaman in June 1755 and was promoted to master's mate within a month. His first ship was HMS *Eagle*, whose lacklustre commander was felicitously replaced in October by the capable and ambitious Captain Hugh Palliser. Five years older than Cook, Palliser was a fellow Yorkshireman and would play a key role in Cook's career and become his lifelong friend and patron.

The Seven Years War (or the French and Indian War as it was known in North America) would not officially begin until the following year, but the continuous friction between Britain and France had already ignited into open warfare. The main aims of the navy at this time was to blockade the French coast and to intercept French ships carrying supplies to or from France's outposts in North America and the East and West Indies. Consequently, Cook's first two years in the navy were mostly spent patrolling the waters around Britain. It was tedious work, until May 1757 when Cook faced enemy fire for the first time.

The *Eagle* was in the Bay of Biscay when it intercepted a French East Indiaman, *Duc d'Aquitaine*, returning from Mauritius. Both ships pounded the other with close-range cannon fire until the French vessel was dismasted, captured and towed to Plymouth, with the English crew relishing the prospect of the prize money that would be divided amongst them. But the *Eagle*'s victory came at a cost. Twelve of Cook's shipmates were dead and 80 were wounded. Cook himself was rewarded with a promotion. He returned to London where he passed his examinations to qualify as a sailing master, which was a senior warrant officer, responsible for the navigation of the ship and for keeping a log book and journal.[1]

This fighting experience, and others that followed, formed Cook as a military man. Like his companions, he viewed France as the enemy and joined in as they boosted their morale by singing patriotic songs making fun of the French and their constant threats (real or imagined) to invade Britain, similar to these lines from 'Heart of Oak' composed a couple of years later:

They swear they'll invade us, these terrible foes;
They frighten our women, our children, and beaus,
But should their flat bottoms in darkness get o'er,
Still Britons they'll find to receive them on shore.

We'll still make them fear, and we'll still make them flee,
And drub 'em on shore as we've drubb'd 'em at sea,
Then cheer up my lads, with one heart let us sing,
Our Soldiers, our Sailors, our Statesmen, our King.

Cook's elevation coincided with another promotion which would have momentous repercussions for the British Empire and for Cook's career. The first two years of the war had gone badly for Britain, but in July 1757 William Pitt the Elder walked through the revolving door of prime ministers and announced his strategy to destroy the French in America.[2] With furious energy and total self-confidence, Pitt persuaded

21. A survey party at work on Isle Madame, Nova Scotia, c.1765.

parliament to fund the fleets and armies he needed to get the job done. James Cook was amongst them and in the early spring of 1758 he made his first Atlantic crossing as master in HMS *Pembroke*.

In May, the *Pembroke* arrived in Halifax, Nova Scotia, the northernmost ice-free port on the Atlantic coast. It was the headquarters of the Royal Navy's North America Station, where Cook would serve for almost five years, without home leave. Within a month, Cook and the *Pembroke* sailed up to Cape Breton Island where they joined the siege of Louisbourg. Here, after weeks of British bombardment, the French finally surrendered on 27 July 1758.

At this point, less than three months after setting foot in America, James Cook had another stroke of luck. A couple of days after the capture of Louisbourg, he was ashore at a nearby cove when he noticed an army officer working at the other end of the beach. The man was manipulating a strange-looking apparatus on a tripod and Cook, ever-curious, approached him. He was Lieutenant Samuel Johannes Holland, an engineer in the Royal Americans, previously of the Dutch artillery. Born and bred in the Netherlands, he had migrated to Britain four years earlier, bringing with him the latest practices of scientific military cartography. It was Holland who had reconnoitered the coast around Louisbourg and drawn up the plan of attack for his commander, James Wolfe.

Holland was the same age as Cook and, like Cook, he was brave, brilliant and ambitious. He was also well-educated, a fine linguist and a talented mathematician. He had a keen eye for talent and gladly explained what he was doing to the eager Yorkshireman. Holland's device was a plane table which allows surveyors to measure angles and plot them directly onto a piece of paper while out in the field. He gave Cook a demonstration, but didn't stop there. Over the following weeks, the generous Dutchman tutored Cook in draughtsmanship and taught him all the best surveying techniques.

It was a turning point in Cook's life. He was hooked. He had learnt some elementary charting skills when he worked for Walker Brothers at Whitby, but now under Holland's instruction he became professional. Cook had found his calling as a nautical survey and cartographer and Holland's instruction was well-timed. From 1759, it was obligatory for captains and masters of naval ships to record useful information whenever they were close to an unfamiliar shore. They were given a remark book which they had to fill with observations of bays and landmarks, shoals and soundings, tides and bearings. This instruction from the Admiralty was prompted by the navy's desperate need for accurate charts of the French and Canadian coasts during the Seven Years War.[3] Master Cook would now supplement his remark book with increasingly proficient charts.

Cook was quick to learn and through the winter months he and Holland worked together to collate and create charts for Britain's next campaign – the conquest of Quebec. Then, in the spring of 1759, Cook was part of the advance reconnaissance party that sailed into the Gulf of St Lawrence and inched its way up the river. Their job was to navigate a safe course to the city of Quebec which lies 360 miles up the St Lawrence River. With the masters of two other vessels, he worked to update their chart and set lines of buoys to mark the channels. They sounded and recorded the labyrinth of reefs, shoals and bars and marked the more dangerous tides and rapids, while dodging constant enemy bombardment. By day, the French fired cannons from the shore, and muskets from their gunboats or 'floating batteries'. By night, they sent flotillas of burning fireships to destroy the British fleet. But by June Cook's job was done and the British Armada of over 200 ships safely made the passage through the notorious channels. The Battle of Quebec took place on 13 September, while the *Pembroke* was anchored off Point Levis on the south bank, opposite Beauport and virtually under the citadel of Quebec.[4]

22. 1759: The Siege of Quebec. At night, the French tried to dislodge the British fleet by sending down fire ships filled with flaming debris.

After the victory at Quebec, Cook was transferred from HMS *Pembroke* to the HMS *Northumberland*, the flagship of Lord Colville, commander-in-chief of the North America Station. Colville encouraged Cook in his hydrographic work and his coastal charts of Nova Scotia and Quebec began to show increasing sophistication, with growing precision and detail. So the budding surveyor was well-prepared when Colville's squadron was suddenly called to Newfoundland.

The French had invaded St John's harbour in mid-1762, forcing the British garrison to surrender. As soon as the news reach London, squadrons were dispatched from England, New York and Halifax. By 18 September, the enemy had fled home to France and St John's was restored to the British. The recapture of St John's was the last battle of the Seven Years War to take place in North America.

Once again, Lady Luck was smiling on Cook. The French attack had brought together three senior men who would have a material impact on Cook's career: Thomas Graves, Lord Colville and Hugh Palliser. In the aftermath of the attack, Graves, the governor of Newfoundland and a naval officer, realized that the lack of reliable charts posed a serious problem for his administration of the island. He wanted to use the few remaining weeks of sunshine to survey Newfoundland's east coast. Lord Colville immediately recommended Master Cook, whose mapping skills had blossomed during the three years he had served under his command. Colville's recommendation was endorsed heartily by Captain Hugh Palliser, who had just arrived with his squadron from England and was able to vouch for his old friend's enterprise and initiative.

Cook spent the next three weeks drawing half a dozen important charts of ports and bays on Newfoundland's east coast. They would put him in a good position as Britain passed from war to peace and the horrors of half-pay.

The war was over, Great Britain had won, and on 7 October 1762 HMS *Northumberland* left St John's and sailed for England. After almost five years in North America, James Cook was going home – to start his new career in the peace-time navy.

13 Cold-War Cartography: Cook Charts Newfoundland and Impresses the Admiralty

Arriving in London on 21 December 1762, Cook set about securing his future. He was fortunate that his skills matched the needs of the time and he had the backing of powerful patrons.

Within two months of his return, Cook married the twenty-year-old Elizabeth Batts whom he had met at The Bell in Wapping while working for Walker Brothers. Elizabeth brought her own strength to their partnership. With Cook so often absent, she bore most of the responsibility for bringing up their children. She was widowed at 37 and the last of her six children died when she was 52. Without partner or descendants, she lived for a further 41 years, until her death 1835, aged 93.

    There was no time for a honeymoon. With the coming of the peace, many ships would be mothballed and their officers put on half-pay or worse. Luckily for Cook, Britain's conquests in North America had delivered boundless territory that now had to be mapped, so there were plenty of jobs for surveyors, both land and marine.

England had undergone a sea change during the five years that Cook was away. In 1760, George II was succeeded by his 22-year-old grandson. George III, the first of

23. Elizabeth Cook (1742–1835) at the age of 81 years.

the Hanoverian monarchs to be born in England, was popular, intelligent, educated and, although widely remembered for going mad, he was remarkably sane for many years. He did not suffer his first bout of illness until 1788.

There were also changes in Whitehall. George Grenville became prime minister on 16 April 1763 and Lord Sandwich was appointed First Lord, for the second time. When the Admiralty Secretary, John Clevland, died in 1764, his deputy Philip Stephens was confirmed as Secretary to the Admiralty, where he remained for the next 36 years. Sandwich and Stephens would become close associates of Cook over the next fifteen years.

Cook was as ambitious as he was talented. He sought not just promotion, but assignments equal to his skills. He knew that such blessings depended on being liked by his senior officers and on patronage from both inside and outside the navy. A week after his marriage, Cook sought and received from Rear Admiral Lord Colville, his commanding officer in North America, a letter of recommendation addressed to the Lords of the Admiralty:

> Mr. Cook, late Master of the *Northumberland,* acquaints me that he has laid before their Lordships all his draughts and observations relative to the river St. Lawrence, part of the coast of Nova Scotia, and of Newfoundland …
>
> I beg leave to inform their Lordships that, from my experience of Mr Cook's genius and capacity, I think him well qualified for the Work he has performed, and for greater undertakings of the same kind. These draughts being made under my own eye, I can venture to say they may be the means of directing many in the right way, but cannot mislead any.[1]

Cook attached Colville's letter to the bundle of his newly finished charts and delivered them to the Admiralty Office. He hoped that Stephens – and perhaps the Lords Commissioners – would agree with Colville that he was qualified for 'greater undertakings', and in fact Cook's first great undertaking was already brewing at the peace negotiations in Paris.

The war had cost France all her territory on the North American mainland, but the Duc de Choiseul made it a precondition to peace that France retain her fishing rights in the North Atlantic. He also demanded a neutral port to replace Louisbourg as an 'abri' or shelter where French fishermen could dry their fish. Choiseul's demands were violently opposed by William Pitt, who was concerned about more than the lucrative fishing trade. Expertise in fisheries increased sea power: the Grand Banks fishery was a nursery for French sailors and, without access to it, Choiseul's campaign to rebuild France's shattered navy would be severely curtailed. Pitt famously declared that he would rather lose the use of his right hand than allow France back into the fishery.[2]

But Pitt was overruled by a more generous cabinet. Choiseul got his concessions, and Britain's sovereignty over the island of Newfoundland was infringed. France retained her fishing rights on the 'Treaty Shore' in the north of the island and gained as its abri the tiny islands of St Pierre and Miquelon, which lie Newfoundland's south coast, separated by a strait about twelve miles wide.

Aware of the danger of having this French outpost on its North American doorstep, Britain insisted that France undertook 'not to fortify the said islands; to erect no buildings upon them but merely for the convenience of the fishery; and to keep upon them a guard of fifty men only for the police'. This was pie in the sky, as the Secretary of State, Lord Egremont, recognized when he bemoaned the 'inconvenience or disadvantage' of having a French base in such close proximity to His Majesty's Northern Colonies.[3]

The islands remained under British control until the official handover, set at three months after ratification of the treaty on 10 March. It was a small window, but the Admiralty was determined to survey and chart the islands while Britain still had the chance. It wanted to know every secret inlet where a French frigate or smuggler's lugger could hide. The governor of Newfoundland, Thomas Graves, was charged with organizing the survey and, thereafter, enforcing the provisions of the treaty.

Graves wrote to the Board of Trade, the body responsible for making the fishery and the colony economically viable, preferably with a profit for the Crown. Graves asked for funding for a small survey vessel and nominated his new friend, James Cook, as the surveyor. The Board of Trade approved and forwarded Graves's request to the Admiralty. There was a fortnight's delay due to a ministerial reshuffle, but on 19 April 1763, James Cook was formally appointed as Surveyor to Newfoundland 'by command of their Lordships [signed] Ph. Stephens'. After farewelling his pregnant wife, Cook departed England on 15 May.

Cook's first assignment in Newfoundland had all the makings of a French farce. When he arrived on the coast, he quickly transferred to a waiting vessel, HMS *Tweed* under Captain Charles Douglas, and sailed across to the harbour at St Pierre. An hour later, an international crisis erupted when the new governor designate, Captain François-Gabriel d'Angeac, arrived with his 200-strong complement of soldiers, merchants, fishermen and their families. The deadline for the handover had passed five days before and d'Angeac demanded to go ashore immediately to claim possession. But Douglas had been ordered to stall the French while Cook completed the survey. For three weeks, the British officers kept the Frenchmen entertained aboard their ship with songs, games and brandy while Cook surveyed the intricate coastline of St Pierre. As soon as that survey was finished, St Pierre was handed over to d'Angeac and Cook set to work on Miquelon. The entire job was completed by the end of July, when the islands were finally ceded to France. Afterwards, Douglas wrote to the Admiralty asking for reimbursement of £50 for the 'extraordinary expenses' he had incurred. The Admiralty was happy to pay him.[4]

Cook stored his sketches, notes and calculations until he found time to make a finished chart of the islands. For now, wanting to make the most of the remaining weeks of summer, he returned to St John's for his next assignment. Although Cook was still officially attached to the *Tweed*, Graves now presented him with a small schooner which Graves had renamed *Grenville* after the prime minister.

The concessions made in the Treaty of Paris inevitably led to disputes at different places around Newfoundland and over the next five years Cook was at the front line of a new cold war as the governor directed him from one trouble spot to the next. Now, Graves sent him up to the northern tip of the island where he was keen to stop the illicit trade in furs and whalebone between the French fishermen and the mainland Indians.[5]

Cook spent the next few weeks surveying the main ports on the Treaty Shore, namely Quirpon, Noddy and Croque Harbours. Then he sailed across the Strait of Belle Isle to the mainland coast of Labrador, where he charted York Harbour (Chateau Bay). It was a superb effort. When the weather closed in in late September, Cook packed up his instruments and sailed back to St John's and then home to England, Elizabeth and his new son James.

Thus a regular, seasonal pattern was established. Cook spent the summer surveying the Newfoundland coast until ice made the work untenable. Then he returned to London for winter, enjoying domestic life and converting his surveys and notes into publishable charts and observations. But his work didn't stop there. Cook's winters in London quickly became as busy as his summers in Canada.

Cook's impressive maps of a strategically important island proved an invaluable means of keeping his name in front of senior crown officers and decision-makers in England, including those at the Admiralty and at the Navy Office in Seething Lane.

Cook gave a particularly fine manuscript copy of his chart of St Pierre and Miquelon to the King. It was the perfect gift. George III had a passion for map-collecting. His tutor had taught him that geography was the science of princes and he understood the political and military importance of his growing collection. Within months of his coronation, he purchased Buckingham House to use as his family home in London and promptly added a magnificent four-room library to the south wing. Its manuscript maps were often more detailed and accurate than other printed maps. This cartographic treasure trove was open to the King's admirals and generals, civil servants and scholars. When John Adams, the future president of the United States, was admitted to the King's library in 1783, he marvelled at the 'Maps, charts, &c. of all his dominions in the four quarters of the world, and models of every fortress in his empire'.[6]

The place names on Cook's charts also provided an excellent opportunity to flatter politicians. Finalizing his plan of York Harbour in Labrador, Cook honoured the minister who had appointed him with Port Sandwich and labelled the arms of the inlet: Grenville Harbour, Temple Bay and Pitts Harbour after the prime minister and his powerful cousinhood. On his map of Quirpon Harbour he named its most important island Graves Island and recommended it for a fort. When he delivered his finished charts to the Admiralty, he was sorry to learn that Graves's term as governor had ended, but was delighted that his replacement was to be his old friend, Hugh Palliser.

Cook's reputation was growing in Whitehall. Just before Christmas, Lord Egmont, who had replaced Sandwich as First Lord, received leaked information from Paris. It warned that the French were planning a resumption of Anglo–French hostilities and 'that Newfoundland should furnish the pretext' for the next war.[7] Egmont promptly called Cook into his office to discuss the sweeping claims being made by the French ambassador.[8] Not many warrant officers are consulted by First Lords of the Admiralty.

The French were making two claims. First, they insisted that they had exclusive rights to Treaty Shore and British fishermen were not allowed there. The second claim concerned the length of the Treaty Shore. The Treaty stated that its western terminus was Point Riche on the island's Northern Peninsula. However, the French argued that 'Point Riche' was really 'Cape Ray' at the south-west corner, so that their fishing rights extended down the entire west coast.

With Egmont's encouragement, Cook turned detective, searching London for old maps and records containing scraps of evidence about historical fishing practices round the island. He also contacted West Country merchants whose families had fished in Newfoundland for decades.[9] After collating all the information, he produced the remarkable map shown in Figure 24.[10] The most interesting aspect of the map is its political content. Cook neatly sets out the British case concerning the Treaty Shore by using different colours to delineate the zones in contention. He uses grey to show the area 'Where the French are allowed to fish' under the Treaty, while the areas where the English had historically fished prior to the Treaty are shown in both red ('English Fisheries for many years') and blue ('English fisheries of late years').

Thanks to Cook's map and other evidence, the Board of Trade was able to rebut the French claims. It proved that the Treaty Shore only extended a few miles down the west coast, and the French had to share that shore with the English fishermen. The need for accurate maps of this shore was now more urgent than ever, so Governor Palliser would direct Cook to continue his work on the north coast when he returned for his second survey season.

In the summer of 1764, Cook returned to Newfoundland as master and commander of the *Grenville*, an appointment Palliser had secured for him while wintering in England. Cook was no longer on secondment, but commander of his own ship and its crew of eighteen men.[11] When he arrived at the northernmost point of the island,

24. The most interesting aspect of Cook's 1763 sketch of Newfoundland is its political content, indicated by the two legends. The first legend, inserted below the title, lists the four colour washes used on the chart – red, blue, grey and yellow – with their meanings explaining the French and English zones. The second legend at the north-east corner summarizes the history of English settlements and fishing practices. Cook evidently knew that his chart would be used in the government's negotiations with France over fishing rights. Courtesy of the National Museum of the Royal Navy.

he showed his pleasure in his new command by naming the nearby inlet 'Cook's Harbour'.[12] Cook rarely sought such immortalization. The few occasions when he did name a place after himself were in celebration of a personal triumph.

His pleasure was short-lived. A few days later Cook took the ship's cutter to make some measurements on shore at a place he would name Unfortunate Cove. Suddenly, a large powder-horn exploded in his hand and 'shattered it in a terrible manner'.[13] His right forearm was a gory mess, with the hand almost torn off, the wrist gashed and his thumb dangling by a tendon. The *Grenville* did not carry a surgeon and Cook might have lost his hand, but his luck held. The crew took Cook back to Noddy Harbour where they found a French fishing vessel which had a surgeon on board. The young man was brought to the *Grenville* where he cleaned, stitched and dressed the wound with remarkable skill. Cook was laid up for a month, but the Frenchman had saved his hand – and his career. Cook was left with a permanent scar between the thumb and forefinger reaching as far as the wrist. This distinctive mark would identify his remains after he was killed in Hawaii fifteen years later.

As soon as the wound had healed sufficiently, Cook doubled back to resume his survey on the west coast down to Ferolle Point. Here he finished for the season and, after calling at St John's, Cook returned to England in his own ship for the first time. He arrived home in mid-December – on the same day that his second son, Nathaniel, was born.

In addition to his charts, Cook took on a much larger project that winter when he persuaded the Navy Board to allow the *Grenville* to be completely overhauled. Not only was she given a new bottom, but the rigging was altered to change her from a schooner into a brig. The work was done at Deptford, where Cook could keep an eye on it and supervise the loading of stores with his characteristic care and attention to detail.

The operation took three months and in April 1765, Cook embarked on his first westbound Atlantic crossing in his own ship. Like most of the fishing fleet making the annual voyage to the Grand Banks, Cook took the direct route from Land's End to Cape Race, the most practical of the westbound routes and much shorter than the southern route. On his first transatlantic crossing back in 1758 as master on the *Pembroke*, Cook's convoy took the traditional southern route – 'head south till the butter melts and then turn right'. It was designed to avoid the harsh conditions of the higher latitudes but was very time-consuming. The convoy ventured almost to the tropics on a voyage lasting 72 days.[14]

Cook made three westward crossings in the *Grenville* and reduced the time to just 23 days, sailing against the combined forces of the prevailing westerly winds and the North Atlantic Current and Gulf Stream. It was an impressive display of speed and efficiency, which would not have gone unnoticed by the navy's top brass.

By the time Cook arrived in Newfoundland in June 1765 for his next survey season, Palliser had received intelligence that the French on St Pierre and Miquelon were violating the terms of the Treaty. French warships had been seen at the islands and there were plans to establish a military and naval base. Furthermore, Frenchmen were not only fishing illegally in the surrounding waters, but they were landing on

Newfoundland's south coast, cutting timber and engaging in contraband trade. Palliser protested vigorously to the resident French administrator, but he knew that the real solution was to send British warships to patrol the waters and to encourage English fisherman into the area. None of this could happen until he had reliable charts of the dangerous and heavily indented coastline. So Palliser asked Cook to suspend his survey of the north coast until he had surveyed the south coast opposite the French islands. No doubt the two friends had some sympathy for William Pitt's objection to allowing enemy occupation of offshore islands.

Consequently, Cook took the *Grenville* to the Burin Peninsula and surveyed west around its southern tip. Here he watched for suspicious activity over on the French islands that lay just twelve miles away, but saw nothing. The ship kept moving west, exploring dozens of narrow inlets, until they reached Hermitage Bay on 11 September. The weather was closing in and it was time to go home.

After his third survey season, Cook returned to London in December 1765. And then, in late February, he learnt that the Royal Society was proposing a joint venture with the Admiralty to send an expedition to the South Pacific to observe the transit of Venus. It was just the sort of epic undertaking that Cook craved, but to gain special notice and preferment he had to attract the attention of the organizers. He was well known at the Admiralty, of course, but unknown to the fellows of the Royal Society. He decided to demonstrate his astronomical proficiency by observing some other predicted celestial phenomenon. Cook had never done such a thing before, but he was good at self-education.

Searching in *Leadbetter's Almanac*, he found that a solar eclipse was due on 5 August 1766. By then, he would be back in Newfoundland and, while it was not strictly relevant to his survey work, he would make time to observe the eclipse while he was there. To get the best result he needed to conduct the observation on land and so he wrote to the Admiralty asking for a tent, which Stephens approved.[15] Cook also took a portable astronomical quadrant fitted with a telescopic sight, made by London's famous instrument-maker, John Bird.

In June 1766, Cook continued his survey of Newfoundland's south coast until, on 23 July, with the eclipse day approaching, Cook left the foggy coast and sailed to the nearby Burgeo Islands where erected the tent, tested his instruments and waited for Tuesday 5 August. The fog had followed him but luckily it cleared on the last day and Cook was able to observe the eclipse of the sun. He carefully recorded his calculations in his notebook and stored it safely before sailing back to the coast to continue the survey. In late September he finished charting the south coast and, with the season over, the *Grenville* returned to St John's.

Entering the harbour on Monday 27 October, they found the *Niger* moored there. Although it would sail for England the following afternoon, it overlapped with the

Grenville for at least 30 hours.[16] While there is no record of Cook actually meeting Banks on this occasion, ships' officers would normally meet to exchange news and mail. If Cook mentioned his observation of the eclipse, it may have been Banks who suggested that Cook should send a report of this astronomical feat to the Royal Society for publication. The two men could not have come from more different backgrounds, but it's possible a chance encounter in the bleak little fishing port laid the foundations of one of history's splendid partnerships.

Cook returned to London in November 1766 only to learn that that his contemporary, Captain Wallis, had departed for New Zealand three months earlier. With ever-steelier resolve and in a bold move for a warrant officer, Cook sent a paper with his observations to the Royal Society. Here it was read to the fellows by the astronomer, Dr John Bevis FRS, who prefaced his remarks by describing Cook as 'a good mathematician and very expert in his business' and noted that his calculations of the eclipse compared most favourably with those of Professor Hornsby himself. His paper was published in the next edition of their prestigious journal, *Philosophical Transactions*.[17] Thus Cook had made his name known to the power-brokers at the Royal Society. They would recognize it when appointing its assistant astronomer the following year. Cook had placed himself in the spotlight and, as he sailed for his fifth survey season – his tenth summer in Canada – he may have hoped it would be his last.

In May 1767, the *Grenville* returned to the south-west corner of Newfoundland. Palliser wanted him to complete the survey of the dangerous west coast and also investigate reports of illicit French activity in the Humber River valley.[18] Cook spent the next four months on this program and, in September, with the weather closing in, he returned St John's to make repairs, then sailed for London.

If Cook had been hoping to command the transit voyage, he must have been disappointed to learn in December that the Royal Society had recommended Dalrymple for this post. Nevertheless, he started preparing for his eleventh season in North America and, as the Admiralty records show, as late as 9 April 1768, Mr Cook wrote requesting a new surgeon's mate for the *Grenville*.[19]

But this time Cook was not returning to the North Atlantic: he was off to the South Pacific. He probably learned of his appointment in late April and by mid-May the Royal Society councillors were extending him the courtesy title of 'Captain', as afforded any rank in command of a vessel. However, the official announcement was not made until 25 May when Master Cook was commissioned First Lieutenant and given command of HMB *Endeavour*.

As luck would have it, Captain Wallis and the *Dolphin* had arrived home five days earlier and announced his discovery of fifteen Pacific islands, including Tahiti. The tricky question as to where the *Endeavour* was going to observe the transit of Venus was now answered.

14 'Greater objects': The Admiralty's Instructions to Cook

After Sir Edward Hawke vetoed Dalrymple's appointment, the Admiralty had to move quickly to find a suitable replacement. The collier chosen by Dalrymple had been brought into the royal dockyards at Deptford to be renamed and it was important that her refit and provisioning be supervised by her commander.

No doubt, as many historians have asserted, it was Philip Stephens who recommended Cook for command of the *Endeavour*.[1] In the twelve years since Cook had joined the navy, there had been nine changes of First Lord at the Admiralty, but Stephens had been there throughout – first as senior clerk, then second secretary and now sole secretary.

Stephens had worked closely with Cook through the five years of the Newfoundland survey. The two men had become friends and there is anecdotal evidence that Cook was a frequent visitor to Stephens's home in Fulham.[2] From his own observations and the reports of others, Stephens knew that through war and peace, Cook had proved himself a courageous and consummate sailor. He had displayed leadership, judgment and initiative. He also had the qualities that make for success – ambition, application, a capacity to take risk, and luck.

More importantly, Cook had displayed another talent, rare among his colleagues: due to his experience at Walker Brothers, he had developed commercial acumen. His annotations and sailing directions are full of commercial judgments, recommending one region for its economic potential, while dismissing another as having nothing to offer. His notes and charts provide an inventory of Newfoundland's natural resources – for the boatbuilding industry, he identifies timber stands of pine, birch, witch hazel and spruce; for the fishing industry, rivers and lakes with salmon and trout, and deep waters with cod, seals and whales; for the fur industry, beavers and otters; for the meat industry, herds of deer and wild geese and ducks. He notes the quality of the soil and even kept his eye out for coal, later reporting that he had found coal deposits in Newfoundland.[3] Even his childhood as a farmer was reflected in his frequent references to 'improving' the places he discovered with seeds and domesticated animals.

Stephens valued Cook's competitive, entrepreneurial instinct, acquired during his years in the seaborne coal trade and the Baltic timber trade.[4] He also believed that Cook's understanding of the geopolitical importance of his work in Newfoundland fitted him for the Admiralty's broader agenda of spearheading Britain's imperial thrust into the Pacific.

Cook was the obvious choice to lead the expedition and Stephens proposed him to the Admiralty Board. No doubt his nomination was supported by Cook's highly placed patrons and friends including Admirals Colville and Saunders, Captain (later Admiral) Thomas Graves and Governor Hugh Palliser. Cook was not the Royal Society's first choice, but he was the Admiralty's.

Next Stephens turned his mind to drafting the instructions for the voyage. He decided to divide them into two sections. The first document would deal with the voyage to Tahiti, while the second would deal with the post-transit agenda.[5] This was not unusual. Separate sets of instructions were useful when a functionary in a foreign port asked too many questions or when a mutinous crew demanded to know when they were heading home. Any document considered too secret could always be thrown overboard.

Both sections of the Admiralty's formal instructions to Cook were marked 'secret', but their broad intent was widely known around London. By mid-August, there were numerous newspaper reports, such as:

> The Gentlemen who are to sail in a few days for George's Land [Tahiti], the newly discovered island in the Pacific Ocean, with the intention to observe the transit of Venus, are likewise, we are told, to attempt some new discoveries in that unknown tract above the latitude 40.[6]

This is an accurate, summary of the *Endeavour*'s formal itinerary. On the first leg, Cook was ordered to arrive at Tahiti 'at least a month or six weeks before the 3rd day of June next' for the scientific purpose of recording the transit. When this was finished, he was to leave Tahiti and head directly south to latitude 40°S, in the hope of bumping into the Southern Continent where he might be able to discover and annex valuable posts on it. If he failed to find it, he was to turn west to New Zealand and check to see if that country was joined to the continent.

The most interesting thing about these written instructions is that they stop in New Zealand. In its previous instructions to Byron and Wallis, who were both senior to Cook, the Admiralty suggested specific routes and ports of call for the homeward leg. Yet this is conspicuously absent from Cook's formal instructions: he was merely told to 'judge the most eligible way of returning home'. But it is unlikely that the Admiralty would leave a newly minted junior officer in a taxpayer-funded vessel without any suggestions as to how best to exploit his unique position in the southwest corner of the Pacific.

There were three possible routes home from New Zealand. The first was to double back to Cape Horn and continue searching for the elusive continent in the higher latitudes of the Pacific. The second was to sail directly west to the Cape of Good Hope, keeping south of New Holland. The third was to go north around New Holland, through the Dutch East Indies, to the Cape of Good Hope. For the Admiralty's strategists, the third possibility had the most appeal. At long last, an English ship would be perfectly positioned to examine the east coast of New Holland and its outliers. But Philip Stephens was not inclined to put such a plan in writing.

In 1889, the historian George Barton, brother of Australia's first prime minister, questioned why the Admiralty did not give instructions 'to Captain Cook, or to some of his contemporaries, to explore those portions of the coast-line [of New Holland] which had not been visited by the Dutch'.[7] It is indeed astonishing that through all Cook's three Pacific voyages, the Admiralty's instructions never mention 'New Holland' or 'Van Diemen's Land'. This seems odd enough in respect of the *Endeavour* voyage (1768–71), when the ship was sent to the Pacific by way of Cape Horn. It is odder still in respect of Cook's second (1772–75) and third (1776–80) voyages when his route to the Pacific was reversed. On these occasions, Cook was instructed to sail round the Cape of Good Hope then follow the southern route under Australia to refresh in New Zealand. Why didn't the Admiralty order Cook, as he brushed past Van Diemen's Land, to make a brief detour to clarify some of the outstanding issues of the *Endeavour* voyage?

Undoubtedly, the Admiralty did issue Cook with instructions for the third leg of the *Endeavour* voyage, but they were oral instructions, not written. Documents are easily copied and leaked and the Admiralty had no wish to alert the Dutch, the Spanish, the French or the East India Company to Britain's investigation of the western Pacific.

Whatever the rules of previous decades, by the mid-eighteenth century the title of first discoverer was no longer regarded as a sufficient legal basis for the acquisition of territory. Even the symbolic act of taking possession was, by itself, inadequate according to Emmerich Vattel, a leading international lawyer of the time:

> All men have an equal right to things which have not yet come into the possession of anyone, and these things belong to the person who first takes possession. When, therefore, a Nation finds a country uninhabited and without an owner, it may lawfully take possession of it, and after it has given sufficient signs of its intention in this respect, it may not be deprived of it by another Nation. In this way navigators setting out upon voyages of discovery and bearing with them a commission from their sovereign, when coming across islands or other uninhabited lands, have taken possession of them in the name of their Nation; and

this title has usually been respected, provided actual possession has followed shortly after.[8]

Vattel went on to explain that discovery alone only established a 'ius ad occupationem', a privilege to take possession by subsequent, effective occupation, in other words, merely an 'inchoate title'.[9] If effective occupation did not occur within a reasonable time, then the temporary bar expires and other States are free to occupy the territory. Consequently, without a program for planting distant garrisons, important discoveries would be better protected by concealment than by publicized annexation.

New Holland already had its European proprietors. For more than two centuries, the great powers had developed an appetite for parcelling out the non-European world amongst themselves. One of the earliest examples of this was the Treaty of Tordesillas (1494), with its line of demarcation running down through the Atlantic Ocean. No one had much idea where the relevant meridian fell, let alone its ante-meridian, but Spain now believed it owned eastern New Holland, while Portugal owned the west. Meanwhile, other rules had evolved as other nations made discoveries and, in the seventeenth century, the Dutch had discovered and named New Holland. The British Admiralty had no wish to offend any of these nations in a period of uneasy peace. They would be told all they needed to know about the trip when Cook returned home.

Although the precise terms of the Admiralty's oral instructions are unknown, Cook later acknowledged that he had known his homeward route for a long time. During his second voyage, he explained that the reason he had failed to chart New Zealand's south-west coast during the *Endeavour* voyage was:

> [I]n my last Voyage I had other and more greater objects in view, viz. the discovery of the whole Eastern Coast of New Holland.[10]

Cook was not the first European sent to examine the east coast of New Holland. Abel Tasman had been ordered to survey it on his second voyage in 1644. William Dampier intended to explore it in 1699. Dr John Campbell had urged the East India Company or the government to investigate it in 1744. And the French government had ordered Bougainville to chart it in 1766. None of them had achieved this task. Apart from whatever commercial and strategic prizes New Holland offered, completing its map would bring glory to the surveyor and to his nation.

The itinerary of the third leg of the voyage was not the only item omitted from the Admiralty's formal instructions. Another was the Admiralty's requirement of cartographic secrecy.

15 'Close and secret in his intentions': Cook, the Admiralty, and Cartographic Secrecy

Satellite imagery and aerial photography have put an end to the age-old practice of cartographic secrecy. For centuries, merchant trading companies and governments tried to suppress geographic knowledge for political or commercial reasons. When King Louis XV's hydrographer, Jacques-Nicolas Bellin, published his collection of sea charts in *Le Neptune Francoise* in 1753, the water depths near the French coast were marked as four or five fathoms. But when Admiral Hawke took soundings during the Seven Years War, prior to his magnificent victory in Quiberon Bay, he found depths of thirteen to fifteen fathoms. The London newspapers roared indignantly: 'Such art do the French use to keep other nations ignorant of their coasts'.[1]

Years earlier, in 1617, the Dutch government censored Willem Blaeu's map of the Strait of Le Maire, when it intervened in a commercial dispute. This alternative route to the Pacific had just been discovered by the Dutch navigators, Schouten and Le Maire, on behalf of the Australische Compagnie, a business rival of the Dutch East India Company (VOC). Their ship had tracked south around Cape Horn on Tierra del Fuego (which they proved to be an island and not the Southern Continent) and, because their route bypassed the Strait of Magellan, it lay outside the limits of the VOC's monopoly zone. Not surprisingly, legal proceedings followed and the government was persuaded to suppress the information. However, the injunction was lifted after twelve months and Blaeu published his new map in 1618.[2]

Earlier still, Queen Isabella of Spain built her colonial headquarters, the Casa de Contratación, in the port of Seville. It became the centre of imperial control over Spanish activities in the New World and housed all the official and secret geographic data coming in from Spain's colonies and expeditions. Returning captains were obliged to come here to deposit their maps of discoveries and new trade routes, then swear not to disclose the information to foreigners or competitors.

Secrecy leads to disinformation by falsification. Maps were published with false geographic information in order to deceive the enemy, as the map historian, J.B. Harley, wrote:

> Throughout the history of modern cartography in the West ... there have been numerous instances of where maps have been falsified, of where they have been censored or kept secret, or of where they have surreptitiously contradicted the rules of their proclaimed scientific status.[3]

The success of such falsification depended on the seductive nature of maps, well described by the geographer J.K. Wright:

> The trim, precise, and clean-cut appearance that a well drawn map presents lends it an air of scientific authenticity that may or may not be deserved.[4]

It was this 'air of scientific authenticity' that made maps such useful political tools. Unlike other documents, maps were usually trusted to be neutral, accurate, authoritative. The reader assumed that the navigator and mapmaker laboured for the common good, producing a factual statement about geographical reality and scientific truth. Yet while the very idea of falsifying a map was met with outrage in gentlemen's clubs and scientific academies, it was seen as a useful tactic in government departments.

During the Second World War, the London Controlling Section concocted false maps and documents to spread disinformation in Operation Mincemeat, Operation Bodyguard and several other hoaxes. One of the most notorious deceptions was a 'secret map' showing Hitler's plans for South America which was given to Franklin Roosevelt. In October 1941, Roosevelt used it to generate domestic support for the Allies, before the Japanese attack on Pearl Harbor ended the argument. The map was supposedly confiscated from a German courier in Buenos Aires, but in fact it had been either forged or doctored by the British Security Coordination unit based in the Rockefeller Center in New York. Roosevelt may not have known of the deceit, but in any event he was political and pragmatic, famously saying: 'I am perfectly willing to mislead and tell untruths if it will help win the war'.[5]

The planting of false maps and documents has long been a legitimate *ruse de guerre*, but such Machiavellian arts were not confined to wartime, particularly in an age when there was very little peacetime. Cartographic secrecy was a weapon for all seasons, to be used against all rivals, political and commercial. Since Elizabethan times, the Crown has suppressed the publication of new geographic knowledge. When Francis Drake sailed on his voyage round the world in 1577, he was given clear instructions that 'none shall make any charts or descriptions of the said voyage'.[6] Furthermore, all charts made or captured from foreigners had to be delivered to the Lords of Her Majesty's Privy Council.[7] Two hundred years later, the Admiralty's instructions to Captain Cook were almost identical.

This is hardly surprising for a nation aspiring to become, and remain, the supreme maritime power. Britain is a small island whose lifeblood was seaborne trade along the world's superhighways of the high seas. British merchants were constantly searching for new trade routes, vying for distant markets and commodities. Before the transoceanic canals of Suez and Panama were built, voyages beyond the almost landlocked Atlantic – to the Far East and the Pacific – were protracted, expensive and dangerous. The early navigators left home with crude or fictitious maps of the world beyond the capes. They returned with newly constructed charts incorporating their hard-won discoveries of coasts, bays, islands, latitudes, longitudes, winds, tides, currents, depths, reefs, gulfs, ice, river mouths, capes and straits. Much of this was eventually published in new maps of the world, expanding the geographic knowledge of humanity and bringing glory to the discoverer and prestige to his nation.

However, diligent navigators returned with much more than just new sweeping coastlines to fill the ocean void. They brought precious intelligence of new sea lanes, shortcuts, insularity, deep harbours, havens of shelter and refreshment: all of it vital for wartime battle and peacetime trade. The British Admiralty had no wish to advertise these critical strategic features until it had worked out a scheme to control them.[8] If Cook discovered a valuable port or channel on the far side of the globe, how could he protect it from the French, short of setting up a permanent military occupation? Secrecy was the only option.

Is it unthinkable that the British Admiralty would order the concealment of discoveries? No. Everyone does it. The royal and corporate shipowners who dispatched the early Spanish, Portuguese and Dutch navigators tried desperately to hide their important discoveries. When NASA sent Apollo 11 to the moon in 1969, it had a fairly open policy about releasing information to the public, not unlike the Admiralty's decision to publish the authorized version of Cook's expeditions. The thinking was that the 'appropriate dissemination of information' would enhance the nation's prestige, boost the government's popularity and encourage taxpayer support for NASA's programs. Even so, Neil Armstrong and his colleagues were NASA employees and were therefore prevented by the National Aeronautics and Space Act of 1958 from revealing classified information, on pain of prosecution. Sensitive material was controlled to protect 'national security', a broad term which extended to economic and political concerns as well as military matters.

In the days when James Cook served in the navy, Britain's Official Secrets Act was still a century away. But it is likely that Cook was required to swear an oath of secrecy before sailing on the *Endeavour*. According to Francis Drake's contemporary, Admiral William Monson, such oaths had been required of seventeenth-century explorers:

> The masters must take an oath to use their best endeavours to advance the voyage,

and
> to keep secret the journal. The plats and cards [charts and sea cards], and all other writings that concern their navigation, must be taken from them and the company at their coming home and sealed up to present to his Majesty.[9]

The continuing need for an oath of secrecy became starkly apparent when, just three months before the *Endeavour* sailed, Samuel Wallis arrived home with the momentous news of his discovery of Tahiti. According to the French ambassador in London, Comte de Guerchy, the *Dolphin*'s crew was taken before a judge of the navy and sworn to secrecy, while the officers took a similar oath at the Admiralty in Whitehall.[10]

Of course, Cook was required to keep a journal on the *Endeavour* voyage. The Admiralty's instructions demanded that he make 'a full account of your Proceedings in the whole Course of your Voyage' and deliver it to the Admiralty Office immediately on returning to England. And of course, the Admiralty's practice of confiscating journals applied to Cook just as it had to Drake. Cook was ordered to maintain secrecy on his return to England by 'taking care before you leave the Vessel to demand from the Officers and Petty Officers the Log Books and Journals they may have Kept, and to seal them up for our inspection and enjoyning them, and the whole Crew, not to divulge where they have been until they shall have Permission so to do'.[11]

Fortunately, Cook hardly needed to swear an oath because he was, by nature, as secretive as the Admiralty could have hoped for. George Forster, the young naturalist who accompanied his father on Cook's second voyage, complained, 'nothing could be more dejecting, than the entire ignorance of our destination, which, without apparent reason was constantly kept a secret to every person in the ship'.[12]

Forster's complaint was echoed by John Elliott, a young midshipman, who wrote that Cook 'only smiled and said nothing, for he was close and secret in his intentions at all times, that not even his first Lieutenant knew, when we left a place, where we should go to next'.[13]

On the face of it, it seems impossible to reconcile Cook's obsession with accuracy with a deliberately fabricated chart. He was a professional, ambitious, curious hydrographer. His whole *raison d'être* was, apparently, to record his observations accurately. However, two imperatives would override this mission: obedience and patriotism.

The Naval Articles demanded obedience. All officers were required to show 'implicit obedience' to their superiors and obey every order and discharge every duty 'with the utmost zeal and alacrity'.[14] Failure to comply with Admiralty orders could mean missing out on promotion or the loss of pay. Neither of these penalties ever threatened Cook. He was the son of a farm labourer who venerated the system which had given him such extraordinary opportunities. He was a servant of the Crown, a naval employee. For most of his naval career, at least until the end of his first Pacific voyage, he obeyed his instructions meticulously, whether he was writing up nautical directions, sketching a chart or sailing to a particular destination. It was only after he had followed his instructions to the letter, that he allowed himself to venture beyond that prescribed point.

Unlike Cook, some of his more cavalier contemporaries ignored their instructions.

Dampier didn't sail south along the east coast of New Holland because he was afraid of the cold. Bougainville didn't explore it because he was afraid of the reef and the voice of God. Instructed to sail north to seek out the Northwest Passage, John Byron sailed west across the Pacific to Indonesia. Wallis didn't investigate the Southern Continent because he was bilious. And when the Comte de Lapérouse doubled the Horn in January 1786, he was instructed to sail west to explore New Holland, but turned north to Alaska instead. If Lapérouse had obeyed his orders, his French ships would have arrived in Australia at least a year before Britain's First Fleet. Cook, however, was the embodiment of obedience, and he sailed exactly where he was told to.

Britain and France were engaged in a struggle for maritime, colonial and commercial supremacy. In the years following the Seven Years War, the theatre for that struggle moved to the Pacific. While some men of science may have thought that scientific truth transcended national boundaries, Cook did not. For more than a decade – in war and peace – he had been fighting the French and his weapon of choice was maps. Where professional accuracy conflicted with the national interest, the latter prevailed.

Consequently, most of the censorship of Cook's journals and charts was not done by any Admiralty officer, but by Cook himself. He concealed important discoveries, as well as some of his actions and motives, by omission or by falsification. Cook's self-censorship is clearly evident in the erasures, deletions, insertions, overwriting, blank spaces, contradictions and fabrications contained in his own journals and charts. It is these that are the focus of the later chapters of this book.

16 Cook Does his Homework: Abel Tasman, Joan Blaeu and the VOC

When Cook was appointed first lieutenant of HMB *Endeavour* in May 1768, he was promptly instructed to 'to use the utmost dispatch in getting her ready for the sea'. This he did with his usual energy and diligence – overseeing the victuallers, sailmakers and carpenters; choosing his crew and attending meetings at the Navy Office in Seething Lane.

But by night, Cook returned to his family in Mile End Road to do his homework. Over the years, Cook had built an impressive library of charts and atlases, textbooks on winds and navigation, and an array of nautical tables. In addition to these, Stephens lent him various collections of travel narratives and voyaging accounts. borrowed from the British Museum and the Admiralty library. Cook's *Endeavour* journal indicates that he was well versed in the sailing accounts of the Spanish, Dutch and English navigators who had preceded him into the Pacific.

The *Endeavour* was not heading off into the unknown. At least two of Cook's destinations were already located and their coordinates known. The first was Tahiti, which Wallis had discovered, and the second was New Zealand, found by Tasman. Even so, Cook was being asked to penetrate the South Pacific to far higher latitudes than any sailor had before him. He was to sail 1500 miles directly south of Tahiti, down to 40°S where Wallis's men had allegedly seen the Southern Continent. But Cook doubted that he would bump into any southern continent. He had long believed that, while a south polar continent may exist, he was unlikely to find it inside the warmer search area nominated by the Admiralty.

Cook was a practical man with little time for the theories of armchair geographers. He preferred to trust the observations of navigators who had doubled the Horn and supplied 248 years of weather reports from Tierra del Fuego. The survivors of Anson's voyage remembered too well the south-westerly gales and huge seas that wreaked havoc on the fleet when it rounded Cape Horn in 1741. If a continent the size of Asia filled the South Pacific as Alexander Dalrymple insisted, then it would block those gales and swells that swept up from the Southern Ocean.

Furthermore, Cook was sceptical about the 'sightings' of earlier navigators, which both Redern and Dalrymple relied on so heavily. Like all seafarers, Cook knew that a smudge on the horizon seen by a tired and homesick sailor had as much chance of being a cloud as a speck of land. When the lookout called 'Land ahead' it was too often that mariner's will-o'-the-wisp, Cape Fly-away.

Of course, reliable James Cook would perform the Admiralty's instructions to the letter. He would search the heavy seas for Wallis's phantom speck seen south of Tahiti and he would hunt for the continental extension of New Zealand, only to prove the non-existence of both. He would even test for an intercontinental current off the coast of Chile, but he did not expect to find one. Cook must have felt that he was being sent on a wild goose chase – more a voyage of elimination than a voyage of discovery. He wanted more than this. He wanted to become a great explorer, using his skills as a marine surveyor. But he needed something to explore.

Philip Stephens gave him this opportunity when he instructed Cook that, after completing his formal work in New Zealand, Cook should survey the east coast of New Holland and return through the Dutch East Indies. This would allow Cook to discover the shape of the unknown coast, its ports of shelter and refreshment, and establish whether or not it joined the known outliers – New Guinea, Vanuatu and Van Diemen's Land. Also, by returning via Batavia, he would make a proper circumnavigation of the globe just as his predecessors Drake, Anson, Byron and Wallis had done

Cook studied the accounts of the Spanish and Dutch navigators who had visited the region, notably Abel Tasman's voyage of 1642–43 when he discovered Van Diemen's Land. Unfortunately, Tasman's journal of this voyage was not available to Cook. The manuscript was filed away in the VOC offices in Amsterdam and wouldn't be printed for another century. However, London's bookshops offered various abridged accounts of the voyage which provided significant geographical detail of Tasman's discoveries, including latitudes and longitudes. Some, such as the work of Dirck Rembrantsz, had been translated into English. Another, not yet translated but available in Dutch, was included in a volume of Francois Valentyn's monumental *Oud en Nieuw Oost-Indien*.[1] Published in 1726, it provided a more detailed version of Tasman's voyage, including maps and drawings, and Joseph Banks carried a copy of it on the *Endeavour*.

As Cook studied the Dutch map, he became puzzled by the direction of Tasman's track. Sailing south-east from Mauritius on a mission to find a continent, Tasman's path was suddenly blocked when he discovered Van Diemen's Land. Faced with the choice of turning left or right, he chose the latter and continued to hug the coast as it turned around its southern point and up the east coast. From here, he surely intended to follow this coast northward as far as possible, to see if it stretched all the way

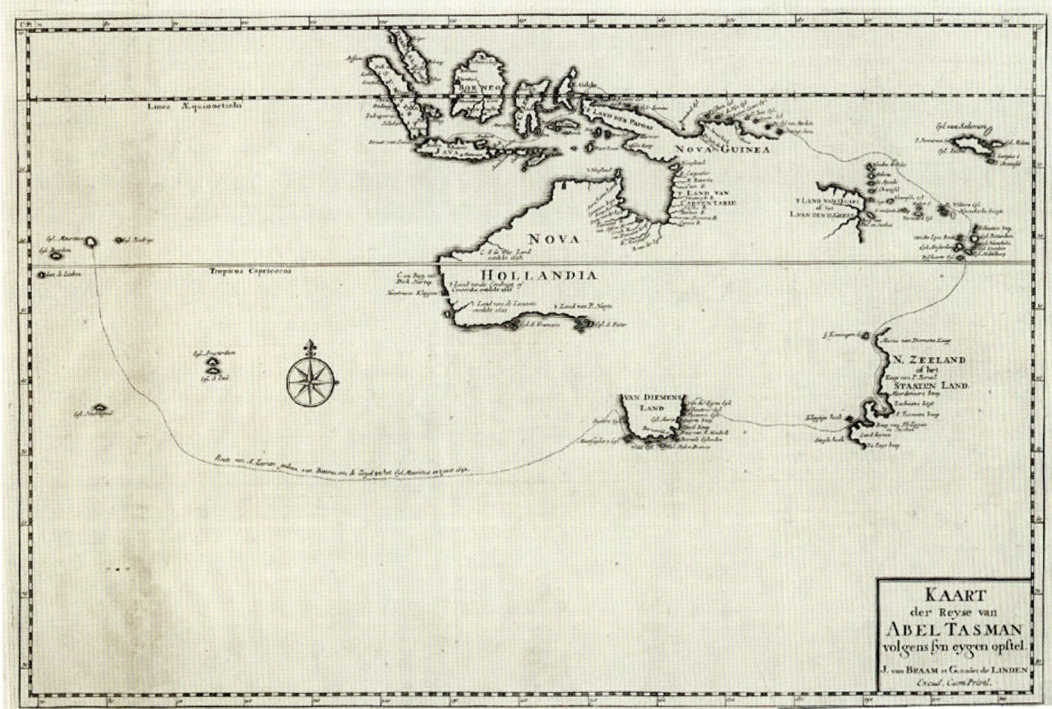

25. This 1726 map, which shows the track of Tasman's voyage from Mauritius in 1642, was included in Banks's library on board the *Endeavour*.

to New Guinea, as seemed tantalizingly likely. Yet when the Dutch ships reached latitude 41°S, Tasman abruptly turned away to the east.

Using his mariner's instinct, Cook tried to guess why the Dutch navigator had suddenly abandoned Van Diemen's Land. Tasman had approached its west coast through the Indian Ocean, running before the wind in the Roaring Forties. Then, as he cruised around the southern tip and turned north, the wild winds dropped for a few days as the ships came under the lee of the east coast. But suddenly, Cook imagined, that protection ended. As the Dutch ships reached latitude 41°S, the coast quickly vanished and the blast of those same Roaring Forties returned. Evidently Tasman had concluded that Van Diemen's Land was just another island, so he turned away to the east to continue his continent hunting. As the historian Günter Schilder writes: 'Tasman in fact sailed along the entire east coast of the island'.[2] The top of that coast is marked by Eddystone Point, where the coast turns away sharply to the north-west. When the Dutch ships reached this corner they were suddenly hit by the howling westerly funnelling through Banks Strait (the southern arm of Bass Strait).

If Cook had had access to Tasman's journal, locked away in Amsterdam, he would have enjoyed seeing his reasoning confirmed. Tasman's entry for 5 December 1642 states: 'the land falls off to the northwest so that here we could no longer keep close to the land, the wind being almost dead against us. Therefore we [decided] to shape the course due east.'³ In fact, Cook did have access to an abridged version of this in Valentyn's book: 'he could no longer keep the land aboard, because the wind was contrary'.⁴

Cook was convinced that Tasman had found a strait and not a bay. Yet the fashionable French maps of the day showed New Holland joined to Van Diemen's Land. Robert de Vaugondy, Philippe Buache and Jacques Bellin all depicted the mainland joined in a vast conglomerate with some or all of its three large outliers – New Guinea, Van Diemen's Land and Quiros's Land of Espiritu Santo.

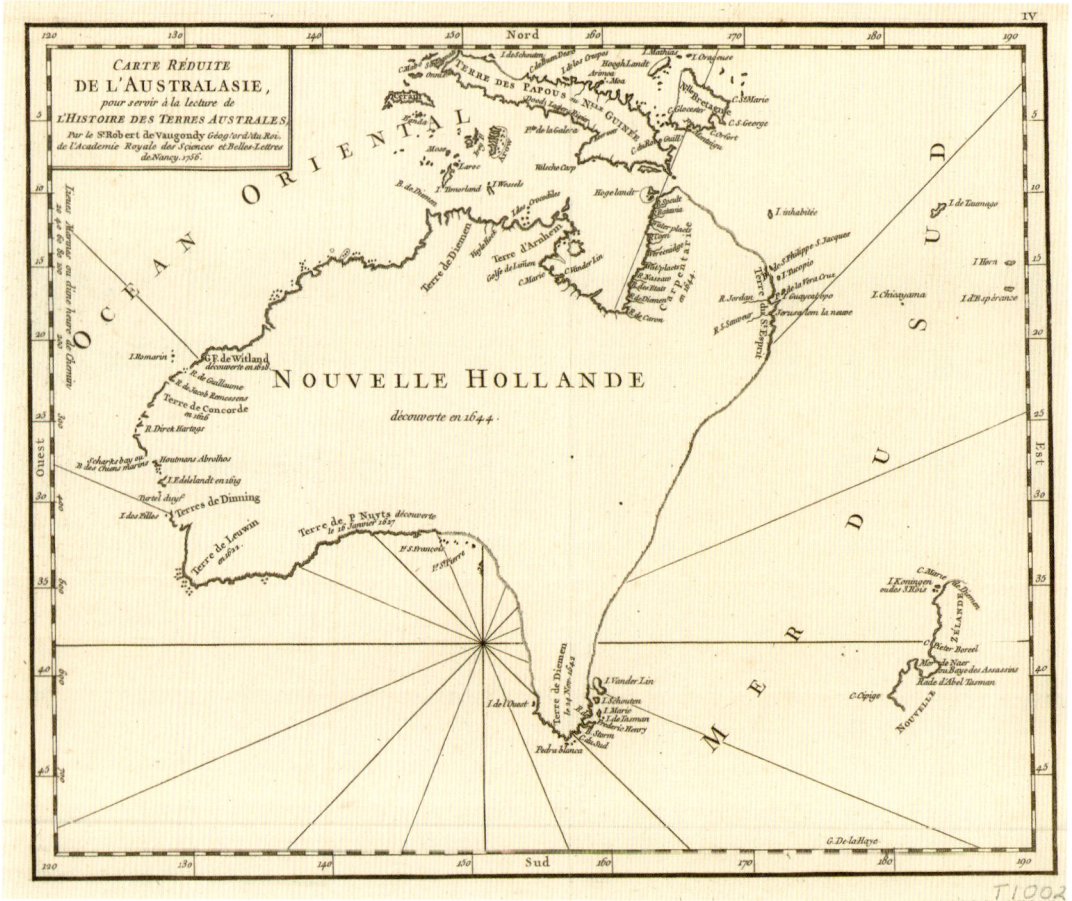

26. In this 1756 French map, Robert de Vaugondy imagines an east coast which joins Van Diemen's Land to Quiros's Land of Espiritu Santo and then onto Carpentaria.

Cook raised these concerns with Philip Stephens during his next visit to the Admiralty Office. Stephens told Cook to take no notice of the fanciful theories and speculative geography of these French cartographers. They had surrendered to the temptation to fill empty spaces and complete unexplored coastlines, and now they published misleading maps of exquisite elegance!

Stephens declared that, as no European navigator had visited the south-west Pacific since Tasman, the only authoritative maps of the region were those made in the wake of his voyages by Joan Blaeu, the official cartographer of the VOC. Blaeu was the only publisher to be granted exclusive access to all the logs, journals, charts and sketches made by Tasman and his crew.[5]

There were plenty of copies of Blaeu's work in circulation by 1768, but Stephens insisted that the best collection of Blaeu's maps were in the Klencke Atlas, now held in the King's new library at Buckingham House. This collection was open to the

27. The Octagon Library was added to Buckingham House in 1766–67. It was here that George III kept his ever-expanding map collection, including the Klencke Atlas.

King's admirals, generals and ministers. Seventy years earlier, William III had invited the English navigator William Dampier to study the Klencke Atlas before he sailed for New Holland with instructions to investigate its east coast. In fact, the king was disappointed when he learnt that, fearing the cold, Dampier had not sailed south around the New Holland to explore the east coast as he had been ordered to do.

Although there is no evidence that Cook actually visited Buckingham House, it is more than likely that he did see the atlas. Philip Stephens would have wanted Cook to see the Klencke Atlas because its enormous size meant that its folios contained more information than ordinary maps. Moreover, the young monarch was very keen about this next Pacific expedition and had already contributed £4000 towards the voyage.

The atlas was so enormous that it took six royal servants to manoeuvre it on to a custom-made frame. The first folio was Joan Blaeu's beautiful wall map of the world in two hemispheres, made in 1648. On this map, New Holland was separated from Van Diemen's Land with a very wide gap. It seemed that Blaeu, like Cook, had interpreted Tasman's journal as describing a passage between the two lands.

The regional maps which followed provided much more detail. The fifth folio was Blaeu's 1659 map of the Oriental or Asiatic Archipelago – *Archipelagus Orientalis sive Asiaticus*. It is a masterpiece, celebrating the extent of Dutch sea power through the Spice Islands and the East Indies. Cook was fascinated to see *Hollandia Nova*, its outline almost complete, dominating the centre of the map. The coasts were dotted with Dutch placenames and, once again, a wide passage separated the incomplete coasts of Van Diemen's Land and New Holland. But what would have interested Cook most was the ship which Blaeu had placed at the western entrance to that passage.

Cook would have seen many old maps where the cartographer had included ships among colourful ornaments of menacing sea monsters and other exotic creatures. Sometimes the ships were merely decorative, but usually they were pictorial signals, providing maritime information. They might indicate safe anchorages, trading destinations, sea routes or navigable waters. Cook would have suspected that Blaeu deliberately placed this ship at the north-west corner of Van Diemen's Land. It signalled that vessels sailing east from the Cape of Good Hope or south from Java would find here a safe passage through to the Pacific Ocean.

Cook told Stephens that he firmly believed that New Holland and Van Diemen's Land were separated by a strait and that he planned to verify it. Stephens might have agreed that a passage was likely. But he also would have urged Cook to do all he could to conceal any insularity from his crew.

Cook needed no instruction about the problem of off-shore islands. He had just spent five years dealing with the consequences of the British cabinet's decision to override William Pitt and allow the French to 'dry their fish' on the islands of St Pierre and Miquelon. Islands were dangerous.

28. Blaeu's large wall map, *Archipelagus Orientalis sive Asiaticus*, 1659, celebrates the extent of Dutch sea power in South-East Asia and contains all the Dutch discoveries in New Holland, Van Diemen's Land and New Zealand. There are half a dozen recorded examples, one being map no. 5 in the Klencke Atlas, now in the British Library, and another in the collection of the National Library of Australia nla.obj-232510007.

17   The Odd Couple: The Relationship Between Cook and Banks

By the beginning of August, it was time to leave. The *Endeavour* had already been taken downriver to the Downs where Cook would join her. After taking leave of his three children and his wife, heavily pregnant with a fourth, he climbed in a coach and was driven to the town of Deal on the Kent coast where he met the ship. After coming aboard, Cook discharged the pilot and made passage around to Plymouth.

Here he was joined by Joseph Banks, the young man he had most likely encountered in Newfoundland two years earlier. Cook was expecting him, having received the Admiralty's orders:

> To receive on board the said Bark ... the said Joseph Banks Esq. and his Suite consisting of eight Persons with their Baggage, bearing them as Supernumer[ar]ies for Victuals only, and Victualling them as the Barks Company during their Continuance on board.[1]

The boyish millionaire had on his payroll a secretary, four servants (who would double as collectors) and two artists: Sydney Parkinson, a natural history draughtsman, and Alexander Buchan for drawing figures and landscapes. In the age before photography, illustrators were essential members of a scientific team. In addition, Daniel Solander obtained leave from the British Museum and joined the party. Banks also sent on board Wallis's goat, two hunting dogs – a spaniel named Lady and a greyhound – plus twenty tons of baggage and equipment, including a dinghy and a library of over 100 books.[2]

How did Cook and Banks get along? Beaglehole has written:

> It appears that Cook and Banks took to each other on sight, which was lucky. Cook was tolerant, with a sense of humour – no doubt he needed it as the ship's company mounted in number – and Banks was really a charming fellow.[3]

Although he doesn't offer any evidence to support this suggestion, Beaglehole is as good a judge as any, having immersed himself in the lives of both men for much of his adult life. If it existed, such a rapport would be a blessing for two people who were to be thrown together for three years – from August 1768 to July 1771 – in the cramped conditions of the great cabin on the *Endeavour*.

However, their rapport is all the more surprising, given that they came from such different backgrounds. Cook was the son of a farm labourer while Banks was a pampered son of the landed gentry. Cook had little formal schooling while Banks had attended Harrow, Eton and Oxford. Cook was married with three children, while Banks was a high-living bachelor about town. And there was a fifteen-year age gap between them.

In fact, there were at least two points of friction between them. The first was Banks's abiding complaint that he had too few opportunities to carry out scientific research, which was his major preoccupation. Of course, at any time he could stand on deck and shoot a bird or net a jellyfish to add to his collection. But Banks's main interest was botany and he wanted to stop at every coast they passed so that he could go ashore and botanize. It took some time for the young man to realize that the captain was not his personal chauffer and had greater priories such as navigation, geographical discovery and the safety of the ship. However, Cook was respectful and kind. He understood Banks's restlessness and always invited 'the gentlemen' – Banks and Solander – to accompany him ashore when the opportunity arose.

A second point of tension between them was Dalrymple's Southern Continent. Put simply, Banks believed it existed and Cook did not, at least not where Dalrymple positioned it in the mid-latitudes between Chile and New Zealand. Judging from their journals, the topic was discussed constantly from the moment the ship doubled the Horn. Up on deck, Cook would point to all the tell-tale factors – currents, swells, prevailing winds – which proved the absence of any land mass over the western horizon, but Banks and his supporters would not give up.

It seems odd that Banks opposed Cook's reasoning for so long. Banks knew that Cook's work was held in the highest regard by Palliser, Sandwich, Stephens and others. Yet Banks clung to the myth until the last possible moment – when the *Endeavour* finally completed the circumnavigation of the 'continent' of New Zealand. Perhaps Banks's refusal to change his mind earlier in the voyage did not mean he mistrusted Cook's judgement. More likely, it was an indication of how desperate Banks was to be the Englishman who found the Southern Continent.

In spite of these differences, Cook and Banks had much in common. It could be said of both men that they had no religion and no politics – absences which would certainly have aided their after-dinner conversation in the close confines of the great cabin. Both were men of ambition, intellect and remorseless application. Both were determined to make their name somehow and both chose the path of exploration.

Another trait they had in common was a fervent patriotism. At home, this would have been irrelevant, but not when they were on a British mission in foreign seas.

29. Portrait of Cook by Nathaniel Dance commissioned by Joseph Banks shortly before Cook departed on his third and final voyage.

When they eventually found out that Bougainville may have beaten them in the Pacific, they both worked to protect British priority.

The *Endeavour* expedition proved more than fruitful – and it made both men's careers. Cook became the most famous Pacific navigator in the world. Banks became the president of the Royal Society and, for the rest of his long life, he ran the 'Ministry of the Pacific' from his house at 32 Soho Square. Here Cook's portrait, commissioned by Banks, hung over the fireplace in the library, reminding Banks and his visitors of their famous voyage. Through the 40 years that Banks outlived Cook, this room became, in the words of Captain James King, 'the common centre of we discoverers'.[4] Banks became the mentor and protector of the sailors and officers of that exclusive club: the men who had sailed with Cook.

Whatever their degree of rapport, it is a great credit to both men that the voyage was the success it was. They learnt from each other, they complemented each other and both allowed the other to shine. Cook, the great navigator, made the voyage successful; Banks, the great promoter, rendered it famous.

18 Ghostly Presence: Cook Disproves Dalrymple's Theory of a Temperate Continent

When HMB *Endeavour* sailed from England on 25 August 1768, a ghostly presence shadowed the voyage: Alexander Dalrymple, who believed in the Southern Continent and was outraged that he was not to lead the expedition that he hoped would discover it. And with eerie precision, much of Cook's voyage shadowed Bougainville, who sailed a year and a half before him. At that moment, Bougainville's French ships were rounding the north-west corner of New Guinea, ten weeks after his men had sighted the coast of Queensland.

Did anyone in Britain know that their arch rival was blazing a trail ahead of Cook? Dalrymple had heard of it from his colleague de Brosses. Being the outspoken patriot, Dalrymple must have discussed this French intelligence with his friends at the Royal Society and elsewhere. The British ambassador in Paris had reported the Frenchman's trip to the Falklands in 1766 and must surely have made enquiries when he failed to return. It seems likely that any information would have been passed on to Stephens. In any event, no one told Captain Cook.

For his part, Cook was not at liberty to chase French ships across the Pacific. He had instructions to arrive at Tahiti some six weeks before the transit of Venus on 3 June 1769. In all, the *Endeavour* voyage would last two years and 46 weeks, about a year longer than the recent voyages of Byron and Wallis. The small bark would circumnavigate the world by way of Madeira, Rio de Janeiro, Tierra del Fuego, Tahiti, New Zealand, New Holland, New Guinea, Batavia, Cape Town and St Helena, arriving home on 13 July 1771.

Heading down the Atlantic, Cook stopped briefly at Madeira to take on beef, vegetables and wine, before arriving at the equator in late October. Here the ship's company prepared for the age-old ducking ritual to mark their crossing of the line. Those who had crossed before, such as Charles Clerke and John Gore, were excused; others, including Cook and Banks, bought their immunity with bottles of rum and

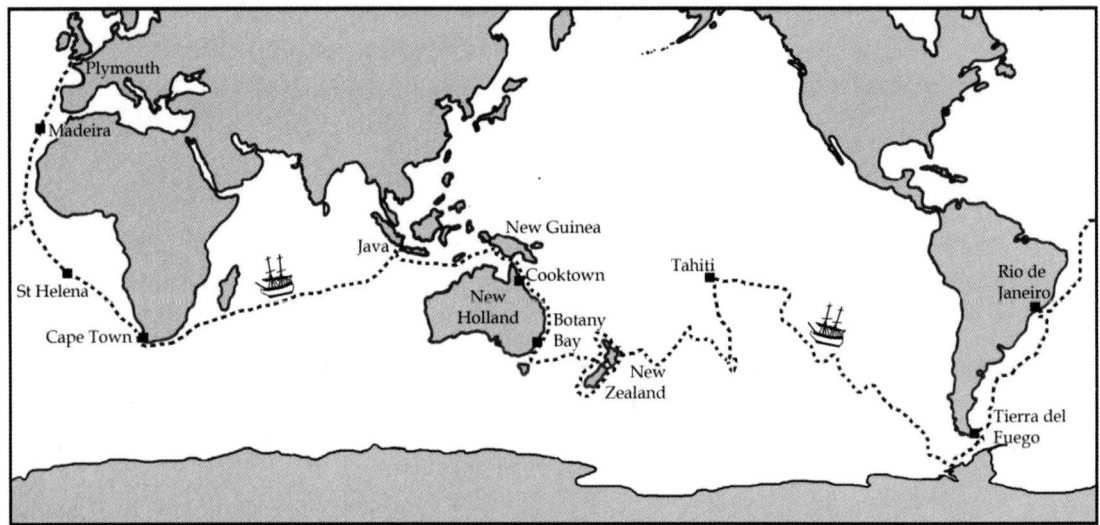

30. Sketch map showing the track of HMB *Endeavour*, 25 August 1768 – 12 July 1771. The website of the National Library of Australia provides daily voyaging maps with companion texts at southseas. nla.gov.au.

brandy. Banks had to pay an additional bottle to free his dogs![1] But 22 men stepped forward and entertained the rest by plunging overboard on the ducking chair, to the shrill call of the bosun's whistle.

Three weeks later they sailed into the harbour of Rio de Janeiro, where Cook wanted to restock with fresh food and livestock and make some repairs. However, his determination to maintain secrecy caused problems when he sent Lieutenant Hicks ahead in the pinnace to the Portuguese headquarters to ask for a pilot. According to both Sydney Parkinson and James Matra, Cook instructed Hicks 'to evade any questions that might be asked concerning our destination or the object of our voyage; or at least to answer them with great reserve'.[2]

Unfortunately, Hicks's evasiveness inflamed the suspicions of the Viceroy, Count Azambuja, who refused to believe their story about watching the transit of Venus and assumed they were smugglers or spies. He issued a prohibition to land so that only those purchasing provisions were permitted to go ashore. After sailing 5000 miles from Plymouth, this three-week shipboard confinement was a bitter blow for the ship's company, all of whom were looking forward to the delights of tropical America. More importantly, if Cook and his men had been free to move about this cosmopolitan city, they may have heard gossip about Bougainville's visit the previous year and his efforts to provision his two ships for an exploratory voyage to the South Pacific.

In spite of the armed surveillance, Joseph Banks and his party managed to escape at night to do some botanizing, as Parkinson records:

[W]e frequently, unknown to the centinel, stole out of the cabin window at midnight, letting ourselves down into a boat by a rope; and, driving away with the tide till we were out of hearing, we then rowed to some unfrequented part of the shore, where we landed, and made excursions up into the country.[3]

These clandestine excursions produced more than 300 specimens, including a colourful woody vine which Banks named *Calyxis ternaria*. This was, of course, the plant discovered a year earlier by Philibert Commerson and Jeanne Baret, who had given it the more glamorous name of *Bougainvillea spectabilis*.

At last, with her stores replenished, the *Endeavour* sailed in early December. In leaving Rio, they left civilization. They would have no communication with the European world until they re-entered it at the Dutch port of Batavia, more than half a world away. Then Captain Cook would again face a barrage of questions from foreign officials, which he would answer just as evasively and with similar results. Cook would make two more global voyages, but he never returned to Rio or to Batavia.

When not laid low by seasickness, Banks and his party continued to add to their collection, using nets, hooks and guns to haul in seaweed, insects, sharks and albatross, much of which was eaten. They shot from the boat, but when the weather permitted, Banks lowered his rowboat – a lighterman's skiff – and paddled round the ship. The evenings were spent drying, storing, drawing, describing and classifying the booty.

By Christmas Day they were off the coast of Argentina, south of Buenos Aires. The captain aided the celebrations by offering an extra tot of rum to each man, as Banks reports:

> All good Christians that is to say all hands get abominably drunk so that at night there was scarce a sober man in the ship, wind thank god very moderate or the lord knows what would have become of us.[4]

At New Year they entered the latitudes of the Falkland Islands, now in a brief period of dual Anglo–Bourbon rule. West Falkland was protected by a British garrison of 25 marines, while East Falkland was still home to some 40 French colonists who had stayed on after Port St Louis was handed over to Spain.[5] Cook knew that beyond these islands lay Cape Circumcision, which French cartographers believed to be the tip of the Southern Continent. But Cook had fixed his course for Tahiti and that investigation would have to wait for a later voyage. As they had refreshed at Rio, Cook saw no reason to stop at the Falklands, which caused some regret in the great cabin. Parkinson had hoped to post letters home to England from the fort in Port Egmont, their last European post office before entering the Pacific. Banks wanted to go ashore to botanize, lamenting that 'I fear I shall not now have a single opportunity of observing the produce of this part of the world'.[6]

Fortunately, the Admiralty had taken note of Wallis's tortuous four-month passage through the Strait of Magellan and had directed Cook to avoid that passage and take the more southerly route around Cape Horn.⁷ This he did successfully, but there was an unfortunate occurrence when they stopped for five days at Good Success Bay in Tierra del Fuego. Banks seized this opportunity to take his plant-collecting party of twelve up into the hills, but the temperature plummeted and his two black servants perished.

The passage round the Horn was easier than expected and on 26 January 1769, Cook entered the vast cauldron of the Pacific Ocean, exactly one year after Bougainville. Although he was past the Horn, Cook continued his south-west course for another four days, sailing some 600 miles down through the Furious Fifties into the Screaming Sixties. They made 'a good westing' as instructed, and reached 60°10'S, the most southerly point of the voyage. Not surprisingly, there was no sign of land.

From this solitary point in the south-east corner of the Pacific Ocean, Cook turned north-west towards Tahiti. It lay 4000 miles away and Cook had two and a half months to get there, according to the Admiralty's timetable:

> taking care however to fall into the parallel of King Georges Island [Tahiti] at least 120 leagues to the eastwards of it and using your best endeavours to arrive there at least a month or six weeks before the 3rd day of June next, that Mr Green and you may have leizure to adjust and try your instruments before the observation.⁸

The business of the transit lay ahead, but for now the conversation in the great cabin was all about continent-hunting. The ship's company quickly divided into two camps – Banks's optimistic 'Continentmongers' and Cook's pessimistic 'No-Continents' – and each was anxious to prove their case. Banks's large library included Dalrymple's pamphlet with its chart of the South Pacific. Banks pointed to the squiggle of coastline marking Fernandez's continent, which they should reach in a few weeks. But Cook preferred the facts provided by wind and waves over the theories proposed in books.

In Cook's experience, the absence of a current indicated an absence of land. On 1 February, before turning north, he hoisted out one of the small boats 'to try if there was any current but found none'. For the rest of the month, he repeated the trial whenever the weather permitted, and the result was always the same. On 1 March he delivered his verdict: there was no continent on the ship's port side:

> [As] we have had no current that hath affected the Ship Since we came into these Seas, this must be a great sign that we have been near no land of any extent, because near land are generally found currents; it is well known that on the East side of the Continent in the North sea [i.e. the Atlantic Ocean] we meet with Currents above 100 Leagues from the Land, and even in the Middle of the Atlantic Ocean between Africa and America are always found currents, and I can see no reason why currents should not be found in this Sea Supposing a Continent or lands lay not far west from us as some have immagine'd, and if such lands was ever seen we cannot be far from it, as we are now 560 Leagues West of the Coast of Chili.⁹

The absence of an offshore current was not Cook's only evidence. He also pointed out that there was nothing blocking the huge swell rolling in from the south-west. At the end of February when the *Endeavour* was 860 miles south of Easter Island, Cook wrote in his journal: 'the SW swell still keeps up notwithstand[ing] the gale hath been over about thirty hours, a proof that there is no land near in that quarter'.

Cook's announcements were not welcomed by the Continentalists. Since rounding the Horn, they had scanned the horizon with mounting gloom. The ship had already crossed the longitude of Fernandez's 'discovery' but still they saw nothing except the boundless sea in every direction. Banks realized the *Endeavour* had been sailing over Dalrymple's promised continent for weeks, slicing a huge chunk from its eastern coast. Losing faith in armchair geographers, he wryly observed:

> I cannot help wondering that we have not yet seen land. It is however some pleasure to be able to disprove that which does not exist but in the opinions of Theoretical writers ... The number of square degrees of their land which we have already chang'd into water sufficiently disproves [their theories].[10]

But the irrepressible Banks could not be gloomy for long. Dalrymple may have been wrong about Fernandez's sighting, but he was right in principle. The Southern Continent's east coast must rise further to the west, as the older charts had predicted. Banks's cheerful confidence sparked a flurry of sightings. At noon on 14 March, the man at the mast called 'Land ahead', but by sunset it was nothing more than a fog bank, another Cape Fly-away. One evening, hopes were raised by a homing flight of shore birds, only to be dashed the following morning. Then on 24 March, just as they crossed the Tropic of Capricorn, there was great excitement when the officer of the watch saw a log of wood pass the ship at 3 a.m. This meant that land was near and the Continentalists wanted to Cook to investigate. But when daylight brought no hint of land, Cook chose to stick to his course – and the Admiralty's timetable.

Banks was disappointed, particularly when he saw some birds that were not the type to venture far from land. Four years later, when Dalrymple read Cook's account of this incident, he furiously criticized Cook's failure to pursue the source of that log of wood in his search for the Southern Continent.[11]

Cook knew only too well that Dalrymple's ghost was aboard the ship and looking over his shoulder. Indeed, Cook's great frustration on the *Endeavour* voyage was that he spent most of it – up to the end of the circumnavigation of New Zealand – proving something he already knew: that there was no habitable continent in the South Pacific. Yet he knew that any short cut or error would be reported back to the Admiralty, and to Dalrymple, as soon as they arrived home. The *Endeavour*'s great cabin could be a lonely place for James Cook.

A few days later, after weeks of coursing north, *Endeavour* finally reached the latitude of Tahiti, which lay beyond the western horizon at the opposite end of the

Tuamotu Archipelago. As Cook turned west to weave a course through this chain of coral atolls, he asked Charles Green to unpack the equipment they had brought to observe the transit of Venus. Then Green and Cook spent the next few days testing and calibrating their instruments in preparation for the main event which was now just two months away.

At this moment scurvy, the scourge of sea, broke out on the vessel. When four of the crew presented with swollen gums and other tell-tale symptoms, the surgeon used all the remedies which the ship was carrying and, remarkably, all the patients recovered. Cook attributed this success to the wort, although it is now known to be as ineffective as an ascorbic as the other elixirs. In fact, the unusually low incidence of scurvy and the men's recovery was undoubtedly due to Cook's passionate insistence on a varied diet, with as much greenstuff as possible, plus a strict regimen of cleanliness and keeping a dry and well-ventilated lower deck.

Meanwhile, the fifth victim – Banks – looked to his private medicine chest. He had packed this in London, following the latest professional advice and sparing no expense. Instead of robs of boiled citrus juice, his chest included several casks of raw lemon and orange juices, preserved in a small amount of brandy. After drinking several doses of the mixture each day, Banks soon reported that 'the effect of this was surprising, in less than a week my gums became as firm as ever'.[12] Surprisingly, Cook makes no mention of Banks's speedy citrus juice recovery. Still, by the time they reached Tahiti Cook could proudly boast 'At this time we had but a very few men upon the Sick list and these had but slite complaints'.[13] Later in the voyage, there were two more outbreaks of scurvy, one in New Zealand and the other in Queensland. But these also were contained and none of those afflicted with scurvy died.

On 4 April a great cheer erupted from the upper deck when Peter Briscoe, Banks's servant, called 'Land ho' from the masthead. He had seen the tiny atoll of Vahitahi – their first landfall in the Pacific. Soon they were surrounded by these low-lying islands and the local people waved from the shore, calling out to the visitors. For a brief moment, Cook considered going ashore and annexing his first discovery, but then decided not to disturb the people, as Banks explains:

> Our situation made it very improper to try them farther, we wanted nothing, the island was too trifling to be an object worth taking possession of; had we therefore out of mere curiosity hoisted out a boat and the natives by attacking us oblige us to destroy some of them, the only reason we could give for it would be the desire of satisfying a useless curiosity. We shall soon by our connections with the inhabitants of Georges Island (who already know our strength and if they do not love us, at least fear us) gain some knowledge of the customs of these savages.[14]

Evidently, the Admiralty's request for annexation was being discussed in the great cabin. However, Cook would have to delay his first possession ceremony until after the transit of Venus. This was because the island of Tahiti had already been claimed in the name of the British Crown, by Tobias Furneaux, on behalf of his ailing captain, Samuel Wallis.

Reaching Tahiti on 13 April 1769, Cook, like Wallis before him, anchored in the sheltered Matavai Bay. The continent debate was suspended for the next three months, to everyone's relief, as they worked and played in this wondrous arcadia.

19 Venus and a Tahitian Holiday

James Cook was the third European captain to visit Tahiti in as many years. The Tahitians had met Samuel Wallis, their first recorded European visitor, in 1767 and Louis Bougainville in 1768 (who had just arrived home in France on 16 March 1769). For the most part, both had been happy encounters, giving no cause to fear these new arrivals. So the people packed their canoes with cocoanuts and breadfruit, and rowed out to greet and barter with their new guests. The fresh fruit was a welcome sight for the crew after weeks at sea and was quickly exchanged for nails and beads. Then, as soon as the anchors were secured, Cook and Banks rowed ashore with a party of marines to take stock of this corner of paradise.

The transit of Venus was not due until Saturday 3 June 1769 and so the Englishmen had more than seven weeks to explore the island and make ready for the viewing. John Gore and Robert Molyneux went to look for Queen Oberea, whom they had met on their previous visit in the *Dolphin*. When they found her court, the Tahitians were delighted to see Toarro (Gore) and Boba (Molyneux) again and to be introduced to their new companions James Cook, whom they called Toote, and Joseph Banks, who was named Tapane.

Others remembered the *Dolphin*'s visit for other reasons. Wilkinson recorded that 'a woman appeared with her child whos father belong to the Dolphin as she told us by sighns and indeed many circumstance make it highly probable'.[1]

Meanwhile, Cook spent a whole day looking for a suitable spot for the observatory, undertaking his Royal Society duties with his usual scrupulous care. After all, the transit of Venus was the *raison d'être* for the voyage and the society had employed him on a separate contract to observe the transit and record the times of the planet's ingress and egress. Charles Green, as the official astronomer to the expedition, was to receive 200 guineas, while Cook would be paid 100 guineas for his report.

Cook selected a sandy spit at the northern headland of Matavai Bay as the best site for observing the transit and named it Point Venus. Here he marked out the ground for the portable observatory, the service tents and the armourer's forge; and then ordered his men to build earthworks and palisades around the perimeter. Fort Venus, which was guarded by six swivel guns, two four-pounders and a squad of marines, protected the delicate scientific instruments from pilferers, and the observers from interruption.

Meanwhile, the *Endeavour* was given a thorough overhaul; later Banks acquired a Polynesian tattoo on his arm like most of the crew.[2] Trade was brisk as the visitors paid for food and cloth with iron nails, hatchets and beads. Cook noted that inflation had set in, with prices considerably higher since the *Dolphin*'s visit two years earlier.[3]

While waiting for the transit, Gore and Banks went hunting with the two dogs. At this point in the story, John Gore deserves a proper introduction as he played an important role in every ship he sailed in, circumnavigating the globe with Byron and Wallis in the *Dolphin*, and with Cook in the *Endeavour*. Ten years later, on the fatal third voyage, after the deaths of Cook and Clerke, it was left to Captain Gore to bring the sad expedition home, completing his fourth circumnavigation.

A year younger than Cook, Gore was born in the British colony of Virginia. He probably first went to sea on a commercial ship in Chesapeake Bay. By the time he was 25, he had joined the British Navy and served as a midshipman in the Seven Years War, during which he forged a friendship with Charles Clerke, a fellow midshipman on the 74 gun-ship HMS *Bellona*. In August 1761, while part of the squadron was blockading the French coast, they spotted the French ship *Courageux* off the coast of Portugal. After chasing the French for fourteen hours, they got within musket-shot and a furious action commenced. Gore was on the gun deck while Clerke was stationed up in the mizzen shrouds. Within nine minutes the *Bellona*'s mizzen mast was shot away and fell over the side, taking the rigging and Clerke with it. Gore rushed to help as Clerke, half-drowned, crawled up the chains. Of those who had been on the mast, he was the only survivor. Soon after, their luck turned and, with half her crew dead or wounded, the *Courageux* surrendered. The *Bellona*'s crew pocketed the prize money, made more valuable by the French ship's cargo of £8500 in specie.

When the peace came, both Gore and Clerke were assigned to Byron's *Dolphin* voyage. On their return, Clerke took leave while Gore stepped back on board the *Dolphin* and circumnavigated the world for a second time with Wallis. After returning to England, Gore was given just three months shore leave, and a promotion, before sailing again as the *Endeavour*'s third lieutenant.

Although he has been referred to as 'a tower of strength in the ship's company, imperturbable and absolutely reliable',[4] his unwavering support of Banks's Continentalist party meant that he was sometimes a thorn in Cook's side during the *Endeavour* voyage.

In fact, there is some evidence of bad relations, recorded a decade after the *Endeavour* voyage. The occasion was a breakfast at Banks's house in Soho Square, and while Solander gossiped about the voyage a colleague jotted down his story:

Gore is the best practical Seaman now in the Navy; Cooke was jealous of him, conscious of not having that thorough stile in naval affairs, nor that determined courage. Gore had a sort of separate command in the vessel being appointed Master Hunter, which gave him superintendance over all the transactions with the Indians. He made use of this sometimes to disobey Cooke; & therefore they hate each other.[5]

No doubt there were tensions between Cook and Gore, but this is a bit harsh. After all, Cook respected Gore enough to take him on the HMS *Resolution* as his first lieutenant of the third voyage. Still, Gore would make quite a nuisance of himself as the *Endeavour* sailed the great empty ocean between Tahiti and New Zealand.

As the transit day approached, instruments were tested for the umpteenth time and a general nervousness gathered pace. When the weather took a turn for the worse, Cook hurried to establish two ancillary observation stations – to the east and west of Point Venus – in case the fort became covered in cloud. The eastern party, led by Lieutenant Hicks, was sent in the pinnace to Taaupiri Island, an islet off Tahiti's east coast. The western party was sent to an islet off Moorea Island, which lies about ten miles north-west of Tahiti. It had four observers led by John Gore and, as they set off in the longboat on 1 June, Banks decided to join them, not as an observer (he was no astronomer) but as the team's caterer, responsible for buying food from the natives. Waving them farewell, Cook may have been pleased to see the backs of the leading Continentalists for a few days.

The Royal Society's official astronomers – Green and Cook – would conduct their observations at the principal station in Fort Venus, where the best instruments were housed. Here they would be assisted by Daniel Solander and the ship's master, Robert Molyneux, both of whom were well experienced in astronomy.

The great day arrived and the weather was perfect. Cook reported:

> This day prov'd as favourable to our purpose as we could wish, not a Clowd was to be seen the whole day and the Air was perfectly clear, so that we had every advantage we could desire in Observing the whole of the passage of the Planet Venus over the Sun's disk.[6]

Soon after daybreak, Green and Cook and their team went out to the fort to take charge of the telescopes, clock, thermometer, quadrant and other cutting-edge scientific instruments which had been set firmly in place. Sentries kept the Tahitians and others away to ensure that the astronomers were not disturbed. Tension increased when the transit began at 9:21 a.m. By midday the temperature on the headland had risen to an exceptional 119°F. Eventually, after six hours, the transit ended at 3:29 p.m., to the enormous relief of everyone.

When the pinnace and the longboat returned, it was clear that all three parties had carried out successful observations. However, Cook, like all astronomers of the day, was confounded by the infamous 'black drop' effect. This made it impossible to time accurately the exact moment of ingress and egress of the planet, so that the duration of

31. Cook and the *Endeavour* crew constructed a fortified observatory at on a sandy spit at the north-east end of Matavai Bay which he named Fort Venus.

the transit – a main aim of the expedition – could not be determined as precisely as had been hoped. Nonetheless, the result was good enough for Professor Thomas Hornsby, after adding the data from the Royal Society's other observing sites in Norway and Canada, to calculate a meaningful figure for the solar parallax.[7]

With the transit business finished, Cook and Banks could turn their attention to solving a mystery. They had noticed that the Tahitians possessed various tools and other items which were European in origin, but very different from their British equivalents. Did this mean that Tahiti had been visited by other foreigners since Wallis discovered the island? One evening, after a man had brought his axe to the forge to be sharpened, the puzzle was debated over dinner, as Banks records:

> Its make was very different from that of our English ones, several gentlemen were of opinion that it was a French one, some went so far as to give it as their opinion that some other ship had been here since the Dolphin.[8]

Although Banks did not agree with them, the gentlemen were right – the axe had been traded by Bougainville. Still, Cook's suspicion grew over the following weeks as the Tahitians told stories of some foreigners who had visited the island about ten to fifteen months earlier. They arrived in two ships and stayed for eight days at a harbour on the east coast. The commander's name was Toottera and there was a woman amongst the crew. The Tahitian chief had asked the strangers to take his brother, Ahutoru, away with them because he wanted to visit their country. The strangers agreed to take him, with a promise to return him home, and then they left the island sailing due west. The Tahitians were giving Cook a succinct and accurate account of Bougainville's expedition.

Alarmed by this, Cook and Banks wanted to know the nationality of the strangers. So they invited a man aboard the *Endeavour* and showed him a large coloured chart displaying the different flags of the maritime nations. When the man picked out the Spanish ensign, Cook was relieved, as he saw no real threat from the local Spanish ships:

> This together with several Articles we have lately seen amongest these people Such as Jackets etc usually worne by Spanish Seamen, proves beyond doubt that they must have been Ships of that Nation and come from some Port on the Coast of South America. [9]

If the Englishmen had guessed that these were in fact Bougainville's French ships, possibly flying the Spanish colours, they may have adopted a speedier itinerary, though not necessarily a better one.

The *Endeavour* spent three months at Tahiti. As she prepared to leave in mid-July, seven weeks after the transit, two Polynesians, Tupaia and his young servant, Taiata, asked to join the ship seeking a passage to Britain. Cook refused them because he doubted that the Navy Board would underwrite the additional cost, but Banks intervened, proposing that they travel as his guests:

> This morn Tupia came on board, he had renewd his resolves of going with us to England, a circumstance which gives me much satisfaction. He is certainly a most proper man, well born, chief Tohowa or priest of this Island, consequently skilld in the mysteries of their religion; but what makes him more than any thing else desirable is his experience in the navigation of these people and knowledge of the islands in these seas; he has told us the names of above 70, the most of which he has been himself at. The Captn refuses to take him on his own account, in my opinion sensibly enough, the government will never in all human probability take any notice of him; I therefore have resolvd to take him. Thank heaven I have a sufficiency.[10]

With his Royal Society duties finished, Cook could embark on his discovery work for the Admiralty.

When Bougainville left Tahiti fifteen months earlier, he headed west and arrived at the Great Barrier Reef just seven weeks later. Sailing a more circuitous route, James Cook took eleven months to reach the same point.

20 Farther South: The Wild Goose Chase for the Southern Continent

The Tahitian holiday was over. The Royal Society's work completed, Cook was no longer tied to a timetable. Now the second set of the Admiralty's not-so-secret instructions came into play. Cook was 'to proceed to the southward in order to make discovery of the Continent above-mentioned until you arrive in the Latitude of 40°, unless you sooner fall in with it'. But first, Cook wanted to investigate the Leeward Islands which the Tahitians said lay about 100 miles north-west of Tahiti.

In mid-July, they reached Huahine and, after exploring the island for a couple of days, sailed across to Raiatea. Cook's instructions authorized him to claim 'such islands as you may discover in the course of your voyage that have not hitherto been discovered by any Europeans'. Believing these islands had not been discovered, Cook chose Raiatea for his first possession ceremony. It was Tupaia's native island and the central island of the group which Cook named the Society Isles because 'they lay contiguous to one another'.[1]

Strictly speaking, the consent of the natives was needed when the land being claimed was inhabited. The Admiralty's instructions implied this and the president of the Royal Society had advised both Banks and Cook that any claim of possession required the voluntary consent of the inhabitants.[2] However, although on one occasion Cook did obtain consent for possession to erect a marker in New Zealand, his journal never mentions either seeking or receiving consent for possession. He probably thought the Admiralty's order was pie in the sky, as he stood on a beach grappling with language and cultural differences, fear and misunderstanding. Alternatively, he may have thought, like his friend William Anderson, surgeon on the *Resolution* on the second and third voyages, that possession ceremonies were 'not only unjust but truly ridiculous, and perhaps fitter to excite laughter than indignation'.[3]

Much has been written about the legality and effectiveness of these preliminary, unilateral claims by European explorers. Suffice to say that, for a pragmatic man like Cook, their primary purpose was not to impose British sovereignty on the local inhabitants, but rather to keep out the French – for as long as possible. In this he was largely successful.

At 1 p.m. on 20 July 1769, he hoisted out the boats and landed on the beach. There, flanked by Banks, Solander, Tupaia and the marines who had rowed them ashore, Cook conducted his first possession ceremony, as Banks describes:

> On landing Tupia repeated the ceremony of praying as at Huahine after which an English Jack was set up on shore and Captn Cooke took possession of this and the other three Islands in sight viz. Huahine, Otahah [Tahaa] and Bola Bola [Bora Bora] for the use of his Britannick majesty.[4]

Parkinson adds that Cook saw very few inhabitants 'and scarce any of distinguished rank amongst them. They behaved so coolly that the captain did not know what to make of them.'[5] It is unlikely the British were unable to find a local leader who was authorized to grant consent.

Eventually, on 9 August, it was time to leave the tropics and head south to resume the business of continent-hunting, much to the delight of Banks and his band of Continentalists. The ship was loaded with 'Hogs Fouls Plantains and Yams' which, as Cook noted wryly, 'will be of very great use to us in case we should not discover any lands in our rout to the Southward'.[6] Cook knew that the only way to slay the myth of a habitable Southern Continent was to physically sail over it on a wild goose chase. Meanwhile, Joseph Banks was feeling almost reckless as he 'launched out into the Ocean in search of what chance and Tupia might direct us to', but the following day the turbulent sea forced him below deck: 'Myself sick all day'.[7]

Tuapia announced that yet another cluster of islands lay ahead. Sure enough, three days later they sighted Rurutu Island, part of the Austral Islands, the most southerly archipelago in today's French Polynesia. When they were unable to land, they left it behind, crossing the Tropic of Capricorn for the third time and entering the emptiest region of the Pacific Ocean. Undaunted, the Continentalists were on high alert and, at 8 a.m. on 16 August, high peaks of land were seen on the eastern horizon. The ship bore away towards them but, after a three-hour chase, the Continentalists agreed that the peaks were clouds. Cook returned to his southward course, beating down into the long hollow swell. Still Banks retained his optimism, despite all the evidence to the contrary: 'A heavy swell from the SW all day, so we are not yet under the Lee of the continent'.[8]

The following week, while albatrosses circled the tiny ship, a party was held to celebrate their first anniversary at sea:

> It was this day a twelvemonth since we left England, in consequence of which a piece of

Cheshire cheese was taken from a locker where it had been reservd for this occasion and a cask of Porter tappd which provd excellently good, so that we livd like English men and drank the health of our friends in England.[9]

Soon after, the Continentalists' hopes were raised again when a piece of rock weed floated past and someone saw what looked like a small land bird. But nothing came of these sightings and they pushed down into the cold and desolate ocean described by Parkinson:

> On the 1st of September, we had hard piercing gales and squalls from the W. and N. W. with violent showers of hail and rain. The sea ran mountain-high, and tossed the ship upon the waves: she rolled so much, that we could get no rest, or scarcely lie in bed, and almost every moveable on board was thrown down, and rolled about from place to place. In brief, a person, who has not been in a storm at sea, cannot form an adequate idea of the situation we were in.[10]

The next day the *Endeavour* reached the required latitude of 40°S and, to the crew's enormous relief, Cook decided they had come far enough:

> At 4 PM being in the Latd. of 40°22'S and having not the least Visible signs of land ... as the weather was so very tempestuous I ... thought it more advisable to stand to the Northward into better weather least we should receive such damages in our sails & rigging as might hinder the further prosecutions of the Voyage.[11]

Cook was the first European to get so far south in the mid-Pacific, but not everyone was happy to abandon the southward search. Soon after returning to England – and having forgotten his seasickness – Banks wrote to his French friend, the Comte de Lauraguais, complaining that: 'we were absurdly forbid to proceed [to a] higher Latitude than 40°'.[12]

The Admiralty had sent Cook 1500 miles south from Tahiti with good reason. He had shown there was no continent here and the *Endeavour* was now in an excellent position to approach the little-known Dutch discoveries in the south-west corner of the Pacific. His instructions continued:

> But not having discover'd it or any Evident signs of it in that Run, you are to proceed in search of it to the Westward between the Latitude before mentioned and the Latitude of 35° until you discover it, or fall in with the Eastern side of the Land discover'd by Tasman and now called New Zeland ... [where] you will explore as much of the Coast as the Condition of the Bark ... will admit of.[13]

Instead of sailing directly west along the fortieth parallel into the raging tempest, Cook set a north-westerly course and spent the month of September beating across 2400 miles of empty sea to the north island of New Zealand. Ten days into this leg there was another call of 'Land ho' from the crow's nest. Once again, they altered course to find it and once again it dissolved into a fog bank. Eventually, signs of land began to pass the ship – seaweed, land birds, sleeping seals and pieces of wood, one of which Banks described as 'part of the produce of our Land of Promise', by which he meant the Southern Continent.

Cook knew he was fast approaching the meridian of longitude that Abel Tasman had recorded for the west coast of New Zealand, so the unknown east coast must be close. It was imperative that they saw the land before they crashed into it, so Cook offered the usual reward:

> The captain apprehended that we were near land, and promised one gallon of rum to the man who should first discover it by day, and two if he discovered it by night; also, that part of the coast of the said land should be named after him.[14]

Cook's call was premature, as New Zealand was further east than he had calculated. His error was partly due to the uncertainties of ocean dead reckoning from his position at Tahiti and partly to the crude longitudes laid down in the old charts.[15] For another week, the *Endeavour* continued westing while tension mounted amongst the crew as eager sailors scanned the horizon, hoping to win the reward. Every distant cloudbank looked like land, only to turn to puff or, as Banks said, 'Our old enemy Cape flyaway'.[16]

The long-awaited cry came at 2 p.m. on Friday 6 October 1769. 'A small boy who was at the mast head Calld out Land,' wrote Banks before climbing up to the mast to see for himself. The small boy was eleven-year-old Nick Young, probably a stowaway, whom Banks had taken under his wing. The lad had spotted a high inland hill which won him his gallon of rum and also his place in history when Cook later named a nearby promontory Young Nick's Head.

The ship erupted in joyful celebration, but not Cook. The captain's immediate responsibility was to determine his landfall longitude, after a three-month passage across the trackless ocean from Tahiti. After hours spent computing log entries and making astronomical observations, he concluded that the ship's longitude by dead reckoning was 3°16' east of the longitude determined by the lunar distance method.[17] He was pleased. This was an acceptable error, easily accrued on a long run out of sight of land with shifting winds and currents. Now, having calculated his first coordinates for New Zealand's east coast, Cook was looking forward to correlating them with Abel Tasman's calculations for the west coast. But the width of the country was unknown and Cook would have to wait until he rounded the coast and intersected Tasman's track. From his landfall near Young Nick's Head, Cook had the choice of sailing north towards Tasman's departure point at Cape Maria van Diemen. Alternatively, he could turn south to search for the eastern entrance of the suggested strait that might flow through to Zeehaen's Bight. First, though, he wanted to refresh his ship and his men.

Curiously, although Cook knew he had reached New Zealand, he doesn't mention this Dutch name in his journal until after leaving the country six months later. He prefers to use the native names, Aeheinomouwe and Tovypoenammu for North and South Island respectively. Similarly, Cook does not mention Abel Tasman's name until the end of the year, and then only incidentally. Even so, as the *Endeavour* approached New Zealand's coast, Cook reached for his extracts of Abel Tasman's journal. They had several versions in the library of the great cabin, including Campbell's latest English translation of Dirck Rembrantsz van Nierop's digest[18] and the account in Valentyn's veritable encyclopaedia of most regions of maritime Asia.[19] With their collections of voyaging accounts, old maps, coordinates and Dutch placenames, these volumes served as Cook's rudimentary Baedeker guidebook for parts of the *Endeavour*'s route from New Zealand to Batavia.

21 North Island: Synchronizing with Tasman and Possession Dilemmas

Meanwhile, crew and civilians cheered and congratulated each other as the land drew near. They had reached their destination, but what was it? Banks and his Continentalists were certain that they had discovered the Antarctic Continent, Terra Australis Incognita. Of course, it was not as large as Dalrymple's Southern Continent, much of which had sunk under the *Endeavour*'s track across the South Pacific. Nonetheless, they believed that Dalrymple was correct in adopting Tasman's first suggestion, that New Zealand was the western side of the legendary continent.

Banks was triumphant. After climbing down from the masthead, he wrote 'all hands seem to agree that this is certainly the Continent we are in search of'. Evidently, the Continentalists were in the majority. Richard Pickersgill, Cook's assistant surveyor, took a clean sheet of paper and began to sketch: 'A Chart of Part of the Southern Continent'.[1] Solander – the most erudite man on the ship – had been cataloguing the plants collected at each landing place using the Linnaean system. Now, giving the 'Southern Continent' its correct scholarly name of Australia, he put aside his list of '*Plantae Otaheitenses*' and started a new list which he titled '*Plantae Australiae*'. His next list would be titled '*Plantae Novae Hollandiae*' when they arrived at their final Pacific destination the following year.[2]

For two days the new land beckoned but the ship was held up by lack of wind. By the time they dropped anchor, expectations had hit fever pitch as men savoured the thrill of taking the Southern Continent for King George III. This posed a dilemma for Cook. On the one hand, if this land was the continent as most of the people believed, then he was bound to 'take possession of convenient situations' of it in accordance with his instructions. On the other hand, if – as he believed – this was an island, then he was not authorized to claim it because it was already discovered by a European. It was, as the Admiralty's instructions stated, 'the land discovered by Tasman and now called New Zealand'.

Even so, Cook was eager to step onto New Zealand soil, conscious of the fact that he would be the first European to do so. He noted in his journal that, while Tasman had found the place, 'he however never landed upon it probably he was discouraged from it by the natives killing 3 or 4 of his people'.[3] It was a nice distinction. Did Tasman's failure to set foot on the island mean that it 'had not hitherto been discover'd by any Europeans' and was therefore eligible for annexation within the terms of the Admiralty's instructions? Perhaps Cook felt that, as the first Europeans to step ashore, his English party must surely acquire some rights. Thus, with a good deal of encouragement from the Continentalists, it seems that he decided to conduct a possession ceremony, continent or not.

Working the *Endeavour* into the bay, Cook saw before him a robust and populous community, judging from the houses, canoes and fortifications that lined the beach. He ordered out the pinnace and yawl and rowed ashore with Banks and Solander and a party of marines. Their purpose was to meet the Maori and purchase fresh food and water, but they failed disastrously. Mistakes and confusion triumphed over good intentions and, in those first two days, six Maori were shot and killed. The only pleasant surprise was finding that Tupaia and the Maori understood each other's language perfectly.

It is a vexed question whether Cook claimed possession at this first landing place.

32. The Maori war canoe, or waka taua, was very large and adorned with elaborate carved designs, paint, and feathers.

Parkinson records that on the second day, 9 October 1769, Captain Cook annexed New Zealand at a ceremony in which he took 'possession of the country, in form, for the king'.[4] No one else reported this event, but their accounts provide enough glimpses of pomp and circumstance to corroborate his statement. Banks tells us that Cook ordered out three boats – the longboat, pinnace and yawl – to carry the dignitaries ashore, protected by an armed escort of marines. After landing on the beach, the marines marched with an English Jack to the river bank where they drew up in formation, to be joined by Cook, Solander, Tupaia and Banks. After the ceremony, Cook initially bestowed the name of Endeavour Bay as a memorial of their first landing place.[5] Only later did he have second thoughts and cross out the name of his ship, substituting the name 'Poverty Bay, because it afforded us no one thing we wanted'. Cook must have wished that the whole, unhappy interlude could be scratched from the record.

Putting Poverty Bay behind him, Cook quickly embarked on his main mission: to prove that New Zealand was an archipelago and not a continent. Tasman's journal offered two contrary suggestions: New Zealand was part of the Southern Continent; or, given the 'flood' or current flowing in from the south-east corner of Zeehaen's Bight, there might be a passage there. Although he failed to investigate it, Tasman was so sure of a passage that his pilot, Visscher, left an opening in the coastline when he mapped Zeehaen's Bight. Even Dalrymple conceded in a footnote in his book that the discovery of such a strait would prove that New Zealand was an archipelago and not a continent.

This 'flood' was, of course, Cook Strait. Tasman had detected it from the west and now, 127 years later, Cook would search for it from the east.[6] But as he sailed south from Poverty Bay, the secretive navigator gives us no clue as to the true purpose of his mission, saying only:

My intention is to fowlow the direction of the Coast to the Southward as far as the Latitude of 40 degr. or 41 degr. and then to return to the northward in case we meet with nothing to incourage us to proceed farther.[7]

Six days later, they reached a headland in latitude 40°34'S, which was Tasman's approximate latitude when anchored in Zeehaen's Bight. Cook found no opening here and his field of vision was blocked by the high mountains of the Tararua Range, 'chequered with snow' and stretching southward along the coast as far as the eye could see. Cook judged that there was no likelihood of a break in this barrier for over 100 miles. If the eastern entrance was so much further south, then Tasman's passage was certainly crooked and probably dangerous. Cook didn't want to risk the ship as this early stage of his mission, so he abandoned his search from the east.

Instead, naming the nearby headland Cape Turnagain, he tacked about and headed north towards Cape Maria van Diemen, Tasman's northernmost landfall in New Zealand. From there, Cook would follow Tasman's track southwards to Zeehaen's Bight – and find the strait through its western entrance. During the next five and a half months, the *Endeavour* circumnavigated the country in a figure of eight pattern, while Cook made running surveys of its coast.

A fortnight later, halfway up the Coromandel Peninsula, Green reminded Cook that the transit of Mercury was predicted for 9 November. More frequent than the transits of Venus, solar transits of Mercury occur about thirteen times a century. Cook wanted to observe this event because he believed it would provide him with a definitive longitude. Needing a land base to set up the equipment, they anchored at the next suitable harbour and named it Mercury Bay. The observations were successful, but once again the eleven-day visit was ruined by a death. When a Maori man came to the ship and stole a coat, the normally good-natured Gore lost his temper and shot him dead. Gore was remorseful, and Cook was annoyed. It was the last Maori life taken on the voyage.

At this point there is another oddity in Cook's journal. On leaving Mercury Bay, Cook interrupted his daily journal entries, as he often did when leaving a significant place, with a long description of the bay and its people, finishing with the sentence: 'Before we left this Bay we cut out upon one of the trees near the watering place, the Ships Name, date etc.' Cook evidently thought that their successful scientific achievement deserved a memorial, so he left his calling card, just as European seafarers had done for centuries when they landed on distant shores. Such inscriptions were seen as a proof of presence and were not, in themselves, claims of possession. This final sentence happened to bring his essay to the end of the page. However, in the bottom margin – using a darker coloured ink and smaller script – Cook has squeezed two more lines:

> [A]nd after displaying the English Colours I took formal posession of the place in the name of His Majesty.[8]

Cook gives no date for this possession ceremony at Mercury Bay. It is not mentioned in his daily entries, nor by Banks, or Parkinson or anyone else. As far as I know, I am the first writer to comment on this apparent addition of the two lines. If they were added later, this was not the only phantom possession ceremony of the *Endeavour* voyage.

Their last two stopovers on the North Island were the Firth of Thames (Hauraki Gulf), followed by the Bay of Islands. In his journal, Cook recommended both places as ideal sites for a British colony.[9] They pushed on northward and, on 9 December, Cook sailed past an opening to a deep, attractive inlet, regular in shape. Being now so close to land's end, there was no time to inspect it, but Cook named this safe-looking anchorage Doubtless Bay. Here 'doubtless' is used as Shakespeare used it, meaning 'secure' or 'free from suspicion'. Amazingly, if Cook had passed Doubtless Bay a week later, he would have been rather less free from suspicion upon finding a French ship anchored there.

Incredibly, the *Endeavour* was not alone in this corner of the Pacific in 1769. Another European ship was rapidly approaching from the west, creating one of history's famous close encounters. The accidental intruder was the *Saint Jean Baptiste*, a merchant vessel commanded by Jean François Marie de Surville. On 16 December, Cook and Surville actually sailed past each other, unknowingly, as they rounded North Cape, heading in opposite directions on almost parallel courses. For an hour or so the ships were incredibly close, with the *Endeavour* positioned about 25 miles north of the *Saint Jean Baptiste*. Yet, even though there were clear patches of sky during that stormy day, the lookouts at the mastheads failed to see each other.

The French vessel had left the Indian port of Pondicherry six months earlier. Surville, a member of a trading syndicate, had been fired up by garbled reports of Samuel Wallis's discovery of Tahiti. Believing the island was fabulously rich, he set out to find it in the eastern Pacific. By the time he reached the Solomon Islands his crew were starving so he turned south, hoping to find food at Tasman's discovery of New Zealand. As he headed down through the Coral Sea, Surville shifted across to the west, which brought him remarkably close to Australia's east coast. In fact, the French were within 100 miles of Sydney Harbour on 4 December, when Surville turned east for New Zealand.[10] Eight days later he reached its north-west corner and hauled around the north coast, looking for a suitable anchorage. It was then that a westerly gale blew up, forcing the oncoming *Endeavour* out to sea, while the *Saint Jean Baptiste* stuck to the coast, so that a historic Anglo–French encounter never took place. The next day, Surville arrived at Doubtless Bay, naming it Lauriston Bay after the governor of Pondicherry, and here the French chaplain celebrated Christmas. A week later, on New Year's Eve, Surville sailed out of the bay bound for South America, 5000 miles away. The Roaring Forties blew the tiny ship directly across the empty sea, removing any lingering ideas about a Great South Land filling the central Pacific. This was the singular, unintended achievement of Surville's voyage; for the rest, it was disastrous. His desperate, scurvy-ridden ship reached the Peruvian coast in April 1770, but Surville drowned in the surf when his boat capsized as he went ashore.

Cook was now wholly focused on finding Cape Maria van Diemen, discovered by Tasman in January 1643. The Dutchman believed, incorrectly, that this headland was the northern extremity of the country and named it after Maria, the wife of Anthony van Diemen, governor of Batavia. For Cook, the crucial importance of this cape was that it would provide him with a fixed datum point. Here, for the first time, the tracks of Cook and Tasman would intersect and, although Tasman had failed to take an observation at the cape, he did record his estimate of its position.[11] Now Cook was determined to fix its position as accurately as the latest navigation techniques would allow. Then he would correlate his coordinates with those of Tasman and compute Tasman's longitude error. With this information, Cook could work out the correct positions of most of Tasman's landfalls in New Zealand and Van Diemen's Land, and calculate the distance between those two Dutch discoveries. As usual, the enigmatic Cook does not explain his purpose in his journal. He merely acknowledges, when he locates them, that Three Kings Island and Cape Maria van Diemen were both discovered by Tasman.

In mid-December, the *Endeavour* reached the northernmost point of the country. It was a significant milestone and deserved a significant name, but the best Cook could manage was North Cape, as his mind was on more important matters. The promontory he wanted, Cape Maria van Diemen, lay just a few miles away to the south-west. It should have been a short, easy sail, but as they rounded North Cape into the Tasman Sea (as it is now called) they were hit by furious gales that threw the ship off course and out to sea. Cook turned the ship and regained the coast – 'much to the credit of our old Collier', Banks applauded – only to be blown out again as soon as the wind returned. It split the foresail, then the mizzen topsail, then most of the other sails, as the men raced to repair them. Day after day Cook battled the storms and driving rains, catching glimpses of the cape as they zigzagged round it, taking sightings from the pitching deck. He would never give up.

On Christmas Eve, there was a lull in the storm and the master of ceremonies, Joseph Banks, took out a boat, shot several gannets and delivered them to the galley. Here the ship's cook baked the birds into a magnificent 'goose pye', the centrepiece of the bacchanalian celebrations that marked their second Christmas at sea. For many it was a two-day bender, as Banks proudly recorded: 'all hands were as drunk as our forefathers used to be upon the like occasion'.[12]

Cook ignored the festivities. Totally immersed in his nautical calculations. In the end, he recorded more than a dozen sightings of Cape Maria van Diemen and eventually fixed its position to his own exacting standards. Beaglehole is impressed: 'the position he fixed was astonishing: two minutes out in latitude, four minutes in longitude'.[13] But Cook's datum point had come at a price: his zigzags round the Cape ate up more than two weeks of the voyage. As Banks remarked, Cape Maria van Diemen is 'our Ne plus ultra'.[14]

Now Cook could turn his attention to his next priority: the strait that would confirm that New Zealand was an archipelago and not a continent.

22 A Transformative Moment: Proving Cook Strait

It was 1770 – Captain Cook's *annus mirabilis*. On New Year's Day, the *Endeavour* turned south and Cook resumed his running survey of the west coast of North Island. In a matter of days, the crew saw the snow-topped peak of a magnificent sleeping volcano with its graceful outline sweeping down to the plains below. Cook named it Mount Egmont and, rounding the spur of land at its base, he found the great gulf of Zeehaen's Bight stretching before him. He followed its shoreline around to the far corner where Abel Tasman had once felt a current flowing from the south-east. Leaving the coast of North Island, Cook sailed across the bight to the heavily serrated coast of South Island which promised a good anchorage. They found a deep inlet running south-west and turned into it. There was an island (Motuara) guarding its entrance where many of the local people were gathered, shouting and waving at the passing ship. Cook would visit the island later, but for now he went across to the opposite shore where he found 'a very snug Cove' which he named Ship Cove. The small bay lies in the lee of Arapawa Island, within the steep, high hills of Queen Charlotte Sound, the easternmost of the Marlborough Sounds on the north coast of New Zealand's South Island. Queen Charlotte Sound would become Cook's Pacific base not only for this voyage, but for all his future campaigns in the South Pacific. It provided a safe shelter where he could careen his ship and rest his men and secure food, fresh water and wood.

As soon as they anchored, the ship was surrounded by four canoes that had followed from the island. These Maoris seemed threatening at first, but Tupia engaged them in conversation and soon an old man asked to come aboard. A rope was thrown to help him onto the deck, where he was greeted enthusiastically and showered with presents. His name was Topaa, apparently the leader of these people, and he became a valuable guide for the visitors through the coming weeks.

The first week of their three-week stay was spent managing the needs of the ship. Cook and his officers allocated the tasks of scrubbing her bottom and caulking her sides, setting up the iron forge to fix the tiller, repairing the rigging, drying the gunpowder, filling the water casks, correcting the ballast, cutting grass for the livestock and wild celery for the crew, chopping wood, fishing and much more. Once the repair and provisioning operations were smoothly underway, Cook took out the boats and went exploring. His most exciting venture took place on Monday 22 January 1770.

That morning, Cook invited Banks and Solander into the pinnace and they rowed south through the labyrinth of islands and peninsulas, searching for Tasman's channel. When this proved impracticable at sea level, Cook looked up to the surrounding ridges which promised a bird's-eye view of this wide aquatic landscape. His boyhood memories of the span of aerial views from Roseberry Topping had never left him. He picked out Kaitapeha ridge which rises to 1268 feet above the south-western end of Arapawa Island and rowed over to it. Leaving the botanists to fossick below, Cook took one of the oarsmen and together they climbed to the top of the hill, now known as Cook's Lookout.

After taking in the panorama with a sweeping gaze, Cook turned to the south-east and saw the Pacific Ocean sparkling in the sunlight, with a channel of water linking it to the Tasman Sea. Later, he wrote in his journal:

> I was abundantly recompenced for the trouble I had in assending the hill, for from it I saw what I took to be the Eastern Sea and a strait or passage from it to the Western Sea.[1]

This was the transforming moment of Cook's life. Here was the strait that proved Cook right and Dalrymple wrong. The lowly farm boy had suspected from the start that there was no continent in the habitable latitudes of the South Pacific. But the aristocratic Dalrymple, with his theoretical modelling, had won over most fellows of the Royal Society, the men at the Admiralty and Mr Banks's popular set on board the *Endeavour*. It had been a lonely voyage for Cook, but now he had proved the non-existence of Dalrymple's Southern Continent on Dalrymple's terms: 'If the flood comes from S.E. it would seem this land was not Continent but Islands'.[2] The weight of Dalrymple and his cronies lifted from his shoulders: he was Cook the Navigator now.

James Cook was not in the habit of stamping his own name on his discoveries, but he was surely entitled to name this waterway Cook Strait. As he ran back down the hill, he allowed himself a rare moment of jubilation which was captured by Banks:

> While Dr Solander and Myself were botanizing the captn went to the top of a hill and in about an hour returnd in high spirits, having seen the Eastern sea and satisfied himself of the existence of a streight communicating with it, the Idea of which had Occurd to us all from Tasmans as well as our own observations.[3]

Here once again, it is only Banks who acknowledges Tasman's role in this pivotal discovery. In Cook's own account of his search for the strait, he never refers to the Dutch navigator.

Four days later, Cook wanted to view the strait again, from a different position.

With Banks and Solander, he rowed east across the sound to the opposite end of Arapawa Island and selected an even higher hill. This time they all climbed to the top and were rewarded with a glorious, uninterrupted view of the strait.

There was nothing more to be done in Queen Charlotte Sound, except to erect some markers. The carpenter prepared two posts, each inscribed with the ship's name and date, and one was planted in Ship Cove. The next day, 31 January, Cook loaded the second marker – and a bottle of wine – into the pinnace and rowed across to Motuara Island at the entrance to the sound, accompanied by Tupaia and William Monkhouse, the surgeon. Curiously, Banks stayed behind even though, as he records, he and Solander did nothing all day, except 'fished a little in the evening and had good sport'.[4]

They landed on the beach and, with Tupaia translating, Cook asked the people if he could erect the marker 'to shew to any ship that might put into this place that we had been here before'. The people agreed and promised never to pull it down. Thereupon, Cook, Tupia, Monkhouse and Topaa, the old man they had met earlier, climbed the highest hill on the island and fixed the post in the ground. Then Cook went further. He hoisted an English Jack, named the inlet Queen Charlotte's Sound and 'took formal possession of it and the adjacent lands in the name and for the use of His Majesty'.[5] Afterwards, they drank Queen Charlotte's health from the bottle of wine and gave the empty bottle to the old man 'with which he was highly pleased'. Commenting on Cook's claim, Beaglehole writes 'how he would have defined "the adjacent lands" may be left in obscurity'.[6]

With their departure imminent, Cook attempted to gather all the information he could about the geography of the coast that lay ahead. Although no European had mapped this land, Cook had learnt from Tupaia's example that the Polynesian people had extensive knowledge of the sea around them. So over the next few days Cook asked Topaa and others to describe the land or lands that lay to the south. Their answers are recorded in various versions by Cook, Banks and Pickersgill. The Maoris said that their country was not part of a continent, but that it consisted of several islands. One of these lay in the north and others to the south, so that the visitors could expect to find at least one more strait after Cook Strait.[7] It was very useful information. Cook thanked them for their guidance and sailed away to complete his chart of New Zealand.

23   Cook Covers his Tracks: Stewart Island Becomes a Peninsula

On 7 February, the *Endeavour* sailed through Cook Strait and re-entered the Pacific, having almost circumnavigated the North Island. The ship had bisected the country but, amazingly, the die-hard Continentalists would not admit defeat. Now they argued that the North Island was joined to their continent by some imagined isthmus that sprung from the short strip of unexamined coast. So Cook felt obliged to turn the ship north for several leagues until they came in sight of Cape Turnagain. At least the exercise gave him the chance to confirm the chain of hills that had blocked his view of Cook Strait four months earlier. And there was amusement all round when they failed to find a sprouting continent:

> I then called the officers upon deck and asked them if they were now satisfied that this land was an Island to which they answer'd in the affirmative and we hauled our wind to' the Eastward. [1]

With that argument settled, Cook turned about to make a clockwise circuit of the South Island. But a week later, the Continentalists were at it again. On the evening of the 15th, someone thought he saw land to the south-east, so the obliging Cook steered towards it through the night. Nothing was found and they returned to the coast, but the following day there was another sighting. John Gore declared that he had seen land in the south-east when he was on the morning watch. Cook was not amused. He was trying to chart the coast and had no wish to chase another cloud. But Gore was insistent and the following morning Cook turned the ship to the south-east. He thought he had little choice, as Banks points out: '[T]he Captn who resolvd that nobody should say he had left land behind unsought for ordered the ship to be steered SE'.[2]

Cook knew that, back in London, Dalrymple was waiting to pounce on any failure to investigate a sighting. So Cook searched the open sea for two days, only to find that 'Mr Gores imaginary land' did not exist. They returned to the coast again.

Unfortunately for Cook's reputation, these distractions took their toll, contributing to the mapping errors he made that week when he twice mistook a peninsula for an island. On 15 February, he saw some people watching the ship from what he thought was an island, which he named Lookers On. But the place was later identified as the Kaikoura Peninsula.[3] Two days later, Cook saw a prominent hill which seemed detached from the coast and he called it Banks Island. Although this hill was originally an off-shore volcanic island, it became tied to the coast long ago and is today Banks Peninsula.[4]

Of course, these are minor errors on the great surveyor's chart of New Zealand. Historians excuse the mistakes by pointing to the particular circumstances, such as the contours of the land and Cook's line of sight and the fact that, in Beaglehole's words: 'Gore was making his presence felt at this time'.[5] Their treatment is understandable, but this generosity stands in stark contrast to their reaction to Cook's far more egregious 'errors' later in the voyage when excuses were harder to find.

As they continued southwards, Banks still cherished strong hopes that this was the Southern Continent but admitted that his party of Continentalists were now in the minority – 'myself and one poor midshipman'. The rest of the men had done with continent-hunting and just wanted to go home to some roast beef and a jug of ale.[6] This seemed possible when they reached the southern tip of South Island in the first week of March and hoped that this was the long-awaited termination of the coast. But when the murk cleared, the lookout at the masthead cried out: 'Land ho!' Lying ahead of them, across Foveaux Strait, lay Stewart Island, New Zealand's third largest island.

It is at this point in the *Endeavour* voyage that Cook's journal becomes so interesting, changing from a journeyman's chronicle to a political document. Initially, Cook observes and records the island's insularity. Then, some weeks later, he changes his mind, alters his journal and charts to depict Stewart Island as a peninsula. Fortunately for the history sleuth, this first attempt at concealment was clumsy and Cook left a trail of evidence showing the discrepancies between his initial observations and his subsequent change of heart.

Even so, this first sally into cartographic falsification was remarkably successful. Historians maintain that Cook's portrayal of Stewart Island as a peninsula, joined to the mainland by a narrow isthmus, is one of Cook's few, significant mistakes. In 1954, R.A. Skelton, cartographic historian and Superintendent of the Map Room at the British Museum, wrote of Cook:

> We can point to only three major mistakes in his charting which he did not himself detect – the delineation of Banks Peninsula (in the South Island of New Zealand) as an island, and of Stewart Island as a peninsula, and the failure to determine the insular character of Tasmania.[7]

Banks Peninsula has been discussed. But did Cook really miss Foveaux Strait in 1770?

On 5 March 1770, the *Endeavour* rounded the south-east corner of the South Island and briefly entered the wide open passage of Foveaux Strait. Cook could see high land to the south which had no visible connection to the mainland in the north. Was this the strait that Topaa and his friends had foreshadowed when they said that not one, but two islands lay to the south? Cook chose not to sail through the strait because he wanted to press on southward until everyone on board was satisfied that they had reached the end of the land. So he tacked about and, for the next five days, followed the coast clockwise round the island, finding no sight of land further south. On three separate occasions, Cook observed and recorded Stewart Island's insularity in his journal and drew the strait on his chart. When they arrived at the western entrance to Foveaux Strait, the crew looked through the opening to the distant eastern entrance and recognized Ruapuke Island, which they had passed five days earlier. Everyone on board could see daylight between Stewart Island and the mainland.[8]

A few weeks later, the circumnavigation of the country was complete and Cook made his first chart of New Zealand (Fig. 33). Significantly, on this chart sections of coast are left blank where the ship was too far from shore for observations to be made. However, although the outline of Stewart Island is incomplete, anyone looking at this first chart could reasonably conclude that it was an island, consistent with Cook's original comments, before Cook changed his mind.

But Stewart Island's insularity didn't last long. Some weeks later, perhaps when sailing towards New Holland, Cook sat at his desk in the great cabin and amended his journal and drew a revised chart where he attached Stewart Island to the mainland, turning it into a peninsula. He had suddenly recalled the Admiralty's policy of disinformation and its instruction to conceal any

33. Before changing his mind: Cook's first manuscript chart, made from his own observations, depicts Stewart Island as an island.

strait separating Van Diemen's Land from New Holland, and thought that Foveaux Strait should be treated the same way.[9]

Why would Cook want to conceal a small strait at the bottom of New Zealand? Cook himself had a ready answer for such a question. Three years later, after allotting two months of his second voyage to mapping the coast of Dusky Sound, Cook wrote: 'although it lies far remote from the trading parts of the world … we can by no means tell what use future ages may make of the discoveries made in the present'.[10]

Cook was working an age when France, Britain's chief enemy, could threaten war over tiny, cold, lucrative Newfoundland. He had just spent five years investigating its economic potential and strategic importance and had seen how troublesome the adjacent French islands had become. If an isthmus had joined St Pierre and Miquelon to Newfoundland, they would never have been ceded to France and French fishermen would have been forced to look further afield for their shelter.

Now, stripped of their colonies in Canada and the Falklands, the French might be searching for a base for a new French Empire in the South Pacific. Britain must not be caught napping again, as it had been when Bougainville established his colony in the Falklands.

Now Cook had found an archipelago with the same valuable products as Newfoundland – fish, whale oil, fur seals, timber. He admired its people, its fertility, its harbours and its geopolitical position in the new emporium of the Pacific. Stewart Island was close to New Zealand, to unexplored Van Diemen's Land, to New Holland and to the fabled Southern Continent, wherever it was, which promised valuable commodities and, more importantly, sophisticated customers eager to purchase Europe's manufactured exports. Furthermore, it lay within cooee of the Spanish colonies of Peru and Chile for the purposes of trade or war. Such a jewel must not be relinquished to Britain's European rivals. Cook had annexed the country in the name of King George III; he recommended it in his journal for colonization; and he decided to use it as his Pacific base on future expeditions.

For the time being, vulnerable Stewart Island could be protected only by concealing its insularity, so Cook altered his records to suggest it was part of the South Island. He was doing what cartographers had done for centuries: falsifying a discovery on behalf of an employer – be it a private trading company such as the Dutch East India Company, or a state's navy – for commercial, political or military reasons. Here, Cook's purpose was to prevent Stewart Island from being used by Britain's enemies as a base for launching attacks against the mainland colony that Cook imagined Britain would plant in New Zealand.

Cook believed he was duty-bound to misrepresent Stewart Island as a peninsula. So he opened his journal at the entry for Sunday 11 March and rubbed out the seven lines describing Foveaux Strait. Then, writing over the erasures, he penned his extraordinary statement which would airbrush the strait from the map for the rest of the century:

> but when I came to lay this land down upon paper from the several bearings I had taken it appear'd that there was but little reason to suppose it an Id. [island]; on the contrary I hardly have a doubt but what it joins to and makes a part of the main land.[11]

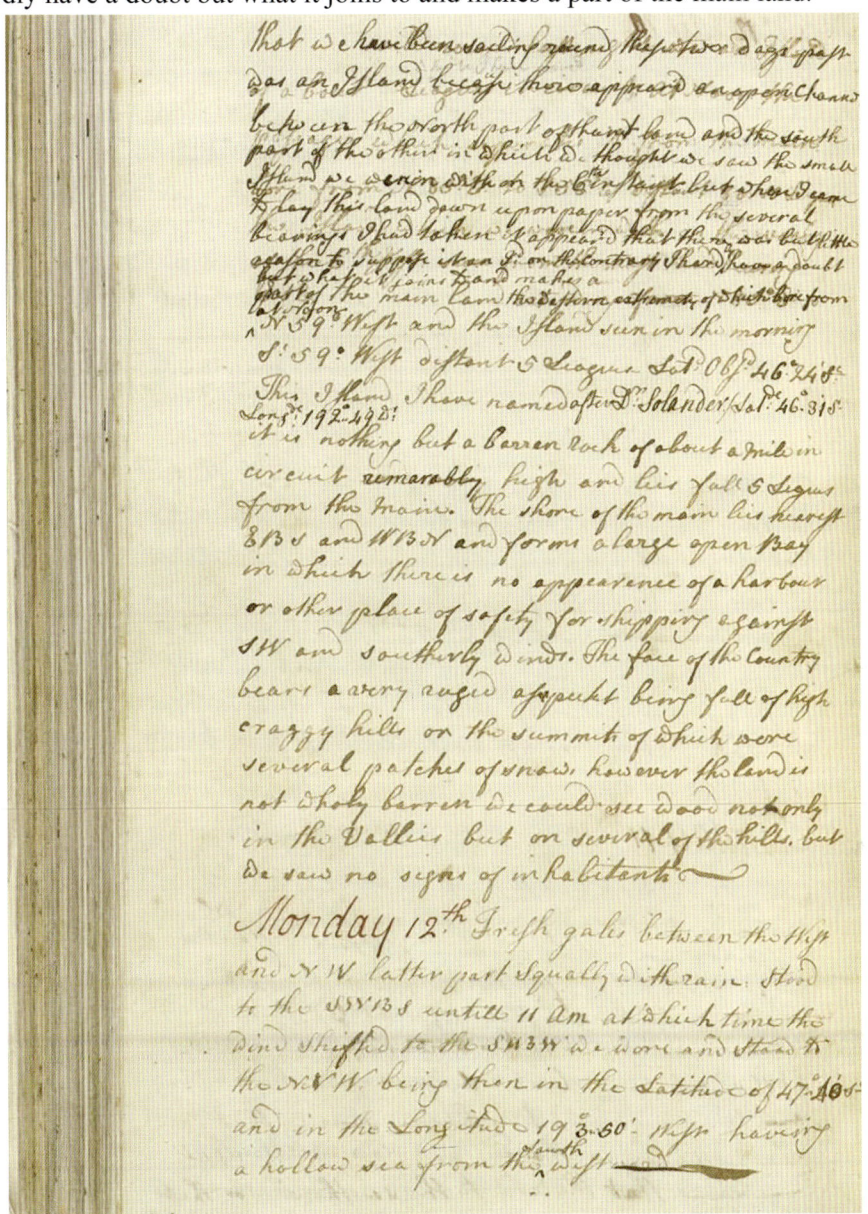

34. Cook's journal entry for 11 March 1770. At the top of the page, Cook has partially erased his seven lines describing the width, length and direction of Foveaux Strait, then over-written them with ten lines describing his subsequent change of mind and asserting a peninsula. National Library of Australia nla.obj-229031188.

More than one scholar has gasped in disbelief at this. Cook's editor, biographer and champion, Beaglehole, struggles to explain his protagonist: 'It is difficult to follow Cook's reasoning here without knowing all that was in his mind. On paper he is unconvincing.'[12] Another New Zealander, Robert McNab – lawyer, politician and historian – was born at Invercargill on the north shore of Foveaux Strait. He knew that the ferry ride from his home to Stewart Island is about the same distance as the ferry trip from Dover to Calais. A 21-mile isthmus across Foveaux Strait was as laughable as a 21-mile isthmus across the English Channel. He knew that the short, straight, wide passage was unmissable in clear weather and that Cook's reclassification of the island as a peninsula was 'incredible'. Still, McNab went along with it because of Cook's unassailable reputation: 'Unless given us in Cook's own words, it would be incredible that he could have made such a mistake – of concluding that it was part of the mainland'.[13]

Having amended his journal, Cook now provided corroborating evidence. He put aside his accurate first chart and drew a less accurate second chart showing New Zealand as two islands, not three. The most interesting feature of the second chart is the droll little isthmus that spans Foveaux Strait. It is reminiscent of the bridge on the willow pattern plate and a baffled Beaglehole describes it as 'a sort of dotted artificial bridge'.

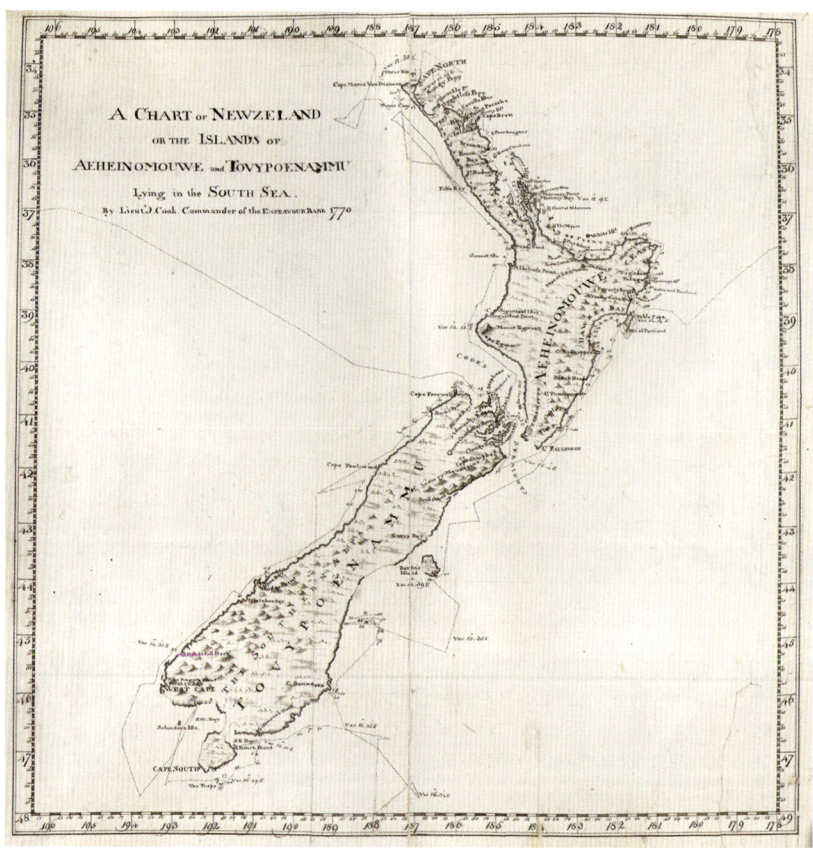

35. After changing his mind: in his second manuscript chart, Cook joins the island to the mainland 'by a sort of dotted artificial bridge', changing Stewart Island into a peninsula.

However, even a dotted isthmus was not sufficient for the Admiralty. When the engraving of this chart was published in Hawkesworth's authorized account, the dots of the isthmus had become solid lines, albeit fainter than the observed coast.[14]

Beaglehole and McNab are two of the few historians to challenge Cook's logic. They recognize the anomaly of Cook, the near-perfect surveyor, drawing a near-perfect chart, only to tarnish it with a glaring, inexplicable error. Yet, as they struggle to explain why Cook changed his mind about the insularity, they cannot conceive that he – or the Admiralty – would deliberately misinform. In the end, they too accept the excuse of a less cynical age: that Cook made a mistake.

Cook's first attempt at falsification was clumsy. His journal and charts contain a trail of documentary evidence for the historical detective to follow. After his initial confident and accurate description of an island, he bungled his efforts to change it to a peninsula. He forgot to delete his three observations of Stewart Island's insularity; the erasure of his seven-line description of the strait is clearly visible; and the logs of the other witnesses contradict him. Still, Cook learnt from these mistakes and his next fabrication would be almost undetectable.

By concealing Foveaux Strait, Cook demonstrated his agreement with the Admiralty's unwritten policy of disinformation. He was not going to let cartographic integrity get in the way of Britain's national interest, but would keep the insularity of New Zealand's third largest island secret until the Admiralty could devise a plan to protect it, should it want to.

Hawkesworth's official account of the *Endeavour* voyage, which includes Cook's charts showing the non-existent isthmus in New Zealand, was published in 1773. It was one of the most popular publications of the eighteenth century and was quickly translated into French, German and Italian. New editions spread rapidly throughout Europe and America and the charts with the curious isthmus spread with them. Before long, the 'dotted artificial bridge' became solid and the bold teardrop at the bottom of New Zealand became a fixture on world maps for decades.

Cook's fabrication worked and Foveaux Strait remained 'undiscovered' for another 34 years until it was found by an American sealer.

36. Cook's dotted isthmus becomes solid in this decorative Italian map.

24   Choosing a Route Home

Cook's work in New Zealand was done. There was no sign of land south of Stewart Island, only the reappearance of the large hollow swell from the south-west, indicating an empty ocean. Even Banks, the last Continentalist standing, ruefully conceded that this meant 'the total demolition of our aerial fabrick called continent'.[1]

Banks found some consolation in the beautiful fiordland of the west coast and asked Cook to stop the ship so that he and Solander could botanize ashore. They had not landed since leaving Queen Charlotte Sound seven weeks earlier. Scanning the craggy shoreline, Banks pointed to several inviting harbours, but Cook refused to enter them. He said that Doubtful Sound was too narrow and dangerous, but this excuse was not true of the other harbours they passed. Banks was furious and clearly the two men quarrelled. The incident is mentioned in both journals.

Of course, the main reason for Cook's refusal to stop was his eagerness to pursue what was sure to be the real prize of this voyage: those 'more greater objects … viz. the discovery of the whole Eastern Coast of New Holland'.[2] But Cook rarely telegraphed his plans.

First, though, he had to find a harbour where he could wood and water the ship before setting out across the Tasman Sea. He sailed north up the dangerous lee shore of the South Island's west coast in half the time he had spent on the opposite coast. The prevailing westerlies and the great swell made it too dangerous to attempt a landing, as Abel Tasman also had found in 1642. It was not until the *Endeavour* turned once again into Zeehean's Bight that they found a safe anchorage in Admiralty Bay, not far from his previous anchorage in Queen Charlotte Sound. The next four days were spent filling the water casks, cutting wood and fishing. Now it was time to depart.

Captain Cook had completed all the tasks of the *Endeavour* expedition. He had observed the transit of Venus, sailed to latitude 40°S in search of the Southern Continent and charted New Zealand's coast.

Yet Cook knew that Dalrymple and his allies would expect him to return via Cape Horn, searching the Pacific in ever higher latitudes for the elusive Southern Continent. Any decision to abandon this search would attract strong criticism from his detractors when he returned to London, as indeed it did. No doubt Cook was also concerned about his crew. The *Endeavour* had been at sea for nineteen months and now, with their mission accomplished, his weary sailors would hope that their captain would choose the shortest – not the longest – route home.

The instructions gave Cook sole authority to make the decision but he decided, wisely, to go through the motions of discussing the options with his officers. Such a diplomatic touch would deflect criticism and spread the responsibility. Therefore, he summoned his officers to the great cabin on the evening of 31 March 1770 to discuss the three possible homeward routes, as Cook artfully recorded:

> To return by the way of Cape Horn was what I most wish'd because by this rout we should have been able to prove the existence or non existence of a Southern Continent which yet remains doubtfull; but in order to ascertain this we must have kept in a high latitude in the very depth of winter but the condition of the ship in every respect was not thought sufficient for such an undertaking. For the same reason the thoughts of proceeding directly to the Cape of Good Hope was laid a side especially as no discovery of any moment could be hoped for in that rout. It was therefore resolved to return by way of the East Indies by the following rout: upon leaving this coast to steer to the westward until we fall in with the East Coast of New Holland and then to follow the deriction of that Coast to the northward.[3]

The shrewd captain invited young Mr Banks, Dalrymple's great supporter, to attend the meeting. Certainly, Banks was abreast of all the arguments and seemed to accept the final decision, albeit reluctantly:

> In doing this, although we hopd to make discoveries more interesting to trade at least than any we had yet made, we were obligd intirely to give up our first grand object, the Southern Continent: this for my own part I confess I could not do without much regret. – That a Southern Continent realy exists, I firmly believe; but if ask'd why I believe so, I confess my reasons are weak.[4]

Evidently Cook hoped that New Holland's proximity to the East Indies might open new commercial opportunities for British trade.

As Cook was preparing to unlock the mysteries of New Holland and change the shape of the Britain's eastern empire, seeds of change were already being sown in her western empire. Earlier that month, on 5 March 1770, five American colonists were shot by British troops during a brawl outside the Customs House in Massachusetts. The incident was quickly dubbed the Boston Massacre.

25 Inventing Promontories, Deleting Coastlines: Cook Lays a False Trail in Bass Strait

Cook's first task in New Holland was to confirm – or otherwise – the existence of Bass Strait. Ever since Abel Tasman's discovery of Van Diemen's Land, the unresolved question of its insularity had become, in the words of George Vancouver (who would sail with Cook on his third voyage), 'a real blot in geography'.[1]

Now, 128 years after Tasman's voyage, Captain Cook was perfectly positioned to expunge the blot. From New Zealand, he had only to sail across the Tasman Sea and clarify the matter, yet he failed in this simple task – or so he would have us believe. Yet it is impossible to accept that the brilliant, curious, ambitious navigator sailed away from the south-east corner of Australia without finding Bass Strait. In fact, the evidence of his journals and charts suggest that Cook did find it and then denied his discovery – a denial he was forced to repeat on his second and third voyages. Thanks to Cook, Tasmania's insularity remained a British state secret until Bass Strait was 'officially' discovered in 1798 – and then the French arrived. How did the great hydrographer engineer this?

With his first concealment behind him, Cook was now better prepared for the task of concealing future strategic discoveries. The fiasco of Foveaux Strait had taught him the virtue of silence. From now on, he would avoid discussing the insularity question with the men on deck, in the hope of minimizing the number of potential witnesses to any strait. Also, he would – as best he could – omit any reference to the insularity question in his journal and on his chart.

Consequently, on leaving New Zealand, Cook writes merely that he intends 'to steer to the westward until we fall in with the east coast of New Holland'.[2] This is as misleading as it is vague. Once again, it is Joseph Banks who gives us details of the discussions taking place in the great cabin. He reveals that Cook's initial plan was to steer a more southerly course to a specific destination in Van Diemen's Land, namely: 'as near as possible to the place where Tasman left it'.[3] This was Eddystone Point, as we saw earlier, and it was from this point that Cook would start his northward survey.

The *Endeavour* left New Zealand at Cape Farewell on 31 March 1770 bound for Van Diemen's Land, but a couple of days later the ship veered north. The sardonic Banks blamed the weary helmsman who wished only to get home to England. Whatever the reason, Cook could have corrected the ship's course and regained the route to Eddystone Point, but he chose not to.

Cook had changed his mind. He knew that if he touched at Eddystone Point, he would have to include that coast on his chart, together with some sort of isthmus joining it to the mainland. But Cook had no wish to repeat the silly, awkward dotted bridge that he had placed across Foveaux Strait on his New Zealand chart. Therefore he kept to the new northerly course and avoided Van Diemen's Land entirely. The *Endeavour* crew never saw Tasmania. It lay below the horizon, far to the south.

Their passage across the Tasman Sea was calm for the first fortnight. Then, as the ship approached Bass Strait, it was suddenly battered by westerly gales, heavy rain and huge seas, as Parkinson recorded:

> we had a broken sea that caused the ship to pitch and roll very much at the same time; we shipped a sea fore and aft, which deluged the decks, and had like to have washed several of us overboard.[4]

Cook doubted that these squalls were coming out of a bay. More likely, they were the Roaring Forties funnelling through a strait.

The following day, Banks spotted some land birds – a sure sign that land was near. But where was it? Once again, Cook turned to the library shelf in the great cabin and reached for Abel Tasman's 1642 journal. After comparing the *Endeavour*'s position with Tasman's coordinates for his final landfall at Eddystone Point, Cook wrote:

> by our longitude we are a degree to the westward of the east side of Vandieman Land according to Tasman's, the first discoverer's, longitude of it, who could not err much in so short a run as from this land to Newzeland, and by our Latitude we could not be above 50 or 55 Leagues to the northward of the place where he took his departure from.[5]

Cook's comparison of latitude and distance is remarkably accurate. Eddystone Point lies on Tasmania's north-eastern tip in 41°S, which was 46 leagues (138 nautical miles) south of the *Endeavour*'s position, so well within his estimate of '50 or 55 Leagues'. However, Cook's comparison of the two longitudes is inaccurate, due to the old navigational problem of longitude error. On that day, the *Endeavour* was positioned a degree to the *east*ward of the longitude for Tasmania's east coast (which Cook may have meant), having sailed a distance of 23°43' from Cape Farewell according to the ship's log.

The ship was approaching Bass Strait, but its north shore was still invisible because of the squally weather. Cook continued westward through the night, adjusting the sails to cope with the furious gales and high seas. Then, in the pre-dawn light of 19 April 1770, his second-in-command, Lieutenant Hicks, cried out 'Land ho' when he saw 'land making high' away to the north-east. It's not known what hill or mountain Hicks glimpsed in the interior of New Holland, but Cook would soon reward Hicks as the 'first discoverer' by naming some other piece of the coast after him.[6]

While the crew rejoiced at making landfall, Cook quietly continued westward. He had the mainland coast off to starboard, Van Diemen's Land away to the south, and the wind in his teeth. He believed he was in a passage, but wanted to make certain. He maintained this westerly course for two more hours, applying his great talent for predicting the trend of a coastline and interpreting the winds and currents. By 8 a.m. he was satisfied and quickly turned the ship around. He did not want to advertise the strait to his crew for any longer than was absolutely necessary.

Even so, if Cook had needed another two hours or another two days to satisfy himself, he would have taken them. If necessary, he could have spent the next two weeks circumnavigating the island, as Bass and Flinders did 29 years later. Cook did not have time to waste, but he did have time to resolve this question and would not leave this coast until he had. He was the famously tenacious surveyor, renowned for his 'indefatigable industry', who had recently allotted almost two weeks to the task of fixing the position of Cape Maria Van Diemen at the northern tip of New Zealand. Apart from keeping his transit appointment in Tahiti, there is no entry anywhere in Cook's journal which suggests he was sailing to a timetable.

Cook had settled the question of the insularity of Van Diemen's Land, but he could not create a documentary record of his discovery. When he wrote up his journal, he knew he had to conceal the strait, but couldn't yet bring himself to tell an outright lie. So he composed a riddle instead:

> [I am] doubtfull whether they are one land or no: however every one who compares this Journal with that of Tasmans will be as good a judge [as] I am, but it is necessary to observe that I do not take the situation of Vandiemen's from the prented Charts but from the extract of Tasmens Journal published by Dirk Rembrantse.[7]

Where was the honest, plain-speaking Yorkshireman now? The historian Professor Ernest Scott has written: 'There can be no doubt that Cook believed at this time that Australia and Tasmania were divided by a strait'.[8] But then the professor hesitates. After making this bald statement of fact, he makes no attempt to explain why Cook shifted from this position of certainty to a position of doubt when he wrote up his journal. Like his fellow historians, McNab and Beaglehole, Scott cannot imagine that Captain Cook would falsify his own clear observations.

Cook's journal entry was clever, but the design of his chart was ingenious. Titled 'A Chart of the Sea Coast of New South Wales or the East Coast of New Holland',[9] it is a

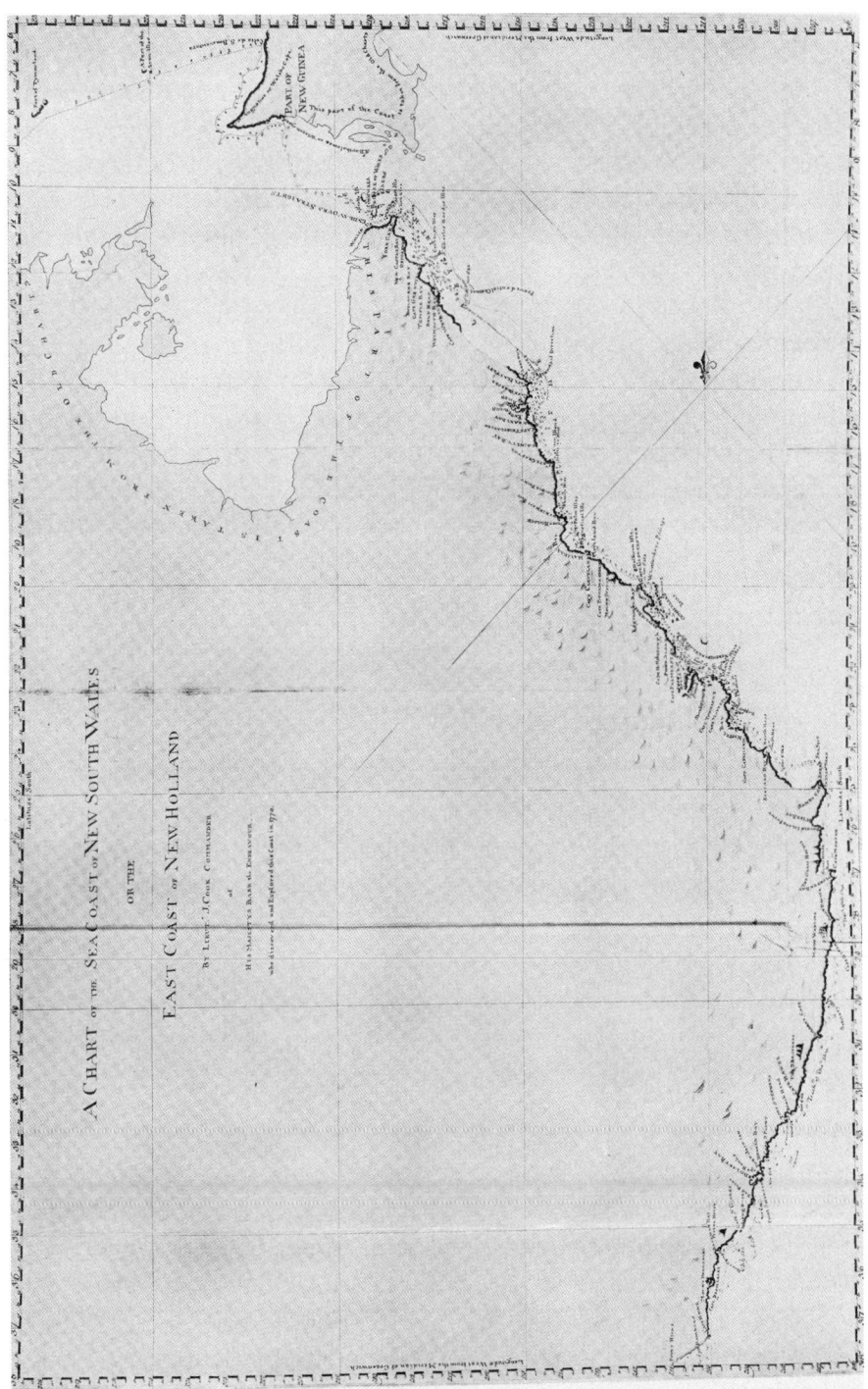

37. Cook's manuscript chart of the Sea Coast of New South Wales is cut short to conceal Bass Strait. National Library of Australia https://nla.gov.au/nla.obj-588080489/view.

masterly survey, but the composition is strangely unbalanced and truncated. At the top of the map, Cook has left a generous space between Cape York, the northern tip of his New South Wales, and the upper edge of the map. He has filled this space with several features which provide a geographical context, including Torres Strait, part of New Guinea, part of Timor and the track of *Endeavour* towards Batavia. He has also pencilled in the entire coast of the Gulf of Carpentaria. Cook never saw this coast, of course, but he copied it from the Dutch charts, as indicated by his perimeter note: 'This part of the coast is taken from the old charts'.

Cook could have done the same thing at the bottom of the map. He could have left a space between the southern point of his survey and the lower edge of the map. He could have filled this space with geographical context by pencilling in the Dutch outline of Van Diemen's Land and showing the final leg of *Endeavour*'s track from New Zealand towards New Holland. But he didn't.

Instead, he chops all that from his chart by making the 38th parallel of latitude

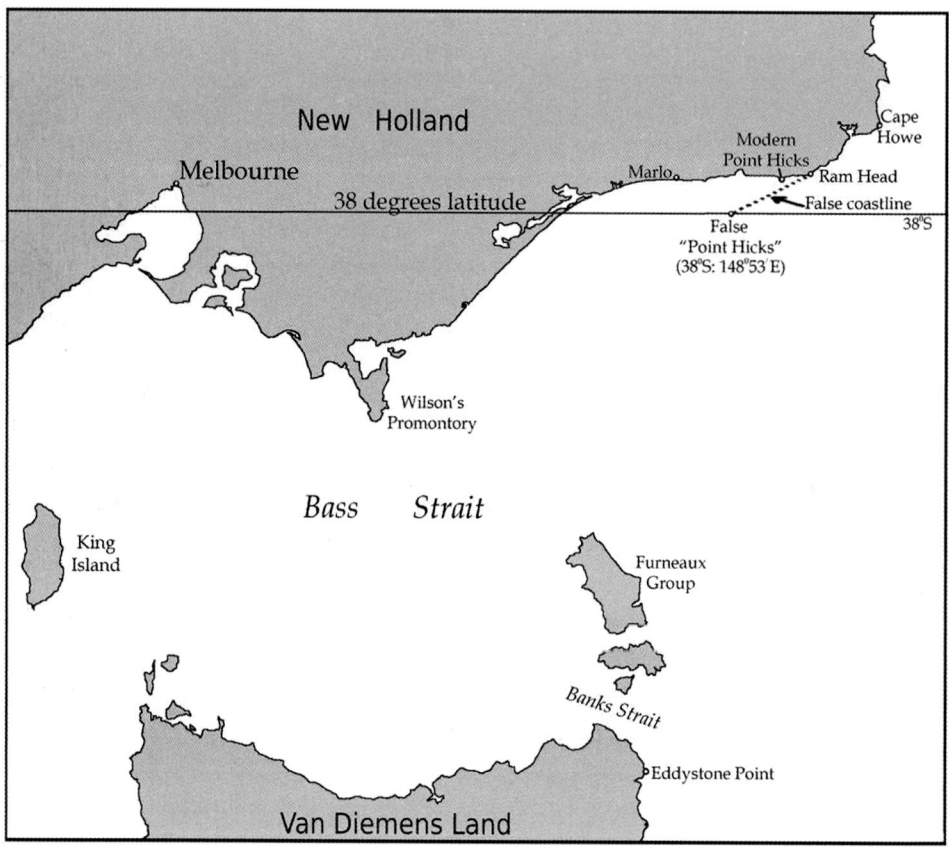

38. Sketch map of Bass Strait and parallel 38 South, showing the waters and context that Cook omits from his truncated chart of the East Coast.

the bottom edge of his map. He leaves no room on the page to show the south coast of the mainland, or the strait, or Van Diemen's Land, or even a dotted isthmus. Then he draws a short diagonal coastline from Cape Howe at the south-east corner of the continent (37°30'S), down to the bottom of the chart at 38°S. The upper section of this coastline is correct, but after Ram Head, the angle should change. At Ram Head the real coast turns west, tracking horizontally along 37°47'S for more than 60 miles. However, Cook does not change the angle. His diagonal coastline continues to the bottom of the chart, travelling over water, not land. Cook has falsified his coast from Ram Head to the bottom – a distance of 47.5 miles (41.4 naut. mi.), based on his logged coordinates.

Having chosen the 38th parallel as the southern limit of his chart, Cook needed a placename to mark the starting point of his east coast survey from that line. So he concocted a mythical promontory, called it Point Hicks, invented its coordinates and wrote in his journal:

> The Southernmost Point of land we had in sight which bore away from us W¼S I judged to lay in the Latitude of 38°0'S and in the Longitude of 211°07'W [148°53'E] from the Meridion of Greenwich. I have named it Point Hicks, because Leuit Hicks was the first who discover'd this land.[10]

When this alleged sighting was made, the *Endeavour* was, according to Cook's log, positioned at lat. 37°58'S, long. 149°21'E, about 30 nautical miles west of the longitude of Cape Howe. From here, he writes, he scanned the western horizon (probably from the masthead) and saw a point of land, lying slightly to the south, which he named Point Hicks. However, no one could have seen such a land feature, because there is nothing but water in that direction for about a hundred miles.

Not surprisingly, after Sydney Town was established, several explorers looked for Cook's 'southernmost point of land'. The first was George Bass during his epic whaleboat journey to Western Port in January 1798. After searching in vain, he declared that Point Hicks was 'a point we could not at all distinguish from the rest of the beach'.[11] Matthew Flinders, who led the first circumnavigation of Australia, also looked for Point Hicks but, unable to find it, he omitted it from all his charts.

No one could find it and its elusiveness soon led to Point Hicks being omitted from most maps until 1970. Then, in commemoration of the bicentenary of Cook's *Endeavour* voyage, the Victorian government renamed a nearby coastal promontory as Point Hicks. It lies on dry land, about 25 miles (22 naut. mi.) north-east of Cook's watery Point Hicks, where it preserves the story of Cook's first landfall in Australia.

Meanwhile, Cook's phantom Point Hicks had generated spirited debate amongst surveyors, navigators and historians for decades.[12] Some have blamed his miscalculation on a compass error, some on a cloud bank, but these excuses only made matters worse. More than a century ago, Professor Scott wrote that such a meteorological mistake 'would be fantastic, even if the observer had been an amateur: but when he was James Cook, the greatest navigator of his age, and one of the greatest of all time, the idea that he mistook a clot of mist for a cape is rather staggering'.[13]

But there was no mistake. Cook's mythical Point Hicks is the lynchpin of his brilliant ruse to conceal Bass Strait. At the stroke of a pen, Cook's false coast turned water into land, removing a large tract of Bass Strait, including the iconic village of Marlo which lies at the mouth of the Snowy River. By deleting these western waters that signalled the entrance to a passage, Cook reinforced the notion the Van Diemen's Land was joined to New Holland, for years to come.

We are left with the impression that Cook saw only the east coast of Australia. He never mentions his landfall on the 'south coast' of the continent, referring only to his visit to the 'east coast of New Holland'. His falsified chart confirms this impression, even though at 8 a.m. on that first day the *Endeavour* was well inside Bass Strait, some 30 nautical miles west of Cape Howe.

Cook had learnt from his mistakes in New Zealand and his strategies for concealing Bass Strait were very successful. He dodged the issue in his journal. He left no space for it on his chart. And he was so adroit in his swift and secret reconnaissance of the strait between 6 a.m. and 8 a.m., that none on board twigged to what was happening. Everyone was distracted by their arrival at New Holland, as Banks records: 'With the first daylight this morn the land was seen, at 10 it was pretty plainly to be observed; it made in sloping hills covered in part with trees or bushes, but interspersed with large tracts of sand'.[14]

The Admiralty evidently approved of Cook's truncated map and even aided and abetted him when preparing the chart for publication. Just as Cook omitted geographical context on the south of his chart, the Admiralty's engraver also removed it from the north and west of the chart. The published version in Hawkesworth shows Cape York at the far north-west corner of the page, leaving no room for Torres Strait or the Gulf of Carpentaria.[15] In the result, some balance has been restored to the composition, so that Cook's truncation is less obvious, and less likely to provoke questions.

No one outside the Admiralty ever guessed that the great navigator had, of course, found Bass Strait in 1770. But secrecy came at a cost. Cook's apparent failure to resolve the big question only encouraged other navigators, English and French, to chase the glory of discovery. Thus the question of the insularity of Van Diemen's Land continued to dog Cook on his next two voyages. On both occasions, instead of entering the Pacific via Cape Horn as he had in the *Endeavour*, he travelled the other way – round the Cape of Good Hope and east into the rising sun. In order to avoid the risk of the crew seeing the strait, the Admiralty never instructed him to revisit Australia as he brushed past it. Yet, each time Van Diemen's Land was visited and each time Cook was again forced to be economical with the truth.

26 Interlude: Hiding Bass Strait for Thirty Years

Cook's second Pacific voyage left England in July 1772 to search the higher latitudes for the Southern Continent and to test John Harrison's chronometer. This time the navy supplied two vessels, the *Resolution* for Captain Cook and the *Adventure* for Captain Tobias Furneaux, who had sailed in the *Dolphin* under Wallis.

From Cape Town, they plunged south in a vain search for Bouvet's Cape Circumcision, then crossed the Antarctic Circle before pack ice and cold forced them north again. The ships managed to stay together for two and a half months, but lost each other on 8 February 1773 in the fog around Kerguelen Island in the Indian Ocean. Cook stayed in the ice and took a southerly route to their rendezvous point in New Zealand, but Tobias Furneaux edged northwards.

Clearly, the problem of Bass Strait and its importance was discussed in both ships. Cook was evidently under pressure to make the detour and resolve the question. Thus, he wrote in his journal, with an eye to his readers, that he was having thoughts of visiting Van Diemen's Land to see if it was joined to New Holland. Yet when Cook wrote this on 17 March 1773, the *Resolution* was positioned a thousand miles directly south of Van Diemen's Land, in the raging westerly winds of the Furious Fifties. From here, he had no chance of reaching Tasmania. Instead, after explaining that the wind prevented such a visit, he continued his north-east course to New Zealand.

Meanwhile, on 9 March, the *Adventure* reached the south-east coast of Van Diemen's Land. Captain Furneaux found an anchorage which he named Adventure Bay and sent an expedition ashore to explore. The men found some huts and saw large fires in the distance, but did not meet any natives. After four days spent refreshing the ship, Furneaux decided to seize his chance:

> Having completed our wood and water, sailed from Adventure bay, intending to coast it up alongshore as high 'till we fell in with the Land seen by Captain Cook and discover whether Van Dieman's Land joins with New Holland.[1]

By midnight on 18 March, the *Adventure* had reached the Bay of Fires and was sailing towards its prominent northern headland. Two hours later the ship was suddenly assaulted by the same ferocious westerly winds that had defeated Tasman in 1642. Furneaux's meagre jottings record: 'at 2, Maintopsail Staysail split all in rags and blew overboard', [2] but his chart tells a more alarming story (Fig. 39) with the ship's track indicating that it was tossed 40 miles out to sea. Furneaux named the headland Eddystone Point, presumably after the notorious Eddystone Rocks in the English Channel 'so called from the great variety of contrary sets of the tide or current in their vicinity'.[3]

Furneaux valiantly regained his course a few hours later and continued north across Banks Strait, past the Furneaux Group of islands, and up into Bass Strait.

Furneaux's journal, unpublished until 1961, provides details of his final hours in Bass Strait which are not included in his authorized 'Narrative'.[4] At 1 p.m. on Friday 19 March, the *Adventure* was off the south-east coast of Flinders Island (as it is now called) and, after sounding just eight fathoms, they headed north into deeper waters. At 4 p.m. they passed Babel Island, then Outer Sister Island (sounding eighteen fathoms) and continued north until the evening. At 7 p.m. they close-reefed the topsails and sounded regularly through the night, measuring 46 fathoms at midnight and 53 fathoms at 2 a.m. By 8 a.m. the ship, in latitude 39°20'S, slightly north of the Kent Group of islands, they sounded 22 fathoms, indicating that the ship had left the deeper water and land lay ahead. Now the weather turned foul and visibility deteriorated, so Furneaux decided to turn east for New Zealand. His unadorned journal entry finishes

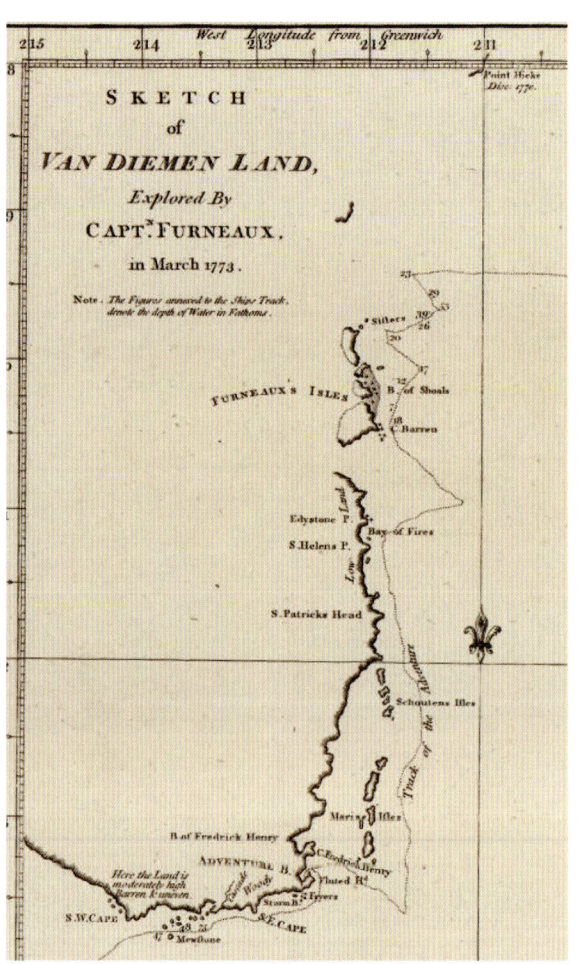

39. In 1773, the Roaring Forties toss Furneaux' ship *Adventure* out to sea near Eddystone Point; and the southern tip of the mainland, Wilson's Promontory, is seen from the masthead in latitude 39°S. National Library of Australia nla.obj-230618345.

here, but Lieutenant James Burney takes up the story:

> at 8 ... we haul'd off & stood for New Zealand – at 9 saw land from the mast head bearing NNW 12 or 14 leagues – this I take to be the south part of New Holland – for it appears very likely to me, that there is a passage between that & Van Diemen's Land.[5]

The weather had cleared sufficiently for the lookout to see a mountainous headland rising in the north-west. Indeed, it was 'the south part of New Holland'. It was Wilson's Promontory which reaches down to 39°08'S, where Furneaux drew it on his chart as the northernmost land they saw.

Twenty-five years later, when Bass was exploring in his whaleboat, he immediately recognized the promontory shown on Furneaux's chart and named it Furneaux's Land as a tribute to its discoverer. He wrote in his journal:

> Its firmness and vast durability make it well worthy of being, what there is great reason to believe it is, the boundary point of a large strait and a corner-stone of this great island, New Holland.[6]

However, when Bass returned to Sydney Town he was dissuaded from using Furneaux's name by Matthew Flinders. Thus the peninsula was renamed Wilson's Promontory, after some forgotten acquaintance.

After recording the strait in his journal, Burney drew a chart of Van Diemen's Land marking in large letters: 'Supposed Streights or Passage'. Other men watching from the deck of the *Adventure* in 1773 detected the strait and some of them recorded their observations.[7]

The astronomer, William Bayly, insisted: 'it seems very evident this is the mouth of a straight which Separates new Holland from Van Diemans Land ... there was a very strong draft of Water directly in shore all the Time we were passing by these broken Islands, which was not the case on any other part of the Coast'.

Richard Hergest, midshipman, wrote on 19 March: 'All the Land which we have passd this Afternoon Appeard to be a Number of Islands if so they are a Strong Confirmation of the Supposed Streights & are in the Mouth of it between Van dieman Land and New Holland'.

Arthur Kempe, first lieutenant, who had sailed with Byron, wrote: 'The opening which we discovered ... I take to be the Streights leading between New Holland and Van Diemen's Land, but this is mere conjecture, as we were not nigh enough to be certain.'

Peter Fannin, the ship's master, drew a chart with the annotation: 'Here appears to be a large River, Deep Bay or perhaps the entrance of Straights between Van Diemans Land & New Holland'.[8]

Presumably if Furneaux was not certain of the passage, he would have investigated further before turning for New Zealand. He had plenty of time on his hands. The

Adventure arrived at the rendezvous point in Queen Charlotte Sound six weeks before the *Resolution*. Cook was still surveying Dusky Sound in the south. On 18 May, a sail was seen entering the bay. The *Adventure* fired an eleven-gun salute which the *Resolution* returned. Then Furneaux went on board to report to Cook after their separation of three and a half months.[9]

The discovery of Bass Strait by Furneaux and his officers was not something that Cook wanted to hear. He examined their journals and charts, writing:

> he supposes that there is a strait or passage behind them [the Furneaux Group] ... When they haul'd up for New Zealand they were in the latitude 39°20'. At that time they saw land from the mast head bearing NNW distant by estimation 12 leagues.

Even in the face of all this evidence, Cook decided

> it is therefore highly probable that the whole is one continued land and that Van Diemens land is a part of New Holland.[10]

Beaglehole is mystified: 'Here again it is rather difficult to follow Cook's reasoning'.[11] But Furneaux understood navy discipline and knew what he had to do. When he wrote his Narrative of the voyage, he stated that Tasmania was indeed a peninsula:

> it is my opinion that there is no Streights between New Holland and Van Dieman's Land, but a very deep bay.[12]

Tobias Furneaux found Bass Strait, but was forced to deny it and his reputation lies in tatters. Beaglehole, who sometimes questioned Cook's reasoning but never imagined that Cook had a secret agenda, wrote of the hapless Furneaux:

> And a really curious man, one feels, would not finally have left the coast of Van Diemen's Land without making certain, from visual evidence, that it was or was not an island, especially knowing what his officers thought on the subject. At the critical moment he clings to assumption, rather than to enquiry; so that he hardly passes into the ranks of the original discoverers.[13]

Furthermore, it was Furneaux's 'corrected' version that enabled Cook to justify his own apparent lack of curiosity:

> I have some were in this Journal mentioned a desire I had of Viseting Vandiemens land in order to inform my self whether or no it made a part of New Holland, but sence Captain Furneaux hath in a great degree cleared up this point I have given up all thoughts of going thither.[14]

This message that the question had been satisfactorily settled by Furneaux was quickly adopted by the Admiralty in a bid to curb further speculation. In the introduction to the official version of Cook's third voyage, published in 1784, the Admiralty's editor wrote:

But what was thus left undetermined by the operations of [Cook's] first voyage, was, in the course of his second, soon cleared up; Captain Furneaux, in the *Adventure*, during his separation from the *Resolution* (a fortunate separation as it thus turned out) in 1773, having explored Van Diemen's Land, from its southern point, along the east coast, far beyond Tasman's station, and on to the latitude 38°, where Captain Cook's examination of it in 1770 had commenced.[15]

Then the Admiralty's engraver added Cook's phantom 'Point Hicks' to Furneaux's chart, although Furneaux himself had not shown it on his manuscript chart.

Still the matter would not rest. Soon after returning to England, Cook received a letter from a young Frenchman requesting advice. Captain Latouche-Tréville was planning a voyage of exploration to that section of the 'undiscovered' south coast of New Holland which neither the Dutch nor the British had seen. Alarm bells surely sounded as Cook feared a French annexation of Bass Strait and the adjacent coasts.

Cook wrote a gracious reply, emphasizing that there was much work to be done elsewhere in the Pacific. In a brief reference to New Holland, he repeated his belief that it was 'a continent which I don't doubt that Van Diemen's land is part, based on what Captain Furneaux has seen of it'.[16] Fortunately for Cook, Latouche's plan was put on the backburner when the Minister of the Marine turned his attention to supporting the rebels in America.

Still the matter would not rest. Three years later, Cook set out on his third Pacific voyage with the HMS *Resolution* and the HMS *Discovery* (Captain Charles Clerke) to search for the Northwest Passage and return Omai to Tahiti. They departed England in July 1776 with instructions to arrive near the Bering Strait by the following June in time for the northern summer. But the expedition quickly fell behind schedule. The ships were late leaving Cape Town and then Cook spent a month exploring the southern Indian Ocean, causing Lieutenant King to fear they 'would hazard ye loss of a season'. In fact, as Beaglehole suggests, Cook probably knew already that he could not meet the Admiralty's unrealistic timetable. In any event, he had no misgivings about making this first detour – or the next one.

The year before, in March 1775, when Cook was at Cape Town on the homeward leg of his second voyage, he met Julien Crozet, the French navigator, who was travelling to Pondicherry. In 1771–73 Crozet had sailed on Marc Joseph Marion Dufresne's expedition south from Mauritius through the Indian and Pacific Oceans. After Marion Dufresne and about twenty of his crew were killed by Maoris in New Zealand, Crozet took command and brought the survivors home. Cook was eager to learn more about the French voyage and so he invited Crozet and his officers to a convivial dinner aboard the *Resolution*.

Crozet obliged his English hosts by telling them stories of their eighteen-month voyage.[17] He spoke of their discoveries of subantarctic islands in the Indian Ocean, their six-day sojourn at Van Diemen's Land and their meetings with the Tasmanian Aboriginal people, the first Europeans to do so. Crozet unfolded his copy of Robert Vaugondy's chart of the Southern Hemisphere recently updated to display the route of his voyage.[18] Cook was filled with curiosity, tinged perhaps with professional and national rivalry. Now on his third voyage, Cook seized his chance to verify the French discoveries in the Indian Ocean. That done, he steered a course for New Zealand 'to recruit our water, take in wood and make hay for the cattle'. But when the thickening fog threatened to separate the two ships, Cook worried that Captain Clerke – like Tasman, Crozet and Furneaux before him – might take his ship to Van Diemen's Land and seize his chance to verify Bass Strait. This must not happen and the only way to prevent it was for Cook to accompany him to the island. Thus, on 7 January 1777, Cook sent a note across to the *Discovery* instructing Clerke to meet him at Furneaux's Adventure Bay.[19]

For three more weeks, the two ships rode the Roaring Forties westwards and arrived at the unscheduled rendezvous on 26 January. The warm sand of the Tasmanian beach felt good after weeks of icy gales in the Southern Ocean, but the men sensed that they were being watched. Sure enough, the following day a small group of men and boys came out of the trees to investigate the new arrivals. Fortunately, it was a friendly and peaceful meeting, as were the two encounters that followed. Cook was greatly pleased by this, particularly after Crozet's report that the French had met local people during their visit, while Furneaux had not. In his journal, Cook described the Tasmanians in great detail, remarking that they seemed quite different from the mainlanders he had met on the *Endeavour* voyage.

Foraging parties were sent out and returned with copious supplies of wood, water, geese and fish. They also found 'plenty of excellent grass for the cattle' on Penguin Island within the bay.[20] Meanwhile, the captain returned to the ship to make some observations and review his itinerary. Cook knew he had lost the season for getting into the high latitudes of the North Pacific by the summer of 1777. The Admiralty's instructions required him to go to the Society Islands

> to land Omiah ... [then] leave those Islands in the beginning of February [1777], or sooner if you shall judge it necessary, and then proceed in as direct a course as you can to the coast of New Albion [North America], endeavouring to fall in with it in the Latitude of 45° 0' North; and taking care, in your way thither, not to lose any time in search of new lands, or to stop at any you may fall in with, unless you find it necessary to recruit your wood and water.[21]

As it was already late January, this was now impossible. Instead, Cook would spend the next ten months cruising amongst the islands of the South Pacific, free to ignore the Admiralty's stipulation not to waste time on new discoveries. He would cross the equator next Christmas and arrive at the Bering Strait for the summer of 1778, a year behind schedule.

Now, thanks to the revised itinerary, Cook had all the time in the world to revisit and clarify those parts of Van Diemen's Land and New Holland which still had question marks hanging over them. Many his companions would soon become famous explorers themselves: William Bligh, George Vancouver, John Ledyard, George Dixon, Nathaniel Portlock, Edward Riou and Joseph Billings. All of them were surely curious to know what lay to the north.

A special plea was made by the men who were visiting Adventure Bay for the second time. William Bayly, James Burney and Richard Hergest all believed that they had seen Bass Strait in 1773 when they sailed into it with Tobias Furneaux, and now they urged Cook to sail north to see it for himself.

But Cook refused to budge. This time, without more humbug, he told a lie (and also omitted Crozet's visit of 1772), writing in his journal:

> Van Diemen Land has been twice visited before, first by Captain Tasman who discovered it in November 1642, and by Captain Furneaux in Mar. 1773. I hardly need say it is the Southern point of New Holland, which if not a continent is one of the largest islands in the world.[22]

Here is Cook's unambiguous declaration that Van Diemen's Land was part of the continent, assuring the world, including the French, that here lay no vulnerable island and no strategic passage. Further enquiry was unnecessary, the matter was finally settled and, with that, the world's greatest hydrographer sailed for New Zealand, where he tarried until the end of February. An exasperated Beaglehole comments:

> We, who know what little difference to the voyage a week's delay would in reality have made, find ourselves regretting, however absurdly, that he did not correct the grand error.[23]

However, Cook's 'grand error' kept Tasmania safe from the French for three decades, though Cook would not know this. Two years after his brief visit to Adventure Bay, James Cook was killed in Hawaii, aged 50.

The next European visitors to the area were the eleven ships of the First Fleet. Sailing round Van Diemen's Land, they passed Eddystone Point in January 1788, and were suddenly hit by 'a perfect hurricane'. Every ship, except the *Sirius*, was damaged, their sails splitting and rigging carried away. Lieutenant William Bradley noted: 'we had a great Sea & think it probable that there may be either a streight or a deep Gulf'.[24]

Over the next decade, this same conclusion was reached by several of the dozens of sea captains who sailed near the strait on their way to and from Sydney. Eventually, the authorities could no longer suppress the fact that Van Diemen's Land was an island. However, before officially announcing the truth, the Admiralty wanted a survey made of the island, before any foreigners or interlopers arrived. So on 7 October 1798, Governor John Hunter sent Matthew Flinders and George Bass in the sloop *Norfolk* to circumnavigate Van Diemen's Land and to make 'such examinations and surveys on the way as circumstances might permit'.[25] Here is an echo of the rush to send Master Cook to survey the islands of St Pierre and Miquelon in Newfoundland before they were handed over to the French 35 years earlier.

Bass and Flinders returned to Sydney in January 1799 and reported the success of their mission. News of Bass Strait was quickly transmitted to Europe, whereupon the French government despatched a reconnaissance expedition of two ships under the command of Nicolas Baudin. He sailed from France in October 1800 with instructions to survey, in particular, the unknown parts of southern New Holland (to be briefly labelled 'Terre Napoleon') and of Van Diemen's Land.[26] When the French ships arrived in Sydney, Baudin's suspicious activities persuaded the new governor, Captain Philip Gidley King, that if he did not send an occupation force to Van Diemen's Land immediately then the French would. King wrote to Lord Hobart, Minister for War and the Colonies in London, warning that:

> [the French] may have some intention of laying claim to Van Diemen's Land, now it is known to be insulated from New Holland ... [I] request Instructions for my conduct in case the latter conjecture should be verified.[27]

But there was no time to wait for instructions from London. In 1803, Governor King sent two vessels to the island to establish Australia's second British colony on the Derwent River at a place called Hobart.

27 Deception at Botany Bay

On 19 April 1770, 30 miles into Bass Strait, Captain Cook completed his investigation of it, and at 8 a.m. he turned the *Endeavour* around and headed back to the east coast. As evening fell, the ship rounded the continent's south-eastern corner, which Cook named Cape Howe, and from here he commenced his epic 2000 mile journey up the east side of the continent. Would it be a continuous coast or a chain of islands? Whatever it was, when Cook's chart was complete and added to the Dutch charts of the north, west and south sides, it would effectively complete the map of New Holland.

The men had not landed for three weeks and so Cook looked out for a good anchorage as they sailed northward. In fact, he passed several promising inlets, including Twofold Bay and Batemans Bay, but chose not to enter them. Soon they reached the great haven of Jervis Bay, today a naval base and the site of the Royal Australian Naval College. With a depth of 27 metres, it is one of the best sheltered and deepest natural harbours in Australia. Although Cook had a good view of it, he made the curious decision not to sail into it, blaming an unfavourable breeze.

But a few days later, another inlet became visible as the sun rose: 'At day light in the morning we discovered a Bay which appeard to be tollerably well sheltered from all winds into which I resolved to go with the Ship'.[1]

The *Endeavour* arrived off Botany Bay at 6 a.m. on Saturday 28 April 1770, but Cook did not enter it at once. There was always the risk with an unexplored bay that a dangerous sandbar – the silt and detritus of aeons – had built up across its mouth, just below the water. So the master, Robert Molyneux, was sent in the pinnace to sound the entrance while the *Endeavour* stayed outside until 1 p.m.

What did *Endeavour* do for these seven hours? Cook writes only that 'we kept turning up with the ship having the wind right out', that is, he kept manoeuvring the ship to remain in the same place. But being active and curious, Cook probably put this time to good use and surely climbed the masthead to study the terrain. Looking through his glass, he could scrutinize the coast as it veered northward, examining the high cliff wall broken by beaches and depressions. Indeed, Cook could have used the opportunity to explore the coast as far as Bondi or beyond, but there is no evidence that he ventured far from Botany Bay that morning.

The men in the pinnace finished sounding the mouth of the bay and returned to the ship with good news: the entrance had a comfortable depth of twelve fathoms as Cook's Chart (Fig. 40) shows.[2] Molyneux also reported seeing a lively group of people on one of the beaches: 'in a cove a little within the harbour they came down to the beach and invited our people to land by many signs and words'.[3] With this encouragement, Cook took the *Endeavour* round the sandstone cliffs of the southern headland and anchored near Molyneux' beach on the south shore.

If Cook was expecting a deep, protected harbour at Botany Bay, he was quickly disappointed. The high balustrades at its entrance gave way to low sandy foreshores and its sea bed shoaled quickly from ten metres at the entrance to a general depth of less than five metres. Fearful of running aground, Cook had to stop the ship even before it had rounded the southern headland. Unable to get close in, he dropped anchor half a mile off the headland now known as the Kurnell Peninsula. Although a deeper channel was soon discovered over on the north side of the bay, Cook did not move the ship to this better mooring. Instead, the *Endeavour*, and her crew, remained stationed on the south side of the bay through the following week. When leaving the ship, they could either wade through the shallows to the beach or use one of the boats – the longboat, pinnace and yawl – to criss-cross the bay as they explored the surrounding country.

After dropping anchor at 1.30 p.m. on Saturday 28 April 1770, the crew sat down to their midday meal. As soon as they had finished eating, Cook organized a landing party of some 30 men including Banks, Solander, Tupaia, and a detachment of marines. Cook wanted to meet the Aboriginal people who had gathered on the beach and hoped that Tupaia would understand their language. At three o'clock the boats were hoisted out and they rowed towards the shore. Family tradition has it that the first to land was able seaman Isaac Smith, the young nephew of Elizabeth Cook. As the pinnace ran up the beach Cook called to him 'You go first', which Isaac did and was promoted to midshipman within the month.[4]

The British tried to communicate with the people on the beach, but they failed in this attempt and in their subsequent attempts that week. None of these early encounters was happy but although shots were fired no one was killed. The only death at Botany Bay was Forby Sutherland – who died of consumption. Cook and his men would have more positive meetings with the people in Queensland a few weeks later. Meanwhile, after searching for fresh water without much success, they returned to the boats.

While his officers put the men to work, Cook climbed to the poop deck and gazed out over the bay. His duty as a naval officer was to discover seaports that promised shelter and refreshment at least and, at best, military and commercial capability. This bay had none of these attributes.

The main problem with Botany Bay was its shallowness. The British navy's men-of-war required a manoeuvring depth of at least 30 feet. Horatio Nelson's HMS *Victory*, which was launched three years before Cook left England, had a draught of 29 feet. Yet most of Botany Bay was less than half this depth. It was useless for military operations and little better for commerce. The *Endeavour*, as an erstwhile collier, had a very shallow draught of fourteen feet, yet Cook chose not to proceed beyond the first headland. In 2005 the *Endeavour* replica ran aground when it approached Cook's anchorage at Kurnell,[5] even though erosion had deepened the bay by about one metre in the intervening centuries.[6]

Another problem was the lack of shelter. Botany Bay is very open and dangerously exposed to strong winds and storm waves. In bad weather, these combine with the shallow water to create conditions as violent and treacherous as the open ocean. These dangers could mean long delays for ships unable to enter or leave except at high tide with a leading wind. This was no good for merchant sailors for whom time was money.

Another crucial problem was the lack of an adequate source of drinking water. After searching on both sides of the bay, Cook was forced to assign a party of men to keep digging holes in the sand until they had filled the ship's casks.

The next disappointment was the soil and surrounds. The low sandy foreshores were interspersed with tidal flats, mangroves and salt marshes, backed by acres of hummocky sand dunes. On the south side, Kurnell Peninsula became a favourite desert location for film producers. In 1940 it was turned into Palestine's Negev Desert to make the war movie *Forty Thousand Horsemen*, the story of the great cavalry charge on Beersheba made by the Australian Light Horse in 1917. Later, these sand dunes became the Sahara Desert in *The Rats of Tobruk* and later still they had a cameo role in the post-apocalyptic film *Mad Max Beyond Thunderdome*.

The bay was circular in shape and had two rivers draining into it – Cooks River in the north and Georges River at the south-west corner. Cook does not mention either river, but the soundings on his chart indicate that the mouths of both were explored. In 1770, the mouth of Cooks River was far more distinctive than it is today. As Cook's chart shows, the river originally flowed into the top of the bay, but after World War II, the mouth of Cooks River was moved two kilometres west to make way for the airport extension, while the rest of the northern shore has been reclaimed and dredged for the container port. Today that wide estuary is buried under Sydney Airport's third parallel runway.

Yet for all its shortcomings, Botany Bay suited James Cook very well. Its unremarkable features meant that any potential spies amongst the crew would return to England with very little information worth selling to France or Spain. So, having found this felicitous anchorage, Cook put his men to work. Some were sent to sound the bay, the armourers heated up the forge, others repaired the sails, went to cut the grass for the livestock, or scrubbed the ship's bottom and cleaned the deck.

Zachary Hicks took charge of the wooding and watering; Banks and Solander

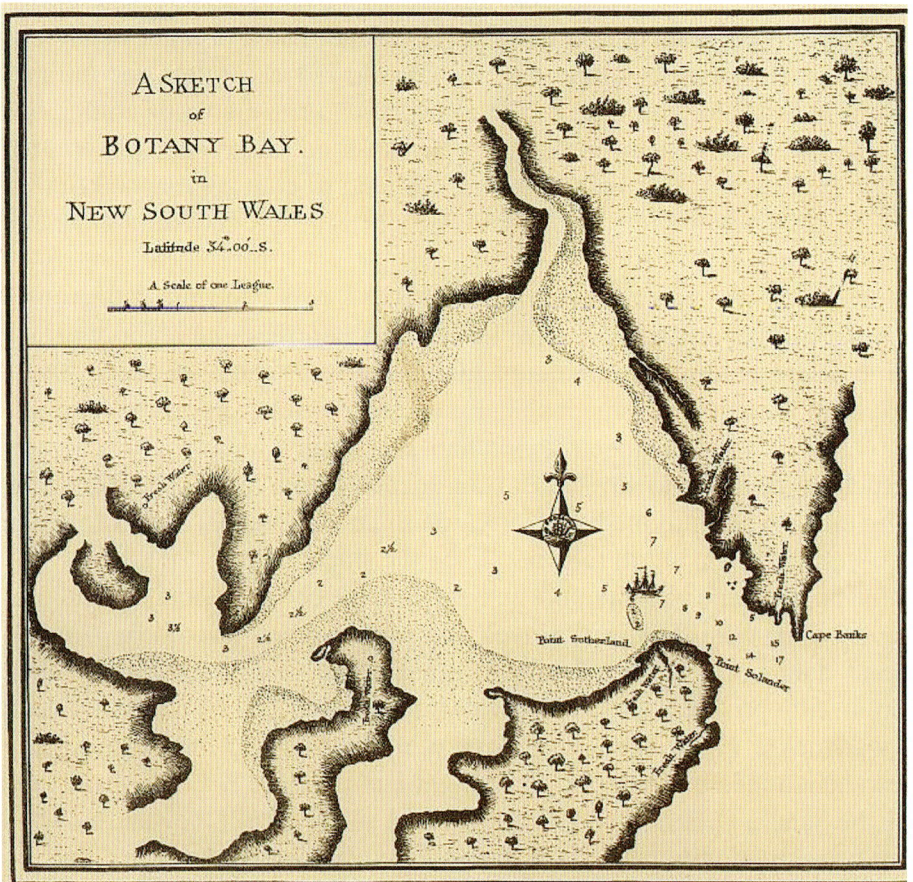

40. Cook's chart of Botany Bay shows the *Endeavour*'s anchorage on the south shore off Point Solander. National Library of Australia nla.obj-231834491.

botanized; John Gore supervised the hunting, fishing and shooting. In fact, Gore's success in catching large numbers of giant stingrays caused Cook to name the inlet Stingray Bay. This was the name remembered by the crew but, about four months later, within the confines of the great cabin, Cook changed the name to Botany Bay.[7]

Some years later, Captain Cook was criticized for extolling the swamps and sand hills around Botany Bay as 'some of the finest meadows in the world'. This criticism was wrong. Cook saw very quickly that Botany Bay was not just singularly inadequate as a naval port, it was dangerous. The phrase 'finest meadows in the world' was not penned by Cook, but by Hawkesworth, his authorized editor, in order to entertain his cultivated readers.[8]

Cook wanted a protected harbour with a deep safe anchorage close to shore, situated near elevated, well-drained land with reliable fresh drinking water. For that, he would have to look elsewhere.

28 'A good Harbour, and several islands': Cook Hides Port Jackson from his Crew

More than one old sea dog has wondered why a mariner as curious and talented as James Cook failed to investigate Sydney Harbour when he sailed past the gap between its majestic headlands on Sunday morning 6 May 1770. After peering through, Cook merely recorded:

> [A]t noon we were ... about 2 or 3 miles from the land and abreast of a bay or harbour wherein there appe[ared] to be safe anchorage which I called Port Jackson. It lies 3 leagues to the northward of Botany Bay.[1]

The view from the ship deserved more than this. It is true that Port Jackson's dog-leg entrance conceals the vast body of the main harbour, which lies behind Bradleys Head and South Head. Even so, a passing sailor catches glimpses of the two smaller arms – North Harbour (Manly) and Middle Harbour (Balmoral) – which display enough clues of its size and grandeur to beckon any experienced mariner inside. From the *Endeavour*, the men could see the rugged, perpendicular cliffs of North and South Heads, with Grotto Point, Dobroyd Head and Middle Head in the background, all of them steep escarpments promising deep water below. After the dangerously shallow Botany Bay, the sight of such a favourable anchorage should have been irresistible to Cook, if he hadn't already seen it.

Cook has been criticized for 'missing' Sydney Harbour in 1770. But there is both documentary and circumstantial evidence to suggest that he had already seen it. While the ship – and the men – were moored in Botany Bay, Cook found Sydney Harbour by walking overland, following Aboriginal tracks connecting the two inlets. He concealed the prize from his crew by not sailing into it, and from his readers by not mentioning it in his journal. But as soon as the *Endeavour* arrived back in England, he rushed to the Admiralty to report his discovery in person.

The clue to Cook's secret discovery is a memorandum written by Captain Arthur

Phillip, governor designate of New South Wales. Before leaving Britain with the First Fleet in May 1787, Phillip discussed his plans with the Home Office, commenting:

> It must be left to me to fix at Botany Bay, if I find it a proper place – if not, to go to a Port a few Leagues to the Northward, where there appear'd to be a good Harbour, and several Islands – as the Natives are very expert in setting fire to the grass, the having an Island to secure our Stock, would be a great advantage, & there is none <u>in or off</u>, Botany Bay.[2]

Here Phillip implies that his notional destination of Botany Bay may not be a proper place, but he knows of 'a good Harbour' nearby. Today there are eight islands in Port Jackson, but in the eighteenth century – before reclamation – there were thirteen. How did Phillip, sitting in London in 1787, know of these islands before he or any other European had entered the harbour?

The first historian to grapple with this question was George Barton, who suggested that Phillip's port 'to the northward' was Port Stephens, near Newcastle.[3] Cook had sailed past that inlet in 1770, noting in his journal: 'at the entrance lay 3 small islands'. However, Port Stephens is too far away. It is located 167 kilometres (30 leagues) north of Botany Bay – not just 'a few leagues' – and the *Endeavour* took five days to reach it.

More recently, Phillip's biographer, Alan Frost, identified the port as Port Jackson, but noted that none of the *Endeavour*'s extant logbooks or journals mentions the islands:

> Phillip's reference to islands in Port Jackson is puzzling, for neither Cook nor Banks mentions them in his journal of the *Endeavour*'s voyage. We can only assume that those on board her noticed more than Cook and Banks recorded, and that Phillip had access to this additional information.[4]

However, as commuters on the Manly ferry know, no one on board the *Endeavour* could have seen the islands while sailing past. Their line of sight was blocked by the high promontory of South Head.

As soon as all eleven ships of the First Fleet had arrived at Botany Bay after their long voyage across the Indian Ocean and were safely anchored near Bare Island on the north shore, Phillip was eager to inspect Cook's port with its 'several islands'.

The last ships arrived on Sunday 20 January 1788 and, at daybreak the following morning, leaving Lieutenant Ball in temporary command of the fleet, Phillip sailed out of Botany Bay with a small reconnaissance party. Knowing they weren't going far, he packed only three days provisions. He travelled in three rigged open boats – two cutters and a long boat – so that by spreading the survey work across three teams and 'by examining several parts of the harbour at once, the greater dispatch might be made'.[5] Evidently Phillip was expecting Port Jackson to be larger and more complex than the simple open bay suggested on Cook's published chart of the east coast.

Sailing through Sydney Heads on Monday afternoon, Phillip's first task was to

41. A view from the lighthouse at South Head looking across to North Head, guarding the entrance to Port Jackson, c.1818.

sound for a sandbar at the entrance. A bar was found but, at a depth of twenty feet, it presented no danger to the eleven ships waiting in Botany Bay.[6] After examining the middle and north arms, they pitched their tents at Camp Cove for the first night. Tuesday was spent rowing and sailing west along the main waterway, taking soundings among the countless bays and promontories. Phillip was anxious to reach the head of the harbour, but the day wasn't long enough. Eventually, he chose a deep cove on the south side which had a freshwater stream flowing into it and where ships could anchor at a half pistol shot from the shore. He named it Sydney Cove and, after breakfast on Wednesday, he hurried back to Botany Bay to gather the fleet and lead it round to the place where he would build the new British colony.

On that Wednesday, anyone watching from the summit of North Head would have been puzzled by the volume of foreign traffic along the coast. As the three little English boats exited the harbour and headed south past Bondi, two large French storeships sailed towards them. Sent by King Louis XVI, these vessels had been exploring the Pacific for two years, under the command of Comte de Lapérouse. Four months earlier, Lapérouse had visited Kamchatka on Russia's Pacific coast to refresh his crews and to collect his mail. This had been sent from Paris via St Petersburg and across Siberia to the governor at Petropavlovsk. One despatch from the Minister of Marine, Maréchal de Castries, informed him that the English newspapers were reporting a plan to occupy Botany Bay. Consequently, Lapérouse was ordered to investigate the bay, instead of New Zealand as originally planned. So Lapérouse left Russia's Far East and sailed south for New Holland. On Wednesday 23 January 1788 he sighted the Australian coast near Narrabeen, which lies about seven miles north of the entrance to Port Jackson.[7] From here, the French ships continued south as instructed, sailing past Sydney Heads and eventually entered Botany Bay, where they gave Phillip a terrible fright.

The fact that Lapérouse sailed past the enticing Sydney Heads, instead of entering them and forestalling the British fleet, is largely thanks to Captain Cook. Cook's singular focus on Botany Bay, which was constantly repeated by the Admiralty, by the London newspapers and by the French minister, ensured that everything else on the east coast – including Port Jackson – remained insignificant for another couple of days. It was a close-run thing.

42. This portrait of a warrior of the Port Jackson region was drawn by Nicolas-Martin Petit, who sailed with Nicolas Baudin. The French expedition stayed in Sydney for five months in 1802.

If Phillip knew about the huge size of the main harbour and its 'several islands' before he left England, then another European had seen them before him. That European could only have been Captain Cook, who told the Admiralty Secretary, Philip Stephens, who told Governor Phillip.

Phillip's memorandum is not the only evidence of Cook's discovery of Sydney Harbour. There is also circumstantial evidence found in Cook's journal and charts, and the role of Botany Bay itself.

Botany Bay was the only place where *Endeavour* stopped on Australia's temperate coast – the climate zone generally favoured by Europeans because of its mild temperatures, free from the heat and diseases of the tropics. A naval captain on a voyage of discovery has a duty to search for ports of shelter and refreshment, places that might also be suitable for future settlement. Yet, during the next seventeen days, Cook travelled non-stop to the Tropic of Capricorn. He sailed past Port Jackson (Sydney Harbour) with all its promise; Broken Bay with its three generous arms of

Pittwater, Brisbane Water and the Hawkesbury River; Newcastle Harbour at the mouth of the Hunter River; Port Stephens; Port Macquarie; Coffs Harbour; and the entrances to the Clarence and Richmond Rivers. Many of these are fine natural harbours with features far superior to Botany Bay in terms of depth, shelter, fresh water, vegetation, food and soils. They surely required investigation after the shortcomings of Botany Bay. But the *Endeavour* entered none of them. Cook had found what he wanted and there was no need for his men to see anything more.

As the *Endeavour* never sailed into Sydney Harbour, the only way Cook could have discovered it is by walking overland from Botany Bay. The two waterways are less than six miles apart as the crow flies. The overland hike would have been easy for man of Cook's height and age. He clearly made one journey, and may have made two. But he does not mention them in his journal.

Historians have found it difficult to determine most of Cook's activities for the eight days he spent at Botany Bay because his journal entries are so vague. One complains: 'We cannot trace the movements of Cook accurately during this week, as his record is indefinite'.[8] Nor is it easy to correlate Cook's record with those of his companions, as another scholar writes 'It is sometimes difficult to get Cook's and Banks's journals to correspond with each other'.[9]

Cook's journal entries for the visit are often not about himself. Instead, he writes about the adventures of his officers and their encounters with the indigenous inhabitants, including meetings when he was not present. He also includes long descriptions of birds and animals, soils and vegetation, some of it copied from Banks's journal.

He says he made many excursions around the bay and into the countryside, sometimes returning to the ship late in the evening. However, he is vague about the routes he took and describes few of the distinctive geographical features he passed. This bay was his only stopover on the temperate coast of a continent where he hoped to make grand discoveries. Yet during this sojourn, Cook appears to have attempted little and achieved less. When the English actor Keith Michell starred in a television series about Cook's visit, the scriptwriter was forced to invent numerous incidents to retain audience interest.

Little wonder that Dr Johnson made his droll assessment of Hawkesworth's rendition of Cook's journal few years later:

> [Johnson]: 'Sir, if you talk of it ... as a book that is to increase human knowledge, I believe there will not be much of that. Hawkesworth can tell only what the voyagers have told him; and they have found very little, only one new animal, I think.' Boswell: 'But many insects, Sir'.[10]

On which day, or days, did Cook walk from Botany Bay to Sydney Harbour? We don't know because he didn't record the event. However, there were plenty of opportunities for him to do so. For example, on the Monday morning, Cook crossed to the north shore 'where I neither met with inhabitants or any thing remarkable'. Again, on the Friday afternoon, Cook took a party over to the north shore and 'made an excursion of 3 or 4 miles into the country or rather along the sea coast. We met with nothing remarkable.' Then on Saturday 5 May – their last full day at Botany Bay – Cook records only that he spent the day exploring: 'I went with a party of men into the country but met with nothing extraordinary'.[11]

The phrase 'nothing remarkable' has a special place in Cook's writings. On the second voyage, when Tobias Furneaux arrived in New Zealand announcing his discovery of Bass Strait, Cook silenced him and wrote: 'he seems to have met with nothing remarkable'.[12]

In truth, Cook's journal was probably written weeks afterwards and then with an eye to obfuscation. His vagueness is deafening. Behind the smokescreen of underachievement, the enterprising, ambitious Cook set out to find a prize to take home to England.

The following portrayal of Cook's discovery is therefore speculative. It is based on a reconstruction of the original pre-settlement environment from the early maps and historical descriptions, before the landscape was altered.

The country on the north shore of Botany Bay is a basin of sand dunes and marshes, slung like a hammock between the three ridges that frame it on the north, west and east, while the south side drops down to the low rocky shoreline. Aboriginal tracks, kept free of brush and boulders, ran along the crest of each ridge, marking the most efficient routes for travelling to neighbouring grounds for trade or ceremony. The northern ridge, which forms the watershed between Port Jackson and Botany Bay and is capped by today's Oxford Street for much of its length, was known by the Aboriginal people as the Maroo.[13] On the western ridge, the Bulanaming track now carries the Princes Highway. On the east, runs the rugged coastal ridge which, following the arrival of Lapérouse and his party would become known as Frenchmans Road.[14]

As soon as he realized that Botany Bay had little to offer, Cook looked further afield. Standing on the poop deck, he could see a broad ridge stretching east–west across the northern horizon, about six miles distant. It seemed to be connected to the high coastal wall that he had observed during the hours spent tacking before entering the bay. Cook decided to do what he always did, since his boyhood adventures on Roseberry Topping. At Queen Charlotte Sound, he had climbed the nearest hill and discovered Cook Strait. Now he would climb to the crest of this northern ridge – modern Bellevue Hill – to see what was on the other side.

He could reach the crest by either the eastern or western ridge – both of which were visible from the bay. Given his eagerness to explore the terrain in Queen Charlotte Sound by climbing a second and bigger hill, it seems likely that he travelled both routes in the course of that week.

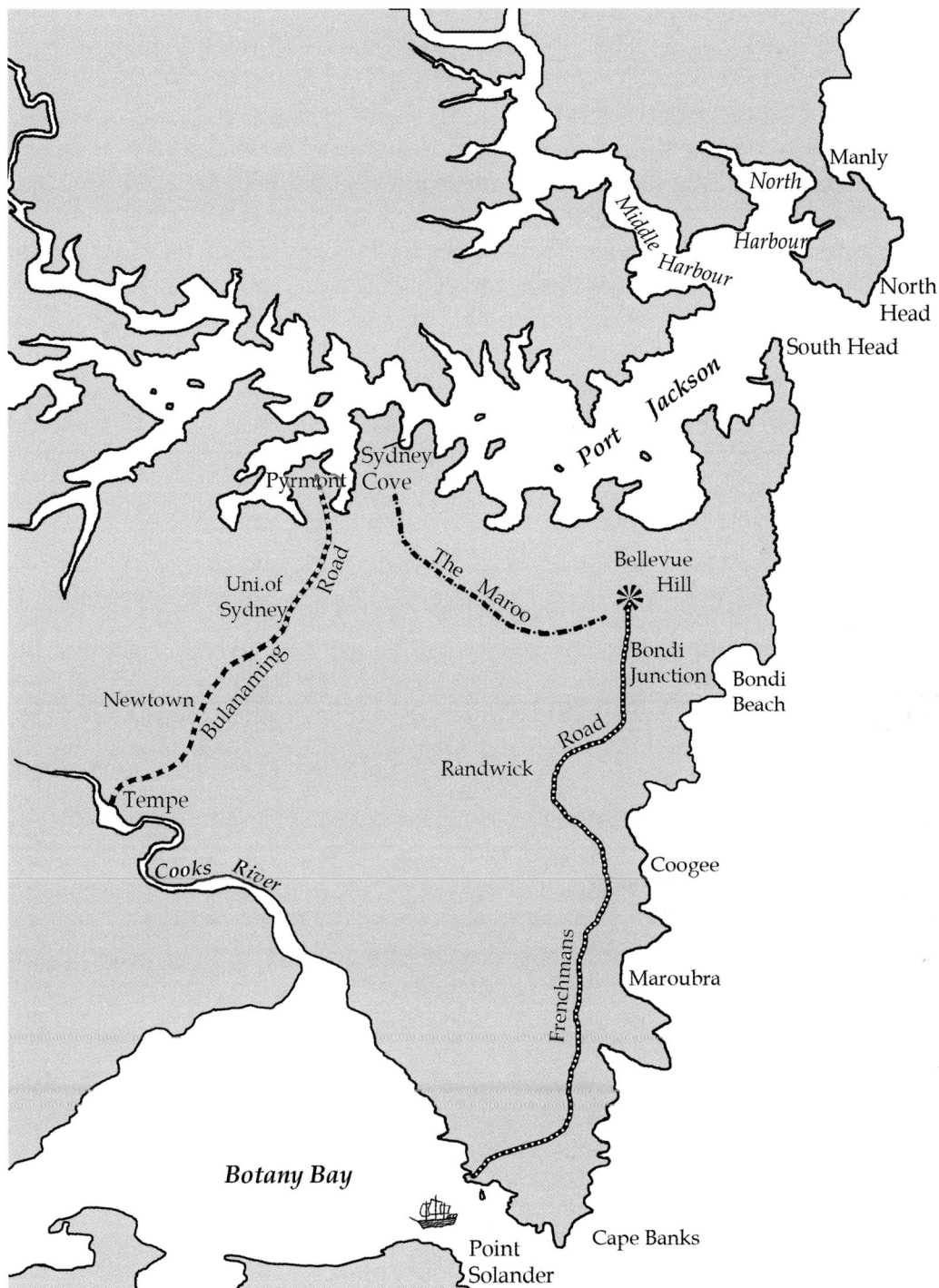

43. Sketch map of the country between Botany Bay and Port Jackson, depicting the three ridges capped by ancient tracks.

Early one morning, Cook asked the rowers to take him across to the northern headland of Botany Bay, which he named Cape Banks. He climbed to the top of the coastal ridge, and after passing Maroubra and Coogee, followed the track through Randwick to today's Bondi Junction, where it meets the eastern end of the Maroo path. The long southern slope rises very gradually up from Botany Bay but here, standing at the top of the hill, Cook surely thought he'd arrived in a naval heaven when he saw the northern slope fall sharply down to the waters of the deep harbour.

Before descending to the shore, Cook hurried up to Bellevue Hill, the highest point on the ridge, where he spent a long time surveying the panorama. From its north east portal in the Pacific Ocean wall, the bays and promontories of Port Jackson extended westward as far as the eye could see, disappearing into the Blue Mountains on the distant horizon. Many islands, including Shark, Clark, Garden and Pinchgut Islands, were dotted about. He would also have seen high cliffs and steep gullies that promised fresh water.

Cook knew that this harbour was a magnificent prize for Britain. When John White, surgeon-general to the First Fleet, first saw the harbour eighteen years later, he wrote:

> Port Jackson I believe to be, without exception, the finest and most extensive harbour in the universe, and at the same time the most secure, being safe from all the winds that blow.[15]

Here a ship could leave the Tasman Sea outside and sail through the mile-wide gap between the headlands into the security of a landlocked harbour, protected from gales and ocean swells by sandstone ridges. With its deep water, ample sea room, many anchorages and straightforward navigation, it can accommodate any number of vessels.

Perhaps, spurred on by this discovery, Cook set out another morning to follow the western track that leads north from Cooks River. The mouth of the river was too boggy to land, but the soundings shown on his chart provide evidence that his boat continued up river for a couple of miles. From here, he could wade ashore in reach of the high, dry knoll on the north bank near today's Tempe train station. From the top of this hill, he could have followed the Bulanaming track northwards through Newtown and up to the site of the University of Sydney, a walk of about six kilometres. From this height, Cook would have seen the upper reaches of Port Jackson fanning out before him. He hurried down the slope, crossed today's Broadway and walked out along the sandstone spine of Pyrmont Peninsula, standing tall before it was diminished by the quarrymen. From that vantage point on the western side of today's Harbour Bridge, surrounded by the waters of the harbour, Cook counted several more islands including Darling, Glebe and Goat Islands.

Then he skirted back around the shore, crossed the path of the Tank Stream and climbed to the start of the northern ridge near Hyde Park. From here, he could see Bellevue Hill at the other end of the Maroo and, turning north, he saw the land in front of him slope down towards Sydney Cove and Bennelong Point, the site of today's Opera House.

If Cook saw both views of the harbour, he would have been even more impressed by its size. But how could he protect it? He couldn't prevent its discovery by some other passing explorer – from France or elsewhere. However, until Britain could protect it by planting a garrison on its shores, he would conceal it by omitting it from his charts. He would definitely not sail into it for his crew to see.

Of all the bays on the east coast, the *Endeavour* visited the one that was the least attractive, yet which lay a stone's throw from the finest harbour in the world. This lucky juxtaposition enabled Cook to park his ship – and its crew – on the south side of the shallow, barren inlet while he made the short walk north. If a sailor was later bribed for information, he'd have nothing valuable to say about Stingray Bay. Cook never bothered to tell the crew when he changed the name to Botany Bay many weeks later.

Botany Bay would become one of the most successful decoys in history, equal to the Greeks' gift of the Wooden Horse to Troy. In the decades following the *Endeavour*'s visit, the term 'Botany Bay' became a coast, a country, a continent in the British consciousness. The inlet was the single focus for all European discourse concerning New Holland. There was little or no discussion about the much richer country Cook saw to the north and south of the bay.

In reality, Botany Bay remained a remote swampy wasteland for decades, while the regular appearance of its name in European newspapers, shipping manifests and history books suggested a metropolis. The phantom colony was initially created by the British authorities as a decoy to protect Sydney Harbour from prying eyes until it could be defended. By then, however, the lyrical name had taken on a life of its own and became synonymous with British Australia for more than a century.

29   From Botany Bay to Cape York: The Map of New Holland Completed

Now it was time to leave Botany Bay and head home. At the end of the week, Cook wrote in his journal:

> During our stay in this Harbour I caused the English Colours to be display'd a shore every day and an inscription to be cut out upon one of the trees near the watering place seting forth the Ships name, date etc.[1]

Unlike the similar entry he wrote at Mercury Bay in New Zealand, on this occasion he did not add a postscript claiming to have taken formal possession of the place. Nor is there any evidence that Cook saw the tree inscription after ordering the carpenter to carve it. With that, the *Endeavour* weighed anchor at 6 a.m. on Sunday 6 May 1770 and resumed the voyage.

The British didn't stop until they reached the Tropic of Capricorn two and a half weeks later. A few miles short of that line, Cook found an inlet which he named Bustard Bay after the bush turkeys found there:

> At Dinner we eat the Bustard we had shot yesterday, it turned out an excellent bird, far the best we all agreed that we have eat since we left England, and as it weighed 15 pounds our Dinner was not only good but plentyfull.[2]

The bay lies 400 kilometres north to today's city of Brisbane. Cook and Banks seized the opportunity to go ashore and spent about six hours looking for food and examining the country. Banks noted the change in vegetation, including the tropical palm trees: 'a sure mark that we were upon the point of leaving the Southern Temperate Zone'.[3] The captain also noticed the change – these tropical waters were becoming shallower. Night sailing was no longer safe and from now they anchored most evenings.[4]

The *Endeavour* continued northward, her bottom occasionally scraping against submerged coral and rocks as she threaded her way through the reefs and islands. Two

44. Looking out to sea through Sydney Heads at a passing northbound ship, by Augustus Earle, 1825.

leadsmen stood in the chains continually casting the lead-lines and calling out the depth of the water. Eventually the ship entered the breathtakingly beautiful Whitsunday Passage where the water is deep and Cook was able to resume night sailing in the clear moonlight: 'we kept under an easy sail and the lead going all night'.[5] But it was a false dawn. Having no knowledge of the earlier experiences of Torres and Bougainville, no one on board imagined that the enormous shelf of the Great Barrier Reef was steadily closing in from the east and the area of safe water was narrowing with every league northward.

A week later, an hour before midnight, the *Endeavour* struck a coral reef and stuck fast. The crew swung into action: the yards and masts were dismantled and heavy articles were thrown overboard to lighten the ship – including six guns and their carriages. Every available man was called to work the pumps, including Joseph Banks: 'myself unused to labour was much fatigued and had laid down to take a little rest'.[6]

The next midday tide was not high enough to float the vessel off, but the midnight tide was. After 23 hours wedged fast on the reef, the *Endeavour* was hauled into deep water. With her bottom bandaged with a fothered sail, the leak plugged fortuitously by a lump of coral that had broken away, and her pumps fully manned, the ship was nursed along the coast while the crew searched for a suitable place to carry out repairs. Eventually, they put into a harbour at the mouth of the Endeavour River, which proved well suited to the purpose. They were confined at this encampment (now Cooktown) for seven weeks and it was here that they first saw kangaroos and learned their Aboriginal name. Repairs that could be made to the ship were done quickly. However, it was not practicable to heave her down to fix her bottom. That would have to wait until Batavia.

By 20 July the *Endeavour* was ready to put to sea, but adverse winds of the monsoonal change delayed their departure for a fortnight. At last, on 4 August, they crossed the bar into the shallow coastal waters and headed north. A hair-raising week followed as Cook picked his way through the winding channels between innumerable shoals, trying desperately to get outside the reef. Eventually, he and Banks rowed in the pinnace to Lizard Island and climbed its highest peak. They were disappointed to find that the reef continued for another seven miles or so, but beyond it there appeared to be a break in the rocks, promising a passage to the open sea. The next day, Cook guided the *Endeavour* through the passage and escaped to the deep ocean. At long last this marked an end to the tedium, anxiety and danger of navigating in shallow water, which had haunted them day and night since crossing the Tropic of Capricorn.

Later that day, Cook resolved another geographical debate when the ship arrived at the latitude of Quiros's elusive Australia del Espiritu Santo, the archipelago now known as the Republic of Vanuatu. It was nowhere in sight and Cook berated the armchair geographers who had joined it to the coast of Queensland. As Torres and Bougainville had already discovered, Vanuatu lies well east of Australia, on the opposite side of the Coral Sea.[7]

Cook was relieved to return to the deep, safer water outside the reef, where the *Endeavour* could return to her normal speed. They could have continued this route to Batavia, turning north around New Guinea as Bougainville had done two years earlier. But that circuitous track promised few new discoveries and would add several weeks to the voyage – a bitter thought for everyone on board. Much more would be gained by verifying the supposed channel now known as Torres Strait, as Banks records:

> The Captn fearfull of going too far from the land, least he should miss an opportunity of examining whether or not the passage which is layed down in some charts between New Holland and New Guinea really existed or not, steered the ship west right in for the land.[8]

Cook had to get back inside the reef as soon as possible so that he did not overshoot the entrance to the strait. So the weary crew enjoyed just two days of freedom from the labyrinth of shoals before they turned back towards the dangerous coast. Now the surf threatened to hurl the *Endeavour* onto the reef, putting the men in more peril than ever before. They searched desperately for an opening to get back inside and eventually found one which, with a sigh of relief, Cook named Providential Channel.

Now inside the reef again, Cook followed the land north for three more days. At last, on 21 August, he reached the top of Australia's east coast: 'the Northern Promontary of this country I have Named York Cape in honour of His late Royal Highness the Duke of York'.[9] Cape York marked the climax of Cook's voyage of discovery. His magnificent chart of the east coast (Fig. 37) supplied the fourth side of the unfinished rectangle that had dogged Dutch maps for more than a century. Cook may not have found the Southern, Antarctic Continent, but he had fully unveiled the fifth.

30 Not Claiming New Holland: What Really Happened at Possession Island

Next comes the curious business of the second of Cook's phantom possession ceremonies. The first was the claim that Cook had taken possession at Mercury Bay, New Zealand (Chapter 21). The second was ostensibly conducted on Possession Island on Wednesday 22 August 1770.[1]

Since arriving in Bass Strait four months earlier, Cook had stepped onto the Australian mainland in five places: Botany Bay, Bustard Bay, Thirsty Sound, Endeavour River, and Point Lookout (north of Cape Flattery). Also, Cook – or one of his crew – had landed on six adjacent tropical islands, usually to climb a hill for a better view or to search for food. Yet Cook did not claim possession at any of these places. None of the journals written by Cook's officers mention an annexation ceremony being held anywhere on Australia's east coast. Yet Cook's own journal and the official records claim that he conducted one here, on an island off the western coast of Cape York, in an area where the Dutch held title as first discoverers, according to the traditional law of European nations.[2]

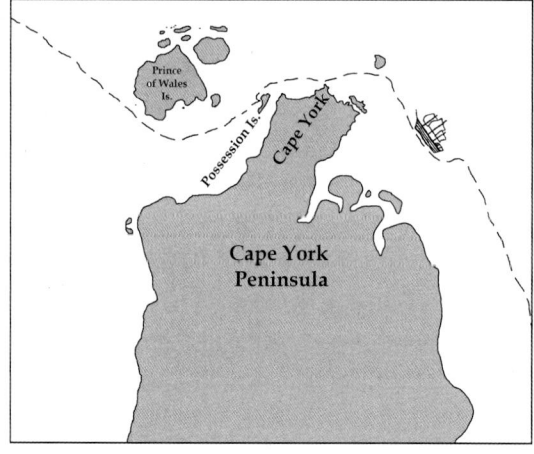

45. Possession Island lies south-west of Cape York, the northernmost tip of Australia.

At this point, it is necessary to bear in mind that Cook's journal is not a single entity. He wrote up a day's events as soon as he could – not necessarily on the day they occurred. Furthermore, he drafted and redrafted his work throughout the voyage, constantly adding and deleting.³ In some instances the alterations are made on the same page so that we can still see his first thought, as in the changes of name from Stingray Bay, through Botanist Bay, to Botany Bay.⁴ In other cases, after a longer redrafting, the page containing his original entry has been thrown away,⁵ so we can only guess what it may have said. Cook retained his holograph journal throughout the voyage and, on returning to London, took it home to his family, after which it disappeared from public knowledge for decades. This final version of Cook's manuscript, known as the Holograph manuscript,⁶ was not finally transcribed and edited until Beaglehole published it in 1955.

During the voyage, when reasonably (though never finally) satisfied with his work, Cook handed this holograph journal to his clerk, Richard Orton, to copy. In fact, Orton made two copies for the Admiralty: the first (the Mitchell MS) was sent ahead from Batavia, and the second (the Admiralty MS) was handed over when the *Endeavour* returned to England. However, none of these three versions were published for over a century. Instead, the Admiralty recruited a ghostwriter, Dr John Hawkesworth, to compose an official narrative of the voyage which was published in 1773.⁷

The motivation and circumstances behind the later revisions of the Possession Island story will be discussed later.⁸ Here, it is more important to consider the contemporaneous accounts of what actually happened on 22 August.

Cook's written instructions relative to specific places go only as far as New Zealand (Chapter 14). Otherwise, the general instruction applied:

> You will also observe with accuracy the Situation of such Islands as you may discover in the Course of your Voyage that have not hitherto been discover'd by any Europeans and take Possession for His Majesty and make Surveys and Draughts of such of them as may appear to be of Consequence, without Suffering yourself however to be thereby diverted from the Object which you are always to have in View, the Discovery of the Southern Continent so often Mentioned.⁹

This did not give him a mandate to claim New Holland, which had already been discovered. Nonetheless, if he wanted to annex the east coast, then Cape York was his last opportunity to do so. Cook was the 'first European discoverer' on the east coast, but he knew he would lose that title after passing Cape York. From there, the coast turned south-west and was recognizably the land of 'Carpentaria' marked on the Dutch charts. In the Arafura Sea, the title of first discoverer belonged to the Dutch navigators who had discovered almost every coast and island between Cape York and Batavia. All the regional maps in the *Endeavour*'s library were festooned with Dutch placenames like Arnhem Land, Carpentaria, Cape Keerweer and Groote Eylandt. In the Eurocentric world of his day, Cook knew he was now entering the domain of the Dutch East Indies.

But in August 1770, Cook had no wish to claim any part of New Holland. So he did not stop the ship at Cape York in order to step ashore with 'the gentlemen' to conduct a possession ceremony.

Cook's only thought during that stressful month was to avoid being wrecked in shallow waters and to reach home as quickly as possible. Rather than taking the long way around the north coast of New Guinea, he hoped to nurse his battered ship through Torres Strait – the supposed gap between New Holland and New Guinea. This meant testing the treacherous shallow waters that had scared away the dozens of Dutch sailors who, for more than 150 years, had searched in vain for the western entrance to the strait. According to Dalrymple's chart, carried on the *Endeavour*, Torres had found a way through from east to west in 1606. Cook hoped to follow him, but the strait was peppered with islands, and Dalrymple's chart did not show Torres's exact path through these: Cook had no guarantee of finding a navigable passage through to the 'Indian Seas'. Tension mounted as all on board feared that they would become embayed and forced to lose many weeks turning back through the shoals and reefs and around New Guinea in order to reach Batavia.

As the *Endeavour* inched westwards, the small boats went ahead to take soundings. It was a noisy business with the lookouts calling from the masthead and gun signals being fired from the ship.

In the early afternoon of 22 August, their path was blocked by the biggest island in the strait, marked on the Dutch maps as Hooghe Eylandt (High Island).[10] Cook would rename it Prince of Wales Island in celebration of the recent eighth birthday (on 12 August) of the King's son, the future King George IV.[11] In order to avoid it, the ship veered southwards into the gulf.

The lookouts at the masthead searched the horizon for a clear passage, but the maze of islands obstructed their view. The captain noticed a group of people at the top of a high hill on a nearby island, attracted by the noise of the signallers' guns. They were armed with lances, although Banks saw that one man carried a bow and arrow, while others wore breastplates made from mother of pearl shell. These items suggested that the people were Melanesian.[12]

Guessing that the locals knew the best lookout, Cook decided to go ashore and climb their hill to get a better view. The pinnace was lowered around 5 p.m. and Cook, Banks and Solander were rowed over to the island with a party of armed marines. Three of the natives ran down to the beach as the boat approached and Cook feared that they might try to prevent their landing. But by the time the party stepped ashore, the natives had gone. Cook chose one marine to accompany him and left the rest on the beach. He then led his small party of Banks, Solander and the musketeer to the top of hill. It rose steeply from the beach to a height of some 70 metres above the water.

Down in the ship, anxious to know if there was a strait and a quick passage home, the crew watched the four small figures standing at the top of the treeless hill. It was a memorable tableau of what was about to become a most memorable day.

Cook was standing on a Melanesian island lying south-west of Cape York, washed by the waters of the gulf and long frequented by Dutch navigators. In all likelihood, many Dutchmen had stood on this very same hill – possibly Abel Tasman himself in 1644 – as they scanned the dangerous waters for a passage through to the Pacific. Perhaps this was Rijders Eylandt, so named by the VOC captain Jean Gonzal during his voyage to Australia in 1756, a mere fourteen years before the *Endeavour*. Possibly Torres had stood here, also searching for a route through to the west.

Cook knew that under the law of nations he had no right to claim this island, writing later: 'I can make no new discovery the honour of which belongs to the Dutch Navigators and as such they may lay Claim to it as their property'.[13]

Later, Cook would reconstruct the events of this day as a possession ceremony, but on the actual day this is what happened. Cook scanned the western horizon. The worst of the shoals were behind them now and he could see a clear passage to the west. He probably handed the telescope to Banks, then Solander, while pointing out the channel they would take to the Indian Ocean. Down on the ship, too far away to hear what their captain was saying, the crew waited for a signal. Another minute passed before Cook held aloft the signal flag he was carrying and ordered the marine to fire three shots into the air. All at once, a tumultuous roar rang out from the deck and the marines on the beach fired off a *feu de joie*.

Sydney Parkinson was watching from the ship and captures the excitement and relief of all on board when they saw and heard Cook's signal:

> The captain, and some others, went up to the top of a hill, and, seeing a clear passage, they hoisted a jack, and fired a volley, which was answered by the marines below, and the marines by three vollies from the ship, and three cheers from the main shrouds.[14]

If there was any hint that the hilltop ceremony was a possession claim, Parkinson would have mentioned it. He reported all the others, even the botched, murderous possession ceremony at Poverty Bay in New Zealand (Chapter 21) that no one else recorded.

Apart from Cook, Banks was the only member of the hilltop party to record the incident. Less exuberant than Parkinson, Banks's journal entry summed up the episode succinctly:

> The hill we were upon was by much the most barren we had been upon; it however gave us the satisfaction of seeing a streight, at least as far as we could see, without any obstruction. In the Even a strong tide made us almost certain.[15]

At that point, Banks was only interested in the discovery of a strait, not in the signalling routine or the cheering that marked the discovery.

So that was all that happened on the hill that day. Neither Banks nor Parkinson make any mention of Cook having carried out a possession ceremony. Neither mentions the name Possession Island. Cook's original record of the event was probably similar to Banks's. However, that's not what the history books say, thanks to Cook's creative journalism. A few weeks later, he was forced to change his journal entry when strategically sensitive information reached him in Batavia (Chapter 32).

For now, all Cook's thoughts were focused on finding a safe passage through Torres Strait and a quick voyage to Batavia. His Holograph entry for that afternoon mentions the word 'Passage' seven times. Although the island became known as Possession Island, a little-known sentence written in Banks's hand, suggests that Cook originally named it Passage Island. This particular piece of manuscript evidence, which has not been published or discussed before, is found only in Banks's copy of extracts from Cook's journal, in one of its various, frequently amended versions.

During the voyage, Cook allowed Banks to copy useful sections of his holograph journal. Banks's abstract has survived as the Grey MS,[16] which provides a snapshot of Cook's journal as it was before he changed it. Beaglehole explains:

> It is in Banks's handwriting, but is clearly not his own composition. It is simply an abstract of Cook's (not the ship's) journal ... The language is all Cook's with a few natural exceptions: thus 'I' becomes 'the Captn'; 'I have named' becomes 'was calld'.[17]

At some stage during the voyage, Banks was copying the last line to Cook's entry for that Wednesday afternoon which was a naming sentence. Banks wrote: 'The island was calld Possession or Passage [interlined] Isle'.[18]

It was not Cook's style to name places in the alternative, so it is unlikely that Cook's entry actually read 'I have named it Possession or Passage Isle'. It is more likely that Cook, in the course of his later revisions, wrote 'I have named it Possession Isle'. Then, when Banks was copying this version, he remembered that this memorable island had earlier been called Passage Isle and made the interlineation.

However, this sentence naming the island on that Wednesday afternoon occurs only in the Grey MS. Either Cook wrote it in an intermediate draft and subsequently deleted it from the Holograph, or Banks, drawing on Cook's mention of 'Possession Island' in his entry for the next day, inserted the names in his abstract of the events of 22 August. But there the sentence is, recording the name Passage Isle.

Cook's first mention of a name for the island occurs the following day when he writes: 'At Noon Possession Island at the SE entrance of the Passage bore N 53° East'.[19]

After anchoring overnight, Cook set a course through to the Indian Ocean. His rediscovery of the strait meant that his crew would be spared the tedious voyage back around New Guinea. After two years at sea, they were heading back to England.

31 Dutch Bureaucracy: Evasiveness and Delay at Batavia

The tedium of the westward journey to Batavia was relieved when, on 16 September 1770, halfway to Java, the island of Timor came into view. Here at Concordia (Kupang) was a Dutch fort and settlement, with the promise of food and European contact. Several officers urged Cook to put into the port for refreshments, but the captain would not, saying:

> this I refuse'd to comply with, knowing that the Dutch look upon all Europeans with a jealous eye that come among these Islands, and our necessities were not so great to oblige me to put into a place where I might expect to be but indifferently treated.[1]

Cook was referring to the treatment of his countryman, William Dampier, in 1699. After surveying the north-west coast of New Holland, Dampier sailed his ship, *Roebuck*, north to Timor in search of fresh water. But the Dutch governor was so suspicious of the Englishman's motives in his precious Spice Islands that he refused to help him, saying: '[Y]ou are come to inspect into our trade and strength, and I will have you therefore be gone with all speed'.[2]

Dampier agreed to keep away from the fort and eventually got his water, but there were significant repercussions in Java. When news of the English expedition reached Batavia, the governor-general promptly despatched two survey expeditions to head off suspected British incursion in his Dutch preserve. One, under Maarten Van Delft, went to New Holland while the other, under Jacob Weyland, went to New Guinea.

Seventy years later, Cook believed that Dutch antagonism was not changed. The *Endeavour* continued west through the archipelago for another week but, with supplies dangerously low, Cook stopped at the island of Savu. Here, with the permission of the VOC's agent they purchased buffaloes, hogs, poultry and palm wine. The quality was poor, but these provisions were welcomed by the crew. Before they left the island, the local rajah requested the gift of an English dog. Joseph Banks obliged by presenting him with his greyhound.[3] This left Lady, the cocker spaniel, as the sole canine companion in the great cabin.

Nine days later, the *Endeavour* turned north into the Sunda Strait that separates the Indonesian islands of Java and Sumatra, and her crew marvelled at the high volcanic island of Krakatoa. Cook was heading for the VOC dockyards at Batavia so that the ship could be properly repaired before attempting the long voyage home. But the feeble winds and contrary currents dogged their progress through the strait, ensuring that another week would pass before they made port.

After maddening delays, the *Endeavour* anchored in Batavia Bay at 4 p.m. on 10 October 1770. Batavia lies on the north coast of Java at the mouth of the Ciliwung River. The town was the heart of the VOC's Asian operations and a centre of international trade. Built around a huge castle and garrison, it was designed as a Dutch town with well-laid out streets, canals and windmills, docks, shipyards, and warehouses. Batavia Castle was the home of the governor-general who, with his Council of the Indies, controlled all the comings and goings in the region down to the smallest minutiae. The spacious bay has numerous islands including Onrust, the great marine depot, and nearby Kuyper's Island, where foreign ships were sent to berth.

But all was not well in Batavia. The *Endeavour* crew, fit and suntanned after their long Queensland holiday, were alarmed by the pallor in the faces of the officials who came aboard, as Banks writes:

46. Batavia, founded in 1619, became the centre of the vast trading empire established by the VOC over Asia and the Orient. Kerry Stokes Collection.

> Both [the officer] and his people were almost as Spectres, no good omen of the healthyness of the country we are arrived at; our people however who truly might be calld rosy and plump, for we had not a sick man among us, Jeerd and flouted much at their brother sea mens white faces.[4]

The Englishmen may have laughed, but before long, they too would be suffering from malaria.

As soon as the anchor was secure, Lieutenant Hicks was sent ashore in the pinnace to report their arrival to the shahbandar (harbourmaster). A few hours later Parkinson was delighted when the pinnace returned to the ship 'loaded with pineapples, plantains, water-melons, and a bundle of London newspapers, which were very acceptable presents'.[5]

The papers were several months old but, after two years out of the world, Cook and his excited officers grabbed them eagerly. In London the coal-heavers, silk-weavers and sailors were striking and rioting; in America the colonists had refused to pay their taxes and war was imminent; the Russians, Poles and Turks were at war; and the navy of Catherine the Great was laying siege to Constantinople. The men on the *Endeavour* were left with no doubt that they had exited the utopian world of the Pacific and were back in the world of European great-power rivalry where secrecy was again paramount.

Earlier that week, following Admiralty instructions, Cook had impounded all the journals and log books (except those belonging to the civilians) and forbidden everyone to divulge where they had been. When a port control officer came on board, he asked the captain to complete a questionnaire, proffering forms printed in English, French and Dutch. But Cook was no more inclined to provide details of his activities to the Dutch authorities at Batavia than he had been to the Portuguese in Rio de Janeiro. The document asked for comprehensive details of the voyage, including placenames and discoveries. Cook refused to answer seven of the nine questions, supplying only the ship's name and destination of England.[6]

And the Dutch interrogation didn't end there according to Johan Stavorinus, commander of the VOC ship *Huis ter Meijen* then anchored in the bay. When the governor asked Cook where the English had travelled since viewing the transit at Tahiti on 3 June 1769, Cook's patriotic reply was 'that they had stayed eight months at that island'.[7] In fact, they had spent only three months there, and most of that prior to the transit. Presumably, Cook wanted the governor-general to conclude that the *Endeavour*'s passage from Tahiti to Batavia had taken only eight or nine months, instead of the fifteen months which were mostly spent exploring the Dutch discoveries in the south-west Pacific. Again, when Cook was asked for the coordinates of Tahiti, Stavorinus records: 'but they would not reveal where it was situated'.[8]

Although there is no available record of this, Cook's reticence may have irritated

Governor Van der Parra. The *Endeavour* had to be emptied, dismantled, careened and refitted. The ship's carpenter reported that parts of the hull had been so badly scraped by rocks and eaten by shipworm that the planks were barely an eighth of an inch thick. Cook submitted a written request for assistance to the Castle and he records that the governor 'received me very politly and told me that I should have every thing I wanted'.[9] Yet nothing happened. There were infuriating formalities, Council meetings, more paperwork, trifling translation errors and maddening bureaucratic delays. More than three weeks passed before the ship could get into the dock on Onrust Island.

Meanwhile, Cook had to notify London of his arrival back in the world. The Admiralty required all its navigators to send reports back to England whenever the opportunity arose, either with a passing ship or on arrival at a European port. This ensured that intelligence was repatriated expeditiously, and safely – even if the navigator was not.

In reality, this directive was honoured as much in the breach as in the observance, and with good reason. A navigator could reasonably assume that any foreign courier would read his report or that it would fall into the wrong hands. With all the uncertainties of eighteenth-century navigation, even a British ship might not be secure. When Byron was on his way to the Pacific in 1765, he sent a final letter back to the Admiralty via his British storeship, saying:

> I have kept a Journal of this Voyage ... I wish'd much to have sent it now but I was afraid to trust it to the Storeship and I have no time to copy it, & I don't chuse any body else should.[10]

Byron was probably justified in not trusting his clerk to copy his journal: later Cook's clerk, Richard Orton, would sell information gleaned from Cook's journals.

Still, the Admiralty had instructed Cook:

> You are to send by all proper Conveyances to the Secretary of the Royal Society Copys of the Observations you shall have made of the Transit of Venus; and you are at the same time to send to our Secretary, for our information, accounts of your Proceedings, and Copys of the Surveys and drawings you shall have made.[11]

Looking around for a 'proper conveyance', Cook noted that sixteen large ships were anchored in the bay. Three of them were English, but none of these was heading home. However, the thirteen VOC vessels were loading their valuable cargos and preparing for the annual return voyage to the Netherlands. The fleet would start leaving in a couple of weeks, but it was customary to despatch a single ship, the voorzeilder (forerunner), a few days ahead of the main convoy. Consequently, when Cook learned that the ship *Vrouwe Kornelia Hillegonda* was about to sail for Texel, he seized the opportunity to write a short note to Philip Stephens. He reported that the *Endeavour* had arrived at Batavia, that it needed repairs after striking 'a Ledge of Rocks', and added that he would send 'an account of the whole Proceedings of the Voyage' with the Dutch fleet that was preparing to sail shortly for the Netherlands.[12] Cook revealed nothing more: there is no mention of places, discoveries or routes taken. Early on 14 October he thrust the letter into the hand of the departing Dutch captain.

This preliminary letter never reached the Admiralty,[13] but its loss didn't matter. Cook sent a longer despatch the following week.

32 Rewriting the Record: Cook's Phantom Possession Ceremony

Cook returned to his damaged ship while Banks and Solander booked into a hotel and hired a pair of carriages. A day or two later, when Banks was out sightseeing with Tupaia, the Englishmen's world was turned upside down. Banks tells the story:

> As I was walking the streets with Tupia a man totaly unknown to me ran out of his house and eagerly acosting me askd if the Indian whoom he saw with me had not been at Batavia before. On my declaring that he had not and asking the reason of so odd a question he told me that a year and a half before Mr De Bougainville had been at Batavia with two French ships, and that with him was an Indian so like this that he had imagind it to be the identical same person had not I informd him to the contrary. On this I enquir'd and found that Mr De Bougainville who was sent out by the French to the Malouine or Fauklands Islands (in order, as they said here, to sell them to the Spanyards) Had gone from thence to the River Plate and afterwards having passd into the South Seas maybee to other Spanish ports, where he and all his people had got an immense deal of Money in new Spanish Dollars, and afterwards came here Across the South seas in which passage he discoverd divers lands unknown before and from one of them brought the Indian in question.
>
> This at once cleard up the account given us by the Indians of Otahite of the two ships which had been there ten Months before us, Vol. I, p. 164 of this Journal. These were undoubtedly the ships of Mr De Bougainville, and the Indian Otourrou [Ahutoru] the Brother of Rette Cheif of Hidea. Even the story of the woman was known here – she it seems was a French woman who Followd a young man sent out in the character of Botanist in mens cloaths. As for the Article of the colours, the Indians might easily be Mistaken or Mr De Bougainville if he had traded in the S. Sea under Spanish colours might chuse to go quite across with them.
>
> As for the Iron which most misled us that he undoubtedly bought in Spanish America. Besides the Botanist mentiond above these ships were furnish'd with one or more Draughtsmen so that they probably have done some part of our work for us.[1]

Not only might the French draughtsmen have done some of Banks's botanical work ahead of him, but Captain Bougainville may also have done some of Captain Cook's discovery work.

Banks surely hurried to the ship and told the captain the dreadful news. Cook was struck dumb – at least on paper. Not a word about Bougainville, or Banks's street encounter, appears in the Batavian section of Cook's journal. It raised too many horrible questions. Did the 'divers lands unknown before' that Bougainville had discovered in the South Seas include the east coast of Australia? Was His Most Christian Majesty Louis XV already reigning over New Holland?

Although his journal does not mention the unwelcome news, Cook moved into damage control immediately. His journal and charts provided all the evidence of his discoveries, so they must be sent to London as soon as possible. Their thoroughness should ensure that Britain's claims would prevail over any competing French claims. His chief problem was New Holland. When he had earlier abstained from claiming that coast, he had not reckoned on being pre-empted by the French. Their presence meant that Britain's claim could no longer be postponed to comply with Whitehall's egg-shell diplomacy with the Dutch Republic. He would have to amend his journal before sending it home with a Dutch courier. The British government would rather incur the displeasure of the Protestant Dutch – whose global power was waning – than be forestalled in New Holland by their still powerful enemy, Catholic France.

Such a political emergency called for swift, decisive action. Showing great ingenuity, Cook made the tactical decision to pretend that he had taken formal possession of New Holland's east coast.

First, he had to work out a time and a place for the possession ceremony. It was easy to invent a ceremony on paper, but more difficult to invent witnesses. Cook could not take the risk that a crew member might later deny the event. Cook had reason to distrust the loyalty and obedience of his crew in the essential matter of keeping strategically sensitive information confidential: Wallis's midshipman, Charles Clerke, who also served on the *Endeavour* as master's mate, is now known to be the source of the unauthorized version of the *Dolphin*'s voyage; two of its crew had offered to sell information to the French chargé d'affaires; Cook's clerk, Richard Orton, on a drunken spree, would later sell details of the *Endeavour* voyage to East India Company captains; an American midshipman on the *Endeavour*, James Matra, would publish an unauthorized account of the voyage. What Cook needed now was a plausible scenario with witnesses he could trust.

He cast his mind back to the excitement generated at Passage Island in the Gulf of Carpentaria when he had signalled his discovery of a channel through to the Indian Ocean. From the ship, his crew would have seen four distant figures and a raised flag, followed by a musket shot. Although it had been little more than a signalling drill, he could easily rewrite it as a possession ceremony. That afternoon, only three people –

Banks, Solander and the marine – had been within earshot and knew that he had not conducted a ceremony. All of them could be sworn to secrecy.

Cook's journal was not a bound book. He wrote on a series of folio double leaves, each of which was folded in two to make four pages. In Batavia, he took a fresh piece of paper and proceeded to draft a new entry for 22 August,[2] the day he had climbed the hill on Passage Island. At the time, possession was the last thing on his mind: he was virtually in the Gulf of Carpentaria – an area that the Dutch held claim to – and he was wholly focused on finding a passage through the perilously shallow waters. However, his 'signalling ceremony' had been witnessed by the entire ship's company, making it a fitting tableau for a possession ceremony. All he had to do was to change the name from Passage Island to Possession Island, include the new name on his chart and write a new script for his journal.

This passage, written in Cook's own hand, is preserved in the Holograph. These 23 handwritten lines are almost poetry, unique in Cook's literary output. The statement is particularly striking because it is far more elaborate than any other possession statement Cook made. During his three Pacific voyages, he recorded only a handful of claims and they all consist of a few stock words which rarely take up more than one short line in his journal.

> Having satisfied myself of the great Probabillity of a Passage, thro' which I intend going with the Ship and therefor may land no more upon this ~~Western~~ Eastern coast of <u>New Holland</u> and on the Western side I can make no new discovery the honour of which belongs to the Dutch Navigators ~~and as such they may lay claim to it as their property~~ but the Eastern Coast from the Latitude of 38° South down to this place I am confident was never seen or viseted by any European before us and ~~therefore by the same Rule belongs to great Brittan~~ Notwithstand I had in the Name of his Majesty taken posession of several places upon this coast I now once more hoisted English Coulers and in the Name of His Majesty King George the Third took posession of the whole Eastern Coast from the above Latitude down to this place by the Name of New Wales together with all the Bays, Harbours Rivers and Islands situate upon the ~~same~~ said coast after which we fired three Volleys of small Arms which were Answered by the like number ~~by~~ from the Ship.[3]

Cook wrote, and amended, his text with a Dutch courier in mind. Initially, he admits the priority of the Dutch on the western side, but claims that 'the same Rule' gives Britain a right to the east coast. Then he deletes the mention of Dutch 'property' and the claim that the east coast 'belongs' to Britain. While Elizabeth Evatt notes both deletions, she merely comments that the original text shows Cook's 'respect for prior discoveries' but offers no explanation for his deletions.[4] Perhaps Cook found his tone too aggressive – 'if the rule says you can have the west, then it says that I can have the east'. Perhaps he simply wanted to avoid any mention of the Dutch having 'property' rights in the matter. Later the Admiralty would water down even Cook's concession to the 'honour' belonging to the Dutch (Chapter 35 and Appendix).

Cook's somewhat superfluous assertion that 'this place I am confident was never seen or viseted by any European before us' betrays the very reason he was now making the claim. For one thing, he had seen Dalrymple's map showing Torres' track, so there was a chance that the Spanish had seen the east coast. Far more urgently, he now had to assume that the French had seen it, as indeed they had. Had Bougainville claimed possession? Cook had found no evidence of this on his voyage along the east coast, but that was probably because he had deliberately bypassed the tempting harbours where Bougainville may have left behind a cairn, or bottle, or inscription. In fact, frightened off by the 'voice of God' from the Barrier Reef, Bougainville had not landed on the coast, but Cook was not to know that.

He tried to minimize his foray onto Dutch territory by claiming only the narrow coastal strip between the mountains and the sea, carefully omitting any east–west coordinates – either for Possession Island itself or for the area of New Holland that he was claiming. Cook also excluded Van Diemen's Land by fixing the southern boundary at parallel 38°S – the same parallel that frames his truncated chart (Fig. 37) concealing Bass Strait. Claiming the continental littoral was scarcely an invasion of the Dutch empire

After considering the possible rights to possession in international law, Cook describes his actual 'ceremony'. Although he asserts here that he took possession at several places along the east coast, there is no record of the annexations in his journal nor in anyone else's journal, and indeed the Admiralty's instructions gave him no authority to claim a country that had already been discovered by Europeans.

Cheers and volleys were not essential at possession ceremonies. What mattered was the consent of the local inhabitants, or markers if uninhabited. Cook may have hoped their omission would go unnoticed.

After describing the ceremony, Cook had to choose a name for his new acquisition. He wanted to assert British priority and continue the European practice of recreating European geography in the New World. This region of that world already boasted New Britain, New Zealand, New Holland, New Guinea and, though Cook may not have known it, New Ireland.

He chose New Wales. On 22 August he had named Prince of Wales Island to commemorate the prince's recent birthday. Calling the coast New Wales would serve to corroborate his claim that the fabricated possession ceremony took place on the same day and while Cook was still at New Holland. The name was altered to New South Wales some time after the *Endeavour* left Batavia, for reasons yet unknown. Perhaps the change was suggested by a nostalgic Joseph Banks, recalling happy summers fishing and hunting at his uncle's house in South Wales.

Cook made sure that the possession ceremony was added in the ship's log[5]:

> At 6 Posession was taken of this country in his Majesty's name and under his coulours; fired several volleys of small arms on the occasion, and cheer'd 3 times, which was answer'd from the ship.[6]

This extant manuscript of the log is not written in Cook's hand, but it 'is certainly the original of a good many of the other extant logs of the voyage'.[7] The small number of logs and journals that were kept by the crew were collected five days before the ship reached Batavia.[8] However, they were returned to their owners later (Hicks's entries extend to mid-March 1771[9]) when, once again, the ship's log was copied. The possession ceremony is mentioned in Hicks's journal,[10] and also in Matra's illicit account published in September 1771,[11] even though neither could have heard Cook's voice from the ship and neither records the place name or says anything more than the ship's log. The journals of the civilians Banks and Parkinson, who recorded the events nearer to the time when they occurred, don't mention the possession ceremony at all. When Banks comes to copy Cook's account into his Grey MS (Chapter 30), the ceremony is mentioned:

> after this we for the last time took possession of all the E Coast of New Holland in his majesties name etc etc & fir'd 3 vollies of small arms which were answer'd from the ship.[12]

Here, Banks is making an abstract of Cook's journal. If Cook had sworn him, Solander and the marine to secrecy, Banks would have felt obliged to record history as Cook wanted. Banks was obedient to Cook in recording the ceremony, but, in his final sentence for that Wednesday afternoon, slipped in the correction 'Passage Isle' as a salute to the truth.

The invented ceremony was an inspired solution but, like most fabrications, there were flaws. The most glaring flaw is the location of the annexation ceremony. As one writer has observed: 'It would have been more correct, dramatically, if the ceremony had been performed on the mainland'.[13]

It would have been more correct, too, if the ceremony had been performed on the east coast of the continent – the coast being annexed – instead of on the west coast of Queensland. The textual evidence shows that Cook at first wrote 'Western coast of New Holland' and then changed it to 'Eastern'. Of course, this could be a slip of the pen, but this passage in the journal is written in an extraordinarily neat and careful hand.

Even Cook's loyal biographer, J.C. Beaglehole, suspected something was amiss. Commenting on Banks's failure to mention the hilltop possession ceremony in his journal entry for 22 August, Beaglehole writes: 'it is curious how casually Banks records what was one of the great moments of the voyage'.[14]

However, Cook was dealing with a crisis. His best option was to place his ceremony on the tiny 'Dutch' island in the Gulf of Carpentaria. Even so, the legal and geographical difficulties raised by this location did not go unnoticed. On the eve of the departure of the First Fleet for New South Wales, a book[15] promoting the new colonial venture included a map of the continent on which Possession Island is relocated north-east of Cape York.[16] In the event, Cook's annexation claim was soon superseded. Eighteen years later, Arthur Phillip stood on the shores of Sydney Harbour and held a real possession ceremony. Instead of just the east coast, Phillip claimed half the continent for Britain, while Lapérouse and his ships cooled their heels in Botany Bay.

Cook's aim was to gain time. If no one denied the ceremony, his fictitious statement of claim would give Britain an inchoate right against her European rivals to occupy the east coast within a reasonable time – he had 'bagged' the east coast for Britain.

And, for all its flaws, his ruse worked. No one doubted that Captain Cook had claimed the east coast in 1770 and in due course the English-born artist, J.A. Gilfillan, commemorated the event in an oil painting (Fig. 47). This fanciful tableau would not have been recognized by Joseph Banks. His memory of that August afternoon was of four people with a signalling flag and one musket on top of a barren hill. He would not

47. This fanciful tableau of Cook's phantom possession ceremony would not have been recognized by Joseph Banks. His memory of that August afternoon was of four people on top of a barren hill.

have recalled a tropical island with all officers present, a troop of marines and Tupaia, in a yellow jacket, holding a tray of goblets.

Cook himself would not have recognized it. His account says nothing about any preparations or fanfare. Instead, his ceremony is the most minimalist of all the ceremonies of the *Endeavour* voyage: no prayer by Tupaia as at Raiatea; no marines in formation as at Poverty Bay; no memorial plaque as at Mercury Bay; no drinking of the king's (or queen's) health as at Queen Charlotte Sound. Evidently Cook hoped that his elaborate possession statement would hide these omissions.

There was no British annexation ceremony in Australia in 1770. And there was no drinking the King's health. That would have to wait until 7 February 1788, nine years after Cook's death.[17]

When Cook had finished writing his revision for 22 August, he gave the manuscript to Orton to copy. Cook would keep his own journal with the ship, Orton's copied journal – minus Cook's handwritten deletions – would be sent to England, and then Orton would start on a new copy of Cook's journal, from the beginning of the voyage. Next, Cook penned two letters, both dated 23 October 1770. The first was a covering letter to Philip Stephens at the Admiralty, giving a brief description of the voyage and stating that copies of his journal and charts were annexed.[18] Cook's second letter was

48. The VOC return fleet sailed from Batavia in late October 1771 under Commander Kelger in the flagship *Kronenburg*. He carried Cook's letters and copies of his journal and charts for delivery to the British Admiralty and the Royal Society.

addressed to the Royal Society, reporting the observation of the transit of Venus and annexing Mr Green's astronomical calculations.[19]

Cook hastily bundled the letters, charts and journal into a parcel, which he sealed and addressed to the Admiralty in London. The parcel was delivered to Frederick Kelger, captain of the *Kronenburg*. The previous day, Cook had gone out into the road to witness the colourful ceremony when Kelger was appointed commodore of the return fleet. The annual fleet of fourteen or fifteen ships sailed home to the Netherlands laden with tons of spices, silks, Chinese porcelain, Japanese lacquerware, tea, coffee, and exotic plants, fruits and animals. This year it would also carry Captain Cook's journal and charts.

Cook's parcel reached London six and a half months later, in the second week of May 1771, beating Cook himself by two months. Despite Cook's concerns, there is no evidence that Captain Kelger broke the seal before delivering it.

Cook watched the *Kronenburg* sail out of the bay, then went across to the Castle to call on the shahbandar. Here, as he had done every day for the last two weeks, he pleaded for the *Endeavour* to be allowed into the wharf at Onrust so the repairs could begin. His pleas grew more urgent, as now he had an even greater crisis on his hands – illness amongst his crew.

33 Plague and Delay at Batavia

Batavia was a death trap in the eighteenth century and the culprit was mosquito-borne malaria. Most newcomers contracted it and more than 50 percent of Europeans died within twelve months of their arrival.[1] Those VOC employees who survived the first year developed an immunity, but remained weak and sickly for years afterwards, as seen in their ghostlike faces. Drained of their natural resistance, they quickly perished from the mildest bout of dysentery or other disease.

Two years earlier, in 1768, Bougainville had aborted his visit as soon as he understood the danger. He hurriedly finished reprovisioning his two ships and fled from the port, writing:

> We had scarce been above eight or ten days at Batavia, when the diseases began to make their appearance. From the best state of health, in all appearance, people were in three days brought to the grave. Several of us fell ill of violent fevers, and our sick found no relief at the hospital. I accelerated as much as I could the dispatch of our affairs; but our sabandar likewise falling sick, and not being able to do any business, we met with difficulties and delays … Almost every officer on board my ship was already sick, or felt a disposition towards it. The number of fluxes had not decreased among the crews, and if we had made a longer stay at Batavia, it would certainly have made greater havock among us than the whole voyage.[2]

Bougainville was lucky. By arriving at Batavia at the end of September, he just dodged the preparations of the VOC return fleet which so delayed Cook two years later. Bougainville escaped after two weeks and most of his men recovered. Of the seven deaths during his voyage, it seems only three occurred after Batavia.[3] Still, Bougainville himself suffered bouts of malaria for the rest of his life and it was an attack that caused his death in 1811 at the age of 82.

Although the fever or 'bloody flux' had not been named as malaria in the eighteenth century, its symptoms had been described. Dr James Lind, the Scottish physician at the Royal Hospital in Portsmouth, had written about this 'true epidemic in the Torrid Zone' and publicized its remedy. In an essay first published in 1757, he declared that the Jesuit's bark (Peruvian bark, cinchona or quinine) was 'universally known, by practitioners of all nations, to be the only sovereign medicine for this most frequent and malignant fever, in those sickly southern climates'.[4]

Before long, Peruvian bark was considered a valuable tonic and cure-all. At the insistence of his sister, Sarah Sophia, Banks took a bottle of bark on his trip to Newfoundland in the summer of 1766 – where it worked miracles.[5] He packed it again for the *Endeavour* voyage.

Although Peruvian bark was an essential item for the mahogany medicine chests of gentlemen adventurers, it was not yet standard navy issue, perhaps because of medical politics and naval economies. Yet it seems that the Navy Board did supply some bark to the *Endeavour*, because there is evidence that both the *Endeavour*'s surgeon, William Monkhouse, and his assistant used it at least once.[6] But whatever the volume supplied, it was not enough to meet the crisis that enveloped the ship's company.

Within two weeks of the *Endeavour* arriving at the port, the sickness appeared. On Friday 26 October Cook ordered tents to be erected on Kuyper's Island for the men who had 'taken ill owing as I suppose to the extreem hot weather'. But soon they were falling like flies. Everyone was sick at one time or another. The first to die was the surgeon, Monkhouse, followed by the Tahitians, Tupaia and Taiata, whose knowledge of the islands and languages of the South Pacific had served the *Endeavour* so well.

By that time, Banks and Solander were so ill that they had rented a country house far from the town. Here, in the care of Malay nurses, they consumed regular decoctions of bark and survived. Cook also became ill. He never mentions it, of course, but Banks records: 'the Captain also was taken ill on board'.[7]

Meanwhile, the waiting continued while the stevedores at Onrust loaded pepper into the VOC ships. By 5 November, the pepper was on its way to Europe and the *Endeavour* was permitted to enter the careening wharf. Work commenced four days later and, after six days of intensive labour, it was completed by 15 November. The workmanship was excellent, Cook was delighted with the result and the ship returned to its berth at Kuyper's Island.

Ideally, the Englishmen would have immediately rerigged the ship, brought the provisions aboard and made their escape. But this was impossible. With so many sick, there was a serious shortage of manpower either to restock the ship or to sail her. Other foreign vessels moved in and out of the port, but not the *Endeavour*. As the weeks passed, Cook hired nineteen additional seamen, mainly British, to assist.

Christmas Day passed, and at last, on Boxing Day 1770, they weighed anchor and sailed out of Batavia Bay. After eleven weeks, Cook had escaped the port, but not its consequences. On the slow passage across the Indian Ocean to Cape Town, the *Endeavour* became a hospital ship, with more than 40 people on the sick list – many of whom would not see England again. Of the 43 men who died during the *Endeavour* voyage, only eight died before Batavia, from accident or malady. Six were buried at Batavia and 29 died after leaving Batavia, all from illness. Remarkably, no one died from scurvy.

Cook never returned to the East Indies. On his next voyage he lost three men through accident, but only one through illness.

Throughout all this, the goat survived. It was partly due to her milk that Cook's crew remained so healthy until Batavia. After she had circumnavigated the world with both Wallis and Cook, Banks ensured that she has a comfortable retirement, until her death a year or so later.

34 Homeward Bound through a Nest of Spies

The coast of Africa loomed on the horizon at the beginning of March. On the 14th, the *Endeavour* anchored in Table Bay and Cook took a coach to Constantia to call upon Rijk Tulbagh, the respected VOC governor of the Cape Colony. The sick were brought ashore for treatment, while those who were well enough helped to provision the ship. When the work was finished, Cook gave his men shore leave – a decision that would turn the homeward leg into a race for the finish.

Cape Town was one of the world's great ports of refreshment and the Englishmen were not surprised to count fifteen foreign ships in the bay: eight Dutch, three Danish and four French vessels which were being loaded with provisions destined for the French colony at nearby Mauritius. The captains of these vessels had heard of Cook's expedition and wanted to know where he had been. However, it was not these foreigners who proved to be the ace spies. That honour went to the enemy within.

During the month that the *Endeavour* spent at Cape Town, four East Indiamen arrived from India and China en route to England. They were the *Admiral Pocock*, Captain Riddell; the *Houghton*, Captain Smith; the *Duke of Gloucester*, Captain Lauder; and the *Europa*, Captain Pelly. When Cook's sailors came ashore, these four captains followed them into the waterfront taverns where they bought them drinks and asked about their adventures and discoveries, as Banks learnt later at St Helena:

> [They] resolvd to steer homewards with all expedition in order (if possible) to bring home the first news of our voyage, as we found that many Particulars of it has transpird and particularly that a copy of the Latitudes and Longitudes of most or all the principal places we had been at had been taken by the Captns Clerk from the Captns own Journals and Given or Sold to one of the India Captns.[1]

The clerk, Richard Orton, was often drunk. Months earlier, parts of his ears had been cut off by an irate shipmate following a drunken binge. He made an easy target for the merchant captains, for whom corporate espionage was a useful means of safeguarding their charter monopoly. Orton had ample opportunity to compile a complete list of the names and coordinates of Cook's discoveries, and sell it to the Company's men. Such tactics were foreshadowed by Alexander Dalrymple, the great apologist for the Honourable East India Company, when he admitted in his pamphlet that the *Endeavour*'s discoveries would 'be an object of great consequence to the company'.[2]

As Banks watched the French ships sail for Mauritius, he dismissed the possibility that France's military ambitions might pose a threat to British India:

> from [Mauritius] it is probable they Meditate some stroke at our East Indian Settlements in the beginning of a future war; which however our India people are not at all alarmed at, trusting intirely to the vast standing armies which they constantly keep up, the support of which in the Bengall alone Costs 840000 eight hundred and forty thousand pounds a Year![3]

However, the French sailors also provided news about Bougainville's expedition, which had called at Mauritius and Cape Town two years earlier. This gossip only increased the Englishmen's fear that France would challenge Britain's Pacific discoveries and the need for haste, as Banks remarked:

> How necessary then will it be for us to publish an account of our voyage as soon as possible after our arrival if we mean that our own country shall have the Honour of our Discoveries![4]

Cook too saw it as a matter of urgency that an account of the voyage be 'published by Authority to fix the prior right of discovery beyond dispute'.[5]

They sailed from the Cape on 15 April and reached the island of St Helena two weeks later. Here Cook was surprised to find a fleet of twelve East Indiamen, including the four vessels he had seen at Cape Town, waiting for naval protection. He was told that their captains feared attack by Spanish warships, after hearing rumours that Britain and Spain were at war over the Falkland Islands. The Admiralty had sent the HMS *Portland* (50 guns) to escort them up the Atlantic, but now a message had arrived saying that the dispute was settled and the fleet could return in safety.

It was here, during his discussions with the merchant captains, that Cook learnt to his chagrin that all the geographical coordinates of his discoveries had been leaked. Now his aim was to beat the fleet and be first home with news of the voyage.

The *Endeavour* sailed with the convoy to Ascension Island. Banks wanted to stop and botanize, but there was no time for that: 'Our Captn however did not chuse to anchor unwilling to give the fleet so much start of him'.[6] But it was no good: the *Endeavour* could not keep up with the other vessels. Cook signalled to the *Portland* whose Captain Elliot, a navy man and trustworthy, came on board. Cook handed him a box of log books, charts and officers' journals and asked that they be delivered to the Admiralty with all speed. In the event, Elliot arrived at the Admiralty only three days before Cook.

The voyage up the Atlantic lasted another two months. They crossed the equator in the middle of May; later that month Lieutenant Hicks, the first of Cook's men to see the Australian coast, died of consumption; then six weeks later Banks's cocker spaniel, Lady, suffered a seizure and died in his cabin. At last, on 10 July, a great cheer went up when the lookout at the masthead announced the coast of Cornwall. Two days later, on Friday 12 July 1771, they passed Dover and arrived in the Downs at 3 p.m. As soon as the anchors were secure, Cook and the gentlemen stepped ashore.

Cook, Banks and Solander landed at Deal on the east coast of Kent and quickly found a post chaise to take them up to London. Cook left the carriage at Whitehall, farewelled his companions of almost three years, and hurried across the road to report to the Admiralty. The two botanists drove on to the West End and greeted the press waiting outside Banks's elegant townhouse at 14 New Burlington Street.

When Cook arrived at the Admiralty Office on that Friday afternoon, Philip Stephens greeted his warmly. He had already received the copy of the journal sent from Batavia two months earlier and Cook's accompanying letter saying:

> Altho' the discoveries made in this Voyage are not great, yet I flatter my self that they are such as may merit the attention of their Lordships, and altho' I have faild in discovering the so much talk'd of southern Continent (which perhaps do not exist) and which I my self had much at heart, yet I am confident that no part of the failure of such discovery Can be laid to my Charge.[7]

Indeed, Cook's recorded discoveries were not great. None of the eight Pacific islands he discovered on the *Endeavour* voyage was as significant as Samuel Wallis's Tahiti; nor had Cook found Terra Australis Incognita. Yet the self-assured navigator had little doubt that his work in New Holland and New Zealand would 'merit the attention of their Lordships'.

But, fortunately, Cook had not recorded all that he knew in his journals, and so Orton had not been able to leak every discovery that Cook had made. Cook told Stephens all about his unrecorded discoveries, including Bass Strait and the deep, natural harbour of Port Jackson, which he believed to be finer than the bay of Trincomalee in Ceylon. Stephens was delighted with his discoveries and congratulated Cook for concealing them so effectively.

As soon as he left the Admiralty building, Cook went home to Assembly Row in Mile End to greet Elizabeth after their three-year separation. Of his four children, James and Nathaniel welcomed him, but little Elizabeth had died three months earlier and the infant Joseph he never knew. Christmas was spent in Yorkshire, where Cook visited his father, James Cook the elder, for the last time. Returning to London at the beginning of January, he started preparing for his next voyage. The first English edition of Bougainville's account of his voyage had just appeared in London and Cook undoubtedly obtained a copy.[8] His earlier fears were partly confirmed and he suspected that French ships had already returned to the South Seas.

He was right. By January 1772, while Cook was buried in paperwork and charts in foggy London, two separate French expeditions were using the southern summer to search for Terra Australis Incognita in the Indian Ocean. The first, commanded by Marion Dufresne, discovered the Crozet Islands, while the second venture, under Yves-Joseph de Kerguelen, found the Kerguelen Islands. By March, both expeditions had landed in Australia. Dufresne arrived on the east coast of Van Diemen's Land and spent some time exploring the land near today's city of Hobart; while, over on the west coast, the captain of Kerguelen's second ship, Louis de Saint Alouarn, arrived off Cape Leeuwin. He followed the coast northward to Dirk Hartog Island, where he claimed the land for France at Baie de Prise de Possession. It was time for James Cook to make his final thrust to find the Great South Land.

On Cook's recommendation, the Navy Board purchased two Whitby colliers, similar to the *Endeavour*, and named them *Drake* and *Raleigh*. But diplomatic heads in Whitehall cautioned against such needless provocation of Spain and they were renamed *Resolution*, to be commanded by Cook, and *Adventure*, to be commanded by Furneaux.[9]

Banks too was eager to start his preparations, but first he had to satisfy the demands of the press for whom his 'first voyage around the world' had become a social and international sensation. On 2 August, Banks was presented to the King at St James's Palace – Cook was presented twelve days later – and in November, Banks and Solander were summoned to Oxford, where both received the honorary Doctorate of Civil Law. Then turning his mind to his next voyage, Banks wrote to a friend saying:

> O how Glorious would it be to set my heel upon ye Pole! and turn myself round 360 degrees in a second.[10]

He gathered together an entourage, larger than last time, so that the *Resolution* had to be reconstructed with an additional upper deck. When this made her so top-heavy that she was in danger of capsizing, the Navy Board ordered that she be returned to her original condition.[11] At this point, Banks went off in a huff and chartered a brig to take his party – including his friend John Gore – on a scientific expedition to Iceland.

Two weeks prior to his departure, Cook received the Admiralty's instructions, most of which he himself had drafted.[12] In an echo of Bougainville's plan conceived a decade earlier, Cook's primary task was to find Bouvet's Cape Circumcision in the South Atlantic and determine whether or not it was joined to Terra Australis Incognita. If it was, then he was to make a thorough survey of the continent and take possession of 'convenient situations' in the name of the King. After that, he was turn east and 'proceed upon farther discoveries … as near to the South Pole as possible'.[13]

On 12 July 1772, Cook and Furneaux left England to begin the second voyage. On the same day, Banks's brig with Solander and Gore on board sailed for Iceland.

35 The Authorized Version – Censorship

Both Bougainville and Cook had kept a journal of their voyages, but, despite the enormous public interest in their discoveries, neither of them would be transcribed and printed. Instead, their manuscripts were confiscated by their government and remained unpublished for 200 years.[1] The admiralties in both France and Britain were eager to assert the priority of their discoveries and enjoy the prestige of publicity, but they also wanted to conceal any knowledge that they didn't want in the public domain. Thus, instead of a book containing the navigator's original journal, the public had to wait for the official, authorized narrative or 'Account'.

Bougainville started preparing the narrative of his voyage soon after his return to France in March 1769. His first version was ready for presentation to King Louis XV in October.[2] He continued working on it through the winter but took a break the following spring when he visited London. Here, on 24 May, he attended a meeting of the Royal Society and reported on his voyage.[3] The other fellows no doubt reminded him that Cook was expected home soon, and Bougainville returned to his desk in Paris with renewed effort. His final manuscript was approved by the Royal Censor's office in January 1771.[4] In May, his narrative, *Voyage autour du monde*, was published in France[5] and eight months later, in January 1772, an English translation by J.R. Forster was available in London.[6]

While Bougainville's journal lay undisturbed in the Archives Nationales in Paris until 1977, the journey of Cook's original journal was more complicated. It seems that, before leaving the Admiralty Office on that first afternoon in 1771, Cook asked Philip Stephens for permission to retain his own manuscript journal as a keepsake, on the promise he would not publish it independently. Stephens agreed as he now held the two copies of the manuscript made by Cook's clerk, Richard Orton. The first was the copy sent home from Batavia, which Stephens had received at his office in May 1771. The second was the new copy which Orton started after Batavia, from the beginning of the voyage through to their arrival in England, when it too was handed over to the Admiralty.

So Cook went home to Mile End Road with his original journal of some 750 pages and presented it to his wife. After Elizabeth Cook died in 1835 it disappeared from public view until 1923 when Sotheby's auctioned it in London. It was purchased by the National Library of Australia and today it is referred to as the Holograph or, simply, as Cook's *Endeavour* journal.[7] The Library has made a digitized version of the whole manuscript available online,[8] as well as a transcribed version.[9] This original journal is especially valuable because it alone contains all Cook's crossings out and corrections, his drafting and redrafting. It is a very carefully written document, strewn with his first thoughts, his second thoughts and his self-censorship.

This is the manuscript which J.C. Beaglehole transcribed, annotated and published in 1955. Beaglehole's scholarly masterpiece gave the public its first opportunity to read Cook's account of the *Endeavour* voyage in his own words. Up until this book, as Beaglehole said, 'for a hundred and twenty years, so far as the first voyage was concerned, Hawkesworth was Cook'.[10]

John Hawkesworth's magnum opus would not appear until 1773, and two years was a long time to wait. With an eager public and money to be made it was inevitable that literary birds of prey would gather.

On 29 August 1771, just six weeks after the *Endeavour*'s return, a curious pamphlet appeared. While not an account of the voyage, it was the first of many entrepreneurial proposals circulated in England over the next fifteen years, all seeking to capitalize on Cook's discoveries in the south-west Pacific. Titled *Plan for Benefiting Distant Unprovided Countries*, it proposed, with rather paternalistic zeal, to undertake the improvement of less developed countries, notably New Zealand. Its authors, Benjamin Franklin and Alexander Dalrymple, concluded:

> It seems a laudable wish, that all the Nations of the Earth were connected by a knowledge of each other, and a mutual exchange of benefits: But a Commercial Nation particularly should wish for a general Civilization of Mankind, since Trade is always carried on to much greater extent with People who have the Arts and Conveniencies of Life, than it can be with naked Savages. We may therefore hope, in this undertaking, to be of some service to our Country [i.e., Britain], as well as to those poor people, who, however distant from us, are in truth related to us, and whose Interests do, in some degree, concern every one who can say, *Homo sum, &c.*[11]

Then, just a month later, the first account, *A journal of a voyage round the world*, was published, illicitly and anonymously, by Becket and de Hondt in the Strand.[12] Historians have long suspected the author to be the American loyalist midshipman, James Mario Matra, and this has now been proved conclusively.[13] To add authenticity, the first edition contained a cheeky dedication to 'the Right Honourable Lords of the Admiralty and to Mr. Banks and Dr. Solander', but the publishers were forced to retract the offending page immediately.

With 130 pages, this was the first extended account of Cook's voyage. It was an instant bestseller in London and quickly seized on by the French. When the second edition of Bougainville's narrative appeared in Paris in 1772, a translated version of Matra's unauthorized account was included as an extra volume.[14]

At about the same time an extraordinary newspaper advertisement appeared in the classified section of London's *Daily Advertiser*:

> In a few days will be published [a book titled] An Abstract of a Voyage round the World, in a Letter from Jos. Banks, Esq. to Count Lauragais, the Original of which is lodged in the Academy of Sciences at Paris.[15]

Banks was aghast. It was true that he had penned a twelve-page letter to his debonair friend Lauraguais, who was then living in London.[16] The Frenchman had been insistent in requesting an account of the voyage and so Banks wrote this short, pithy summary of his adventures in the Pacific. It was intended as a private letter and Banks never imagined that Lauraguais would abuse it by taking it to a printer to get it published. After reading the advertisement, Banks stormed around to the printer's premises, bought the impression plate and destroyed it, before any copies found their way to London's booksellers.[17]

The next embarrassment was the brother of the late Sydney Parkinson, Banks's young artist who died in Batavia. Stanfield Parkinson announced his intention to produce a posthumous journal, much to the annoyance of the Admiralty. However, the project was temporarily frustrated when Banks and Hawkesworth applied to Chancery for an injunction which was not lifted until after Hawkesworth's own volumes appeared.

Meanwhile, in the autumn of 1771, Lord Sandwich (now enjoying his third stint as First Lord of the Admiralty) invited a ghostwriter, Dr John Hawkesworth, to transform the records of all the recent Pacific voyages into a series of entertaining narratives. He was given access to all the collected logs and journals, including Orton's copy of Cook's journal, while Joseph Banks obligingly lent a copy of his *Endeavour* journal. With these at his elbow, Hawkesworth constructed his narrative by amalgamating extracts from the various journals, interspersed with his own reflections weighted with literary and classical allusions.

Published in June 1773, Hawkesworth's *Voyages in the Southern Hemisphere* consists of three beautiful volumes filled with exciting descriptions and engravings of newly discovered places, peoples and customs. Volume I contains the edited accounts of the voyages of Cook's predecessors, Byron, Wallis and Carteret, while volumes II and III are dedicated wholly to Cook's *Endeavour* voyage.[18]

Hawkesworth's eagerly awaited narrative was a popular success, but he had his critics. The main criticism was that readers could not separate Hawkesworth's editorial flourishes from the words of Cook or the words of Banks. The editor had decided to use the first person so that the awkward jumble is retold through Cook's mouth. The work was published while Cook was absent on his second voyage, but when he learnt of it he was so horrified and embarrassed by the inaccuracies and misrepresentations that he wrote an angry denunciation of the narrative in his next journal:

> It was not less mortifying to me when I first read it, which was not till I arrived now at the Cape of Good Hope; for I never had the perusal of the Manuscript nor did I ever hear the whole of it read in the mode it was written, notwithstanding what Dr Hawkesworth has said to the Contrary in the Interduction ... How these things came to be thus misrepresented, I can not say, as they came not from me.[19]

Hawkesworth never read this because he died five months after publishing. However, Cook's outburst is testimony to the fact that Hawkesworth's official account was a very unreliable record of what Cook actually wrote.

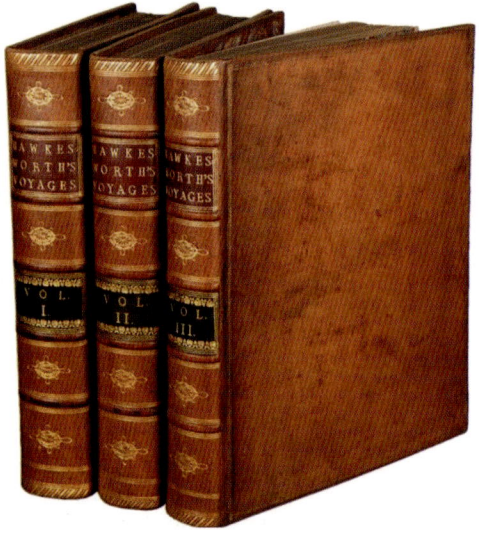

49. Hawkesworth's officially sanctioned *Voyages*, which appeared in June 1773, provided the only version of Britain's mid-eighteenth-century voyages for over a century. Volume I contains the edited accounts of the voyages of Byron, Wallis and Cartert, while volumes II and III are dedicated wholly to Cook's *Endeavour* voyage. Hawkesworth died shortly after publication, and the Admiralty appointed Dr John Douglas, Canon of Windsor, to edit Cook's journals for the second and third voyages.

Yet Hawkesworth's pastiche, with all its errors and omissions, had a great impact on the European mind simply because it was the only available version of the *Endeavour* voyage for over a century. Eventually, in 1893 Admiral William Wharton put together a new edition of the *Endeavour* journal using both of Orton's inadequate and inaccurate copies of Cook's journal.[20] But it had little impact.

When Beaglehole's transcription of Cook's manuscript is compared with the Admiralty's authorized version, it becomes clear that the discrepancies go much further than matters of style. Words have been altered, so that Cook's facts have been changed, as well as his meaning and intent. In short, Cook's text – already heavily self-censored – was further censored in 1773. The censor would not have been Hawkesworth himself, as he was simply a journalist improving on a good story. The censor was most likely Philip Stephens.

One example of the censor's handiwork is the 'possession statement' written by

Cook at Batavia. His original words – discussed in Chapter 32 and the Appendix – can now be compared to the Hawkesworth version:

> As I was now about to quit the eastern coast of New Holland, which I had coasted from latitude 38 to this place, and which I am confident no European had ever seen before, I once more hoisted English colours, and though I had already taken possession of several particular parts, I now took possession of the whole eastern coast, from latitude 38° to this place, latitude 10 ½ S. in right of his Majesty King George the Third, by the name of NEW SOUTH WALES, with all the bays, harbours, rivers, and islands situated upon it: we then fired three vollies of small arms, which were answered by the same number from the ship. Having performed this ceremony upon the island, which we called POSSESSION ISLAND, we reimbarked in our boat.[21]

This official 1773 version differs from Cook's manuscript in several places. The words 'about to quit the eastern coast' have been added to reinforce the pretence that the supposed ceremony took place on the east coast. For further validation, the last sentence has been invented by the Admiralty. It does not appear in the Holograph or in either of Orton's copies, and looks like Admiralty language. Cook's journals always spoke of 'taking possession', not possession 'ceremonies'. Hawkesworth generally follows Cook's practice and this is the only occasion where he talks of performing a possession ceremony.

More significant is the omission of Cook's words:

> on the Western side I can make no new discovery the honour of which belongs to the Dutch navigators.[22]

The Admiralty wanted no truck with Cook's acknowledgment of Dutch priority by right of discovery, even though Britain did not deny it. Whitehall wanted to avoid any unnecessary confrontation with Holland, which was much better as a friend than an enemy. Better not even to mention the idea of New Holland 'belonging' to the Dutch.

In fact, Whitehall's misgivings about the legitimacy of Britain's title over a nominally Dutch New Holland persisted for decades. As late as 1824, John Barrow, the Admiralty Secretary, reminded a colleague that the Dutch had a potential claim to Australia:

> it would be well to bear in mind that they would have a justifiable plea, in planting an establishment on any part of the Northern Coast of the latter, in our own example of taking possession of the Eastern Coast and the Island of Van Diemen, the original discovery of which by the Dutch is not disputed. Indeed I believe it is admitted, tho' not provided for (that I am aware of) in the Law of nations, that Occupancy is a stronger title than priority of discovery; but be this as it may, in the present instance our own Conduct might be quoted against us.[23]

And it wasn't only Cook's text that was concealed and censored. The original maps and charts drawn by Cook and his men were also deposited in the Admiralty's vaults and remained unpublished in their manuscript form for more than a century. The few charts chosen for inclusion in Hawkesworth were altered.[24] After selecting the handmade chart, a 'fair copy' of it was redrawn to the Admiralty's specifications. This was the version delivered to a London engraver who cut a mirror image of the map into a copper plate and prepared it for printing. Eventually, in 1955, reproductions of Cook's original charts were published in R.A. Skelton's portfolio that accompanied Beaglehole's edition of Cook's journals.[25] Thirty years later, the Hakluyt Society published the comprehensive collection of Cook's maps and charts.[26]

Comparing Cook's originals with Hawkesworth's maps shows that the Admiralty deliberately altered or refined Cook's charts to conceal politically sensitive discoveries. Cook's manuscript map of Stewart Island uses a dotted line to suggest an isthmus joining the island to the mainland. Hawkesworth's engraved map replaces this with a solid – if lighter – line. This device hid Stewart Island's insularity for decades.

As for Bass Strait, Cook had edited the southern part of his map of the east coast of New Holland, cutting short his chart at the 38th parallel (Fig. 37). He thus avoided giving any context for this part of his map in order to hide the existence of Bass Strait. The Admiralty aided him in this deception: Hawkesworth's version of the east coast of New South Wales shows Cape York at the far north-west corner of the page, leaving no room for the Torres Strait or the Gulf of Carpentaria.[27] This made Cook's truncation of the bottom of his map less obvious, and less likely to provoke questions about what lay between the *Endeavour*'s landfall and Van Diemen's Land. The repositioning of the published map not only helped to conceal the insularity of Van Diemen's Land, but it was also aimed at avoiding any suggestions that Cook had trespassed on territory where the Dutch held a prior claim – either in Van Diemen's Land or on the coast of Carpentaria.

But it was the French, not the Dutch, who were Britain's greatest rivals in exploring the Southern Seas at this point. Bougainville, Surville, Marion Dufresne, Lapérouse, Kerguelen and Baudin traversed much the same area as Cook. How did France react to these decades of subterfuge? After Cook's discoveries in 1770, Bass Strait was officially 'discovered' in 1798 and Foveaux Strait a decade later. When this latter news reached Europe, it seems that a French agent gained access to Cook's original charts, held under wraps at the Admiralty Office in Whitehall. As he examined them, it became obvious that these hand-drawn charts differed significantly from the engraved versions published in Hawkesworth almost 40 years earlier.

The French were outraged, charging the English with the contemptible crimes of concealing discoveries and fabricating false charts. In 1810, the bureaucrat Victor-Donatien de Musset-Pathay, wrote:

It is known that in the last century the English performed many maritime expeditions, the object of which was the improvement of the astronomical, natural, and physical sciences, and principally the discovery of new countries. In this respect, the learned world owes their gratitude for so laudable an undertaking; but this sentiment is eradicated by the well-defined certainty, that they wished to concentrate in their island the fruits of all their discoveries, and prohibited every kind of communication, even those relative to the sciences and arts, which all civilized nations never refuse, whether in peace or in war. The privation of a good may be a positive evil; but the English have even gone farther. Not content with prohibiting these communications to the continental powers, and wishing not to have the air of refusing them, they adopted a means which might occasion a real evil. This was to print false accounts, and charts full of errors, of their voyages, and to hawk them on the continent. When these charts were compared with those preserved in London, the fraud was discovered in all its blackness.[28]

Here was further evidence of perfidious Albion to add to the wrongs and humiliation of the Seven Years War, on top of the French losses at Crecy, Poitiers and Agincourt. As Napoleon put it to General Augereau: 'We have six centuries of insults to avenge'.[29]

Here was justification for the governor at Île de France (Mauritius) having arrested and detained Matthew Flinders for six and a half years so that Baudin's expeditioners could be first into print. In 1807, François Péron published the first volume of his *Voyage de decouvertes*,[30] presenting half of New Holland's south coast – from the head of the Great Australian Bight to Wilson's Promontory – as Terre Napoleon and peppering it with French placenames like Golfe Josephine, Golfe Bonaparte, Île Decrès and Cap des Adieux.

Peron's book caused great indignation in England. One reviewer (believed to be John Barrow, Secretary to the Admiralty) hit back, championing the confined Flinders and accusing the French of stooping 'to pluck the laurels from a brother's brow ... for the purpose of setting up a claim, at some future day, to this part of New Holland'.[31]

Worse was to come in 1811 when Louis Freycinet published his map titled 'Carte générale de la Nouvelle Hollande'. It was the first complete map of the continent, beating Flinders's map by three years.[32]

But Freycinet's Atlas was France's last hurrah. While Napoleon was defeated at Waterloo and exiled to St Helena, the settlements in New South Wales would continue to grow. Britain had won New Holland and so began a century when Britannia ruled the waves.

James Cook had played a pivotal role in Britain's winning maritime dominion – both in what he discovered and what he concealed. He was serving his country at a time when France and Britain were enemies in a cold war and rivals in an age of imperial expansion. As in the Cold War between the Western Powers and the USSR, secrecy, spies and fake documents were the name of the game.

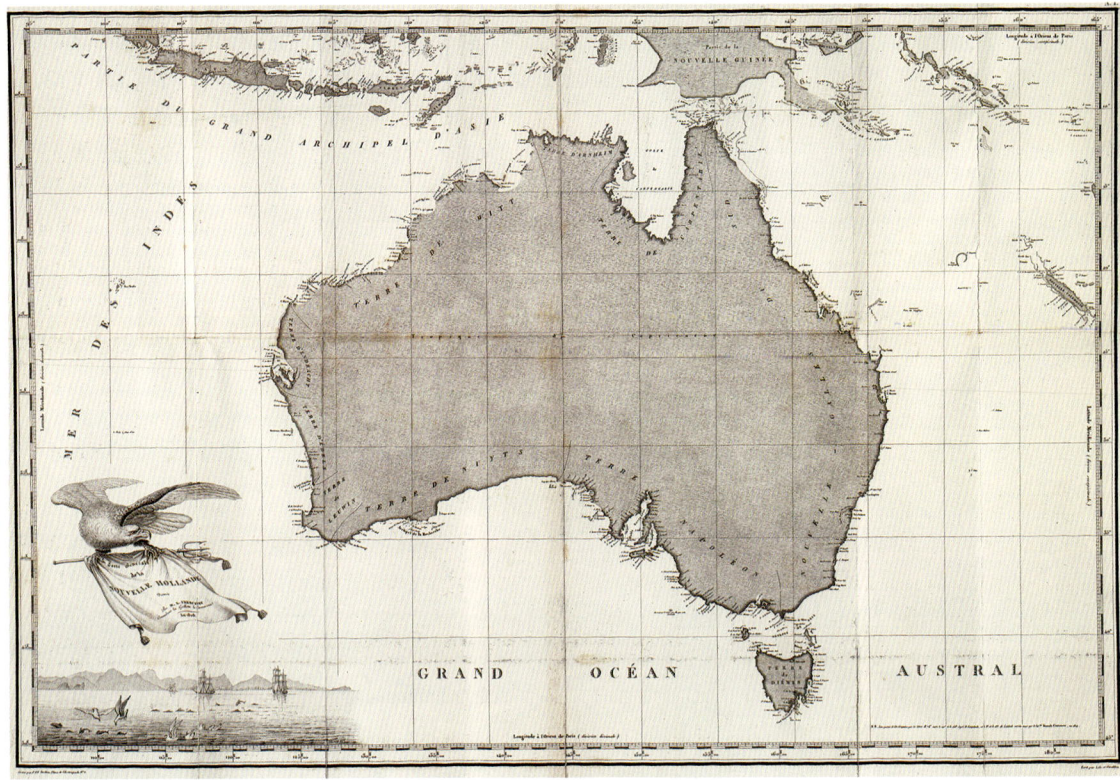

50. The first modern map of the Australian continent, Louis Freycinet's chart was published in France in 1811, three years before Flinders's map. It appeared in the official account of the 1801–04 French voyage to Australia commanded by Nicolas Baudin. National Library of Australia nla.obj-230971556.

Moreover, Cook's falsifications, and those of other explorers, were not designed to hide dangers that might harm other mariners. Navigators did not deliberately hide reefs and shoals. Cook disguised the existence of straits, made false claims of insularity, rewrote the record to suggest that he had conducted possession ceremonies when he had not. But these were strategic matters. Cook was a loyal and obedient patriot in a time of tension between the European powers. He was prepared to lie for the sake of his country. And Hawkesworth's charts and authorized account show that the Admiralty itself was prepared to refine and embellish upon these lies.

For its part, the Admiralty – in the person of Philip Stephens – continued to show its appreciation of Cook's fidelity and enterprise. When Cook asked for an assurance that he could expect to resume his comfortable retirement, Stephens wrote:

> [My Lords Commissioners] will on your return from the Voyage re-appoint you to the [Greenwich] Hospital or if that cannot with propriety be effected they will recommend you to His Majesty for some other Mark of his Royal favor.[33]

On 6 July 1776, when sending Cook some very secret instructions for the third voyage, Stephens wrote, in language which was, for him, full of emotion: '[I] most heartily wish you a successful Voyage, and am with great esteem ... etc.'[34]

Stephens, no doubt regretfully, was also a member of the Advisory Committee, established by Lord Sandwich in 1780, to oversee the publication of the official account of Cook's last Pacific voyage.[35] When Stephens departed the secretary's office in 1795, aged 71, he took with him Orton's first copy of Cook's journal which had been sent from Batavia.[36] It went with his estate to Viscount Ranelagh, the husband of Stephens's illegitimate daughter who died in childbirth. It is now held in the State Library of New South Wales.

On 23 November 1775 the full significance of Cook's contributions to navigation and exploration was recognized when he was nominated as a Fellow of the Royal Society.

> Captain James Cook of Mile-end, a gentleman skilfull in astronomy, & the successful conductor of two important voyages for the discovery of unknown countries, by which geography & natural history have been greatly advantaged and improved, being desirous of the honour of becoming a member of this Society, we whose names are underwritten, do, from our personal knowledge testify, that we believe him deserving of such honour, and that he will become a worthy & useful member.[37]

Beaglehole comments:

> It was an election to which the philosophers were more than usually attentive, and his nomination was a fitting one ... The signatures that followed were a coruscation, twenty-five in number as against the more usual three to half-dozen that nominated, beginning with Banks, Solander ... and Stephens.[38]

Cook has always been credited with establishing that New Zealand was not a continent, with mapping the east coast of New Holland, and being the first to chart a route through Torres Strait. However, some of Cook's fabrications – especially the hiding of Foveaux and Bass Straits – have led to him being criticized for his errors. The true story, revealed in the alterations he and the Admiralty made to his journals and charts, or deduced by the fact that Arthur Phillip knew, before he had seen it, that Sydney Harbour contained islands, shows that Cook was, if anything, an even greater navigator, hydrographer and cartographer than has been believed. This book's forensic examination of the paper trail also proves that he was a more consummate politician than his admirers have so far suspected.

After reading Hawkesworth, Cook may have hoped that one day, when tensions reduced, he would be able to publish his own journal and set the record straight by correcting the lies told on behalf of the Admiralty. But he died in Kealakekua Bay, Hawaii, on 14 February 1779, before he had the chance to do so.

51. James Cook's election certificate to the Royal Society, 1775–76.

Appendix – An Analysis of Captain Cook's Possession Speech Discussed in Chapters 32 and 35

Cooks Holograph version

Hawkesworth's official version, authorized by the Admiralty

A [the Lands laying to the NW of this passage were composed of a number of Island of various extent both for height and circuit rainged one be hind a nother as far to the Northward and Westward as I could see which could not be less than 12 or 14 Leagues.]

[The land to the north west of it consisted of a great number of islands of various extent, and different heights, ranged one behind another, as far to the northward and westward as I could see, which could not be less than thirteen leagues.]

B Having satisfied myself of the great Probabillity of a Passage, thro' which I intend going withthe Ship and there^for may land no more upon this ~~Western~~ Eastern coast of New Holland and on the Western side I can make no new discovery the honour of which belongs to the Dutch Navigators ~~and as such they may lay claim to it as their property~~

C but the Eastern Coast from the Latitude of 38° South down to this place I am confident was never seen or viseted by any European before ^us and ~~therefore by the same Rule belongs to great Brittan~~

As I was now about to quit the eastern coast of New Holland, which I had coasted from latitude 38 to this place, and which I am confident no European had ever seen before

D Notwithstand I had in the Name of his Majesty taken posession of several places upon this coast I now once more hoisted English Coulers and

As I was now about to quit the eastern coast of New Holland, which I had coasted from latitude 38 to this place, and which I am confident no European had ever seen before,

E in the Name of His Majesty King George the Third took posession of the whole Eastern Coast from the above Latitude down to this place by the name of New South ^Wales

I now took possession of the whole eastern coast, from latitude 38° to this place, latitude 10 ½ S. in right of his Majesty King George the Third, by the name of NEW SOUTH WALES,

F together with all the Bays, Harbours Rivers and Islands situate upon the ~~same~~ ^said coast after which we fired three Volleys of small Arms which were An the like number by ^from the Ship

with all the bays, harbours, rivers, and islands situated upon it: we then fired three vollies of small arms, which were answered by the same number from the ship.

G this done we set out for the Ship but were some time in geting on board on account of a very rappid Ebb Tide which set NE out of the Passage.

Select Bibliography

Anson, George, *A Voyage round the World in the Years 1740–1744. Compiled by Richard Walter, Chaplain to his Majesty's Ship the 'Centurion'*, London, John and Paul Knapton, 1748.
Arlidge, Allan, 'Cook as a Commander: As his Naval Contemporaries Saw Him', *Cook's Log*, Vol. 27, No. 4, 2004. Available at https://www.captaincooksociety.com/home/detail/cook-as-a-commander-as-his-naval-contemporaries-saw-him
Atkinson, Alan, *The Europeans in Australia: A History*, Vol. 1, Melbourne, Oxford University Press, 1997.
Banks, Joseph, *The Endeavour Journal of Joseph Banks: 1768–1771*, 2 vols, ed. by J.C. Beaglehole, Sydney, Angus & Robertson, 1962.
Banks, Joseph, *The Letters of Sir Joseph Banks: A Selection, 1768–1820*, ed. by Neil Chambers, London, Imperial College Press, 2000.
Barton, George Burnett, *History of New South Wales from the Records*, Sydney, Charles Potter, Government Printer, 1889, Vol. 1. Available at https://archive.org/details/historynewsouth00bartgoog
Bass, George, 'Journal of a Whaleboat Voyage', printed in *HRNSW*, Vol. 3.
Baudin, Nicolas, *The Journal of Post Captain Nicolas Baudin, Commander-in-Chief of the Corvettes Géographe and Naturaliste*, trans. by Christine Cornell, Adelaide, Libraries Board of South Australia, 1974.
Baugh, Daniel, 'Seapower and Science: The Motives for Pacific Exploration', in Derek Howse, ed., *Background to Discovery: Pacific Exploration from Dampier to Cook*, Berkeley, University of California Press, 1990.
Beaglehole, John Cawte, *The Life of Captain James Cook*, California, Stanford University Press, 1974.
Beaglehole, J.C., 'Some Problems of Editing Cook's Journals', *Historical Studies Australia and New Zealand*, Vol. 8, No. 29, 1957. Available at http://nzetc.victoria.ac.nz/tm/scholarly/tei-BeaSome-t1-body1.html
Beaglehole, J.C., ed., *The Journals of Captain James Cook*, Vol. 1: *The Voyage of the Endeavour, 1768–1771*, Cambridge, Hakluyt Society, 1955, reprinted 1968.
Beaglehole, J.C., ed., *The Journals of Captain James Cook*, Vol. 2: *The Voyage of the Resolution and Adventure, 1772–1775*, Cambridge, Hakluyt Society, 1961, reprinted 1969.
Beaglehole, J.C., ed., *The Journals of Captain James Cook*, Vol. 3: *The Voyage of the Resolution and Discovery, 1776–1780*, Parts I and II, Cambridge, Hakluyt Society, 1961, reprinted 1969.
Bertie, Charles H., 'Captain Cook and Botany Bay', *Journal of the Royal Australian Historical Society*, Vol. 10, Part 5, 1924.
Black, Jeremy, 'Ideology, History, Xenophobia and the World of Print in Eighteenth-Century England', in Jeremy Black and Jeremy Gregory, eds, *Culture, Politics and Society in Britain, 1660–1800*, Manchester, 1991.
Blainey, Geoffrey, *The Tyranny of Distance*, revised edition, Melbourne, Sun Books, 1983 (f.p. 1967).
Bougainville, Louis-Antoine, *The Pacific Journal of Louis-Antoine de Bougainville, 1767–1768*, trans. and ed. by John Dunmore, London, Hakluyt Society, 2002.
Bougainville, Louis (Lewis), *A voyage round the world 1766–1769*, trans. by J.R. Forster, London, Norse, 1772.
Bougainville, Louis-Antoine, *Voyage autour du monde, par la frégate du Roi La Boudeuse en 1766–1769*, Paris, Chez Saillant & Nyon, 1771.
Brosses, Charles de, *Histoire des navigations aux Terres Australes*, 3 vols, Paris, Durand, 1756.
Burney, James, *A Chronological History of the Discoveries in the South Sea or Pacific Ocean*, Vol. 3: *1620–1688*, London, 1813.
Byron, John, *Byron's Journal of his Circumnavigation 1764–1766*, ed. by Robert E. Gallagher, Cambridge, Hakluyt Society, 1964.
Cameron-Ash, M., 'French Mischief: A Foxy Map of New Holland', *The Globe*, No. 68, 2011.
Cameron-Ash, M., 'Whitehall's Secrets and Captain Cook', *Cook's Log*, Vol. 38, No. 2, 2015.
Cameron-Ash, M., 'Political Captain Cook', *The Globe*, No. 75, 2014.
Campbell, John, *Navigantium atque itinerantium bibliotheca*, 2 vols, London, 1744–1748.
Carrington, Hugh, *Life of Captain Cook*, London, Sidgwick & Jackson, 1939.
Carter, Harold B., 'The Royal Society and the Voyage of H.M.S. *Endeavour* 1768–71', *Notes and Records of the Royal Society*, Vol. 49, No. 2, 1995.
Carter, Harold B., *Sir Joseph Banks, 1743–1820*, London, British Museum (Natural History), 1988.
Clark, C.M.H., *A History of Australia*, Vol. 1, Melbourne University Press, 1977 (f.p. 1962).
Cobban, Alfred, *Ambassadors and Secret Agents: The Diplomacy of the First Earl of Malmesbury at the Hague*, London, Jonathan Cape, 1954.
Cock, Randolph, 'Precursors of Cook: The Voyages of the Dolphin, 1764–8', *The Mariner's Mirror*, Vol. 85, No. 1, 1999.

Colley, Linda, *Britons: Forging the Nation, 1707–1837*, New Haven, Yale University Press, 2009 (f.p. 1992).
Cook, Andrew S., Alexander Dalrymple (1737–1808), Hydrographer to the East India Company and to the Admiralty, as Publisher: A Catalogue of Books and Charts, 3 vols, PhD thesis, University of St Andrews, 1993.
Cook, James, Journal of H.M.S. Endeavour, 1768-1771, Holograph MS at National Library of Australia, Canberra; digitized version available at nla.obj-228958440; transcript (as daily entries) available at southseas.nla.gov.au; transcribed, edited and published in Beaglehole, *Journals* I, 1955 (listed above).
Cook, James and Furneaux, Tobias, *A Voyage towards the South Pole ... in His Majesty's Ships the Resolution and Adventure, 1772–1775*, ed. by John Douglas, London, 1777.
Cook, James and King, James, *A Voyage to the Pacific Ocean ... In His Majesty's Ships the Resolution and Discovery, 1776–1780*, ed. by John Douglas, London, 1784.
Corney, B.G., ed., *The Quest and Occupation of Tahiti by Emissaries of Spain During the Years 1772–1776*, 3 vols, London, Hakluyt Society, 1913–1919.
Crimmin, Patricia K., Admiralty Administration, 1783–1806, MA thesis, University of London, 1965.
Dalrymple, Alexander, *An Account of the discoveries made in the South Pacifick Ocean, 1767*, reissued with an essay by Andrew Cook, Sydney, Australian National Maritime Museum, 1996.
Dalrymple, Alexander, 'Memoirs of Alexander Dalrymple Esq.', *European Magazine*, Vol. 42, 1802, pp. 323–7* and 421–4.
David, Andrew, *The Charts and Coastal Views of Captain Cook's Voyages*, 3 vols, London, Hakluyt Society, 1988–1997.
David, Andrew, 'Further Light on James Cook's Survey of Newfoundland', *International Hydrographic Review*, Vol. 1, No. 2, December 2000.
Day, David, *Claiming a Continent: A New History of Australia*, Sydney, HarperCollins, 2001 (f.p. 1996).
Dunmore, John, *French Explorers in the Pacific*, Vol. I: *The Eighteenth Century*, Oxford, Clarendon Press, 1965.
Dunmore, John, *Storms and Dreams: The Life of Louis de Bougainville*, Fairbanks, University of Alaska Press, 2007.
Eccleston, Gregory C., *The Early Charting of Victoria's Coastline*, ANZ Map Society, 2012. Available at https://www.anzmaps.org/other-publications/
Edwards, Philip, *The Story of the Voyage: Sea-Narratives in Eighteenth-Century England*, Cambridge, Cambridge University Press, 1997 (f.p. 1994).
Fisher, R. and Johnston, H., eds, *Captain James Cook and his Times*, Seattle, University of Washington Press, 1979.
Fleming, Fergus, *Barrow's Boys: A Stirring Story of Daring, Fortitude, and Outright Lunacy*, London, Granta Books, 1998.
Flinders, Matthew, *A Voyage to Terra Australis, 1801–1803, in His Majesty's ship the Investigator*, 2 vols, London, G. and W. Nicol, 1814.
Forster, George, *A Voyage Round the World*, 2 vols, ed. by Nicholas Thomas and Oliver Berghof, Honolulu, University of Hawai'i Press, 2000.
Frost, Alan, *Arthur Phillip, 1738–1814: His Voyaging*, Melbourne, Oxford University Press, 1987.
Frost, Alan, *The Precarious Life of James Mario Matra: Voyager with Cook, American Loyalist, Servant of Empire*, Melbourne, The Miegunyah Press, 1995.
Frost, Alan and Williams, G., 'The Beginnings of Britain's Exploration of the Pacific Ocean in the Eighteenth Century', *Mariner's Mirror*, Vol. 83, 1997.
Frost, Alan, 'Shaking off the Spanish Yoke: British Schemes to Revolutionize Spanish America, 1739–1807', in M. Lincoln, ed., *Science and Exploration*.
Fry, Howard T., *Alexander Dalrymple (1737–1808) and the Expansion of British Trade*, Toronto, Royal Commonwealth Society, 1970.
Fry, Howard T., 'Alexander Dalrymple and Captain Cook: The Creative Interplay of Two Careers', in R. Fisher and H. Johnston, eds, *Captain James Cook and his Times*.
Gascoigne, John, *Joseph Banks and the English Enlightenment: Useful Knowledge and Polite Culture*, Cambridge, Cambridge University Press, 1994.
Gaziello, Catherine, *L'expédition de Lapérouse, 1785-1788: réplique française aux voyages de Cook*, Paris, Comité des travaux historiques et scientifiques, 1984.
Geikie, Archibald, *Annals of the Royal Society Club: The Record of a London Dining-Club in the Eighteenth and Nineteenth Centuries*, London, Macmillan, 1917.
George, King of Great Britain, *The Correspondence of King George the Third from 1760 to December 1783, Printed from the Original Papers in the Royal Archives*, 6 vols, ed. by Sir John Fortescue, London, Macmillan and Co., 1927.
Goebel, Julius, *The Struggle for the Falkland Islands: A Study in Legal and Diplomatic History*, New Haven, Yale University Press, 1982 (f.p. 1927).
Grenville-Temple, Richard, *The Grenville Papers*, ed. by W.J. Smith, 4 vols, London, John Murray, 1852.
Grewe, Wilhelm G., *The Epochs of International Law*, trans. and revised by M. Byers, Berlin, De Gruyter, 2001.
Hansen, Dagny B., 'Captain James Cook's First Stop on the Northwest Coast – by Chance or by Chart?', *Pacific Historical*

Review, Vol. 62, No. 4, 1993.

Harley, J.B., *The New Nature of Maps: Essays in the History of Cartography*, ed. by Paul Laxton, Baltimore, Johns Hopkins University Press, 2001.

Hawkesworth, John, *An Account of the Voyages undertaken by the order of his present Majesty for making Discoveries in the Southern Hemisphere, And successively performed by commodore Byron, Captain Wallis, Captain Carteret, and Captain Cook, in the Dolphin, the Swallow, and the Endeavour: drawn up from the Journals which were kept by the several Commanders, And from the Papers of Joseph Banks, Esq*, 3 vols, Vol. 1, London, Strahan and Cadell, 1773.

Hawkesworth, John, *An Account of a Voyage round the World, 1768-1771, by Lieutenant James Cook, Commander of his Majesty's Bark the Endeavour*; Vols. 2 and 3, London, Strahan and Cadell, 1773.

Historical Records of Australia, ed. by Frederick Watson, Series I, Vols 1–10; Series III, Vol. 5, Sydney, Library Committee of the Commonwealth Parliament, 1914–25.

Historical Records of New South Wales, ed. by F.M. Bladen, Vols 1–6, Sydney, Charles Potter, Government Printer, 1893.

Hodson, Christopher, *The Acadian Diaspora: An Eighteenth-Century History*, New York, Oxford University Press, 2012.

Hooker, Brian, 'James Cook's Secret Search in 1769', *Mariner's Mirror*, Vol. 87, No. 3, 2001.

Hooker, Brian, 'Two Sets of Tasman Longitudes in Seventeenth and Eighteenth Century Maps', *Geographical Journal*, Vol. 156, No. 1, March 1990.

Hooker, Brian, A multiplicity of prime meridians: detecting faulty longitudinal placement of coastlines in early hybrid maps 2006, online at http://zeehaen.tripod.com/unpub_2/multitude_meridians.htm

Horner, Frank, *The French Reconnaissance: Baudin in Australia 1801–1803*, Carlton, Vic.: Melbourne University Press, 1987.

Huxtable, G. and Jackson, I., 'Journey to Work: James Cook's Transatlantic Voyages in the Grenville 1764–1767', *The Journal of Navigation*, Vol. 63, 2010.

Johnson, A.J.C., Charting the Imperial Will: Colonial Administration and the General Survey of British North America, 1764–1775, PhD thesis, University of Exeter, 2011.

Keir, Bill, 'Captain Cook's Longitude Determinations and the Transit of Mercury — Common Assumptions Questioned', *Journal of the Royal Society of New Zealand*, Vol. 40, 2010.

Kennedy, Brian E., 'Anglo–French Rivalry in Southeast Asia 1763–93: Some Repercussions', *Journal of Southeast Asian Studies*, Vol. 4, No. 2, September 1973.

King, Robert, J., 'Dutch Claims to New Holland and the British Colonization in 1788', Australia on the Map, Australasian Hydrographic Society, 2008. Available at australiaonthemap.org.au

King, Robert J., 'What Brought Laperouse to Botany Bay?', *Journal of the Royal Australian Historical Society*, Vol. 85, Part 2, 1999.

Kohl, J.G., *A Descriptive Catalogue of Those Maps, Charts, and Surveys Relating to America Which are Mentioned in Volume III of Hakluyt's Great Work*, Washington, Henry Polkinhorn, 1857.

La Pérouse, Jean-François de Galaup, comte de, *The Journal of Jean-François de Galaup de la Pérouse, 1785–1788*, trans. and ed. by John Dunmore, 2 vols, London, Hakluyt Society, 1994–1995.

Laver, Roberto C., *The Falklands/Malvinas Case: Breaking the Deadlock in the Anglo–Argentine Sovereignty Dispute*, The Hague, Martinus Nijhoff, 2001.

Lincoln, Margarette, ed., *Science and Exploration in the Pacific: European Voyages to the Southern Oceans in the Eighteenth Century*, Woodbridge, Suffolk, Boydell Press, National Maritime Museum, 1998.

Lipscombe, Trevor, 'The Point Hicks Controversy: The Clouded Facts', *Victorian Historical Journal*, Vol. 85, No. 2, December 2014.

Lysaght, Averil M., *Joseph Banks in Newfoundland and Labrador, 1766: His Diary, Manuscripts and Collections*, Berkeley, University of California Press, 1971.

Mackay, David, *In the Wake of Cook: Exploration, Science and Empire, 1780–1801*, Wellington, Victoria University Press, 1985.

Maffeo, Steven E., *Most Secret and Confidential: Intelligence in the Age of Nelson*, London, Chatham Publishing, 2000.

Marshall, John B., 'The Handwriting of Joseph Banks, his Scientific Staff and Amanuenses', *Bulletin of the British Museum* (Natural History), Botany series, Vol. 6, No. 1, 1978.

Martin-Allanic, J.E., *Bougainville navigateur et les découvertes de son temps*, 2 vols, Paris, P.U.F., 1964.

Matra, James Mario, *A journal of a voyage round the world, in His Majesty's ship Endeavour, 1768–1771*, London, Becket, 1771, reproduced in Alan Frost, *The Precarious life of James Mario Matra*.

McLeod, Anne Byrne, The Mid-Eighteenth Century Navy from the Perspective of Captain Thomas Burnett and his Peers, PhD thesis, University of Exeter, 2011.

McLynn, Frank, *Captain Cook: Master of the Seas*, New Haven, Yale University Press, 2011.

McNab, Robert, *From Tasman to Marsden: A History of Northern New Zealand from 1642 to 1818*, Dunedin, 1914, facsim

reprint, Christchurch [N.Z.]: Cadsonbury Publications, 1996.
McNab, Robert, *Murihiku: A History of the South Island of New Zealand and the Islands Adjacent and Lying to the South, from 1642 to 1835*, Wellington, N.Z., Whitcombe & Tombs, 1909.
Monmonier, Mark S., *How to Lie with Maps*, 2nd ed., Chicago, University of Chicago Press, 1996.
Namier, Lewis and Brooke, John, *The History of Parliament: The House of Commons 1754–1790*, Vol. 1, London, HMSO, 1964. Available at http://www.historyofparliamentonline.org
National Library of Australia, *Mapping our World: Terra Incognita to Australia*, Canberra, National Library of Australia, 2013.
Nugent, Maria, *Captain Cook was Here*, Cambridge, Cambridge University Press, 2009.
O'Brian, Patrick, *Joseph Banks: A Life*, London, C. Harvill, 1987.
Orchiston, Wayne, 'James Cook's 1769 Transit of Venus Expedition to Tahiti', in D.W. Kurtz, ed., *Transits of Venus: New Views of the Solar System and Galaxy*, Proceedings IAU Colloquium No. 196, 2004.
O'Sullivan, Dan, *In Search of Captain Cook: Exploring the Man Through his own Words*, London, I.B. Tauris, 2008.
Parkin, Ray, *HM Bark Endeavour: Her Place in Australian History*, The Miegunyah Press, Melbourne, 2003 (f.p. 1997).
Parkinson, Sydney, *A journal of a voyage to the South Seas, in his Majesty's ship, the Endeavour*, London, printed for Stanfield Parkinson, the editor, 1773.
Péron, François, *French Designs on Colonial New South Wales: François Péron's Memoir on the English Settlements in New Holland, Van Diemen's Land and the Archipelagos of the Great Pacific Ocean*, trans. and ed. with an introduction, notes and appendices by Jean Fornasiero and John West-Sooby, Adelaide, SA, The Friends of the State Library of South Australia Inc., 2016 (f.p. 2014).
Perry, T.M. and Dorothy Prescott, eds, *A Guide to Maps of Australia in Books Published 1780–1830: An Annotated Cartobibliography*, Canberra, National Library of Australia, 1996.
Phillip, Arthur, Comments on a draft of his instructions, c. 11 April 1787, Colonial Office Records, The National Archives, Kew, U.K., TNA CO 201/2, f. 128-131.
Protos, Alec, *The Road to Botany Bay: The Story of Frenchmans Road Randwick through the Journals of Lapérouse and the First Fleet writers*, rev. ed., Sydney, Randwick and District Historical Society, 2000.
Renaut, Francis P., *Le secret service de l'Amirauté britannique au temps de la guerre d'Amérique: 1776–1783, d'après des documents retrouvés dans les archives britanniques*, Paris, Éditions du Graouli, 1936.
Robertson, George, *The Discovery of Tahiti: A Journal of the Second Voyage of H.M.S. Dolphin ... Under the Command of Captain Wallis, 1766–1768*, ed. by Hugh Carrington, London, Hakluyt Society, 1948.
Robson, John, *Captain Cook's War and Peace: The Royal Navy Years 1755–1768*, Sydney, UNSW Press, 2009.
Robson, John, 'James Cook's Contribution to the Mapping of Newfoundland and Newfoundland's Contribution to the Career of James Cook', *Association of Canadian Map Libraries and Archives Bulletin*, Vol. 124, 2005.
Rodger, N.A.M., *The Insatiable Earl: A Life of John Montagu, Fourth Earl of Sandwich 1718–1792*, London, HarperCollins, 1993.
Roy, P.S. and Crawford, E.A., *Holocene Geological Evolution of the Southern Botany Bay – Kurnel Region, Central New South Wales Coast*, Sydney, Department of Mineral Resources, 1979.
Sankey, Margaret, 'The Cartography of the Baudin Expedition: Louis Freycinet's Map of New Holland', Australia on the Map Division of the Australasian Hydrographic Society, 2012. Available at http://www.australiaonthemap.org.au/the-cartography-of-the-baudin-expedition-louis-freycinets-map-of-new-holland/
Savill, Merilyn, Empiricism, Enlightenment and Aesthetics: Engravings from the 'Endeavour' Voyage, 1768–1771, PhD thesis, University of Auckland, 2011.
Schilder, Günter, *Australia Unveiled: The Share of the Dutch Navigators in the Discovery of Australia*, trans. by Olaf Richter, Amsterdam, Theatrum Orbis Terrarum, 1975.
Scott, Ernest, *Terre Napoleon: A History of French Explorations and Projects in Australia*, London, Methuen, 1910.
Scott, H.M., 'The Importance of Bourbon Naval Reconstruction to the Strategy of Choiseul after the Seven Years' War', *International History Review*, Vol. 1, No. 1, 1979.
Skelton, R.A., ed., *Charts and Views Drawn by Cook and his Officers and Reproduced from the Original Manuscripts*, Cambridge, Hakluyt Society, 1955. Available at https://nla.gov.au/nla.obj-588086057/view.
Skelton, R.A., 'Captain James Cook as a Hydrographer', *Mariner's Mirror*, Vol. 40, 1954.
Skelton, R.A., *Looking at an Early Map*, Lawrence, University of Kansas Publications, Library Series No. 17, 1965.
Spate, O.H.K., *The Spanish Lake*, Canberra, Australian National University Press, 1979.
Stephensen, P.R., *The History and Description of Sydney Harbour*, Adelaide, Rigby, 1966.
Surville, Jean de, *The Expedition of the St. Jean-Baptiste to the Pacific, 1769–1770*, ed. and trans. by John Dunmore, London, Hakluyt Society, 1981.
Tabouis, Geneviève, *Perfidious Albion – Entente Cordiale*, trans. by J.A.D. Dempsey, London, Eyre & Spottiswoode, 1938.

Taillemite, Étienne, ed., *Bougainville et ses compagnons autour du monde, 1766–1769: Journaux de navigation*, 2 vols, Paris, Imprimerie nationale, 1977.

Tasman, Abel Janszoon, The Huydecoper (Huijdecoper) Journal, 1642–1643, Mitchell Library, State Library of New South Wales, Sydney, Safe 1/72., ed. and trans. by P.K. Roest. Available at http://acms.sl.nsw.gov.au/_transcript/2014/D32685/a287.html

Tebel, René, *Das Schiff im Kartenbild des Mittelalters und der frühen Neuzeit. Kartographische Zeugnisse aus sieben Jahrhunderten als maritimhistorische Bildquellen*, Bremerhaven, Deutschen Schiffahrtsmuseum, 2012.

Tombs, Robert and Isabelle, *That Sweet Enemy: The French and the British from the Sun King to the Present*, Alfred A. Knopf, New York, 2007.

Valentyn, Francois, *Oud en nieuw Oost-Indien*, 5 vols, Dordrecht, J. van Braam, 1724–26, Vol. 3.

Wallis, Helen, 'Publication of Cook's Journals: Some New Sources and Assessments', *Pacific Studies*, Vol. 1, No. 2, 1978.

Wallis, Helen, ed., *Carteret's Voyage Round the World 1766–1769*, 2 vols, Cambridge, Hakluyt Society, 1965.

Webb, Adrian, The Expansion of British Naval Hydrographic Administration, 1808–1829, PhD thesis, University of Exeter, 2010.

West-Sooby, John, ed., *Discovery and Empire: The French in the South Seas*, Adelaide, University of Adelaide Press, 2013.

Wharton, W.J.L., ed., *Captain Cook's Journal During his First Voyage Round the World*, London, 1893.

Whitely, W.H., 'James Cook and British Policy in the Newfoundland Fisheries, 1763–7', *Canadian Historical Review*, Vol. 54, No. 3, 1973.

Wickwire, F.B., 'Admiralty Secretaries and the British Civil Service', *Huntington Library Quarterly*, Vol. 28, No. 3, 1965.

Williams, Glyndwr, ed., *Captain Cook: Explorations and Reassessments*, Woodbridge, England, Boydell Press, 2004.

Maps and Illustrations

Frontispiece. John Hamilton Mortimer, *Captain James Cook, Sir Joseph Banks, Lord Sandwich, Dr Daniel Solander and Dr John Hawkesworth*, 1771, National Library of Australia nla.obj-135646842.
1. Allan Ramsay, *George III*, c.1761–62, Royal Collection Trust, © Her Majesty Queen Elizabeth II 2017.
2. Artist unknown, 'The Royal Society's House in Crane Court', from W. Thornbury, *Old and New London: A Narrative of its History, its People and its Places*, London, Cassel, 1873, Vol. 1, p. 108.
3. 'Sphere of the Winds', in *Astronomia: Teutsch astronomei* published by Cyriaco Jacob zum Barth, Frankfurt, 1545, National Library of Australia nla.obj-230899009.
4. Sigismund von Redern, *Hemisphere Meridional*, Berlin, 1762, National Library of Australia nla.obj-232150652.
5. Sketch map of Abel Tasman's voyage, 1642–44, orig. by author, graphic by D. Fraser @CartoDavid.
6. Artist unknown, 'Vue de la Baye de l'Est de la plus grande des Iles Malouines', in Dom Pernety, *Journal historique d'un voyage aux Isles Malouines fait en 1763 et 1764*, Vol. 2, Plate IX, Berlin, http://gallica.bnf.fr/ark:/12148/btv1b2000062z/f11.item.
7. Julien Leopold Boilly, 'Bougainville', from *Le Plutarque français*, Paris, 1846, p. 433 nla.obj-296177252.
8. Artist unknown, [Miniature portrait of Philip Stephens], c.1770, © National Maritime Museum, Greenwich, London.
9. Thomas Rowlandson (artist), Henry Melville (engraver), *The Admiralty – board room meeting of the Lords of the Admiralty*, published in *London Interiors*, 1845, Vol. I, p. 180.
10. J. Hall, 'A representation of the surrender of the island of Otaheite to Captain Wallis by the supposed Queen Oberea', published in Hawkesworth, Vol. I, Plate 22, London, 1773, National Library of Australia nla.obj-135963681.
11. Artist unknown, 'Monsieur Bougainville Hoisting the French Colours on a Small Rock near Cape forward in the Streights of Magellan', from D. Henry (ed.), *An Historical Account of All the Voyages Round the World performed by English Navigators*, London, 1773, Vol. 4, p. 194. National Library of Australia nla.obj-136033966.
12. Jan van Ryne (artist), Robert Sayer (printer), Fort St George on the Coromandel coast belonging to the East India Company of England, 1754, © National Maritime Museum, Greenwich, London.
13. Alexander Dalrymple, *Chart of the South Pacifick Ocean, pointing out the discoveries made therein previous to 1764*, London 1767. State Library of New South Wales, Call No. Q77/41.
14. Thomas Luny, *The Bark, Earl of Pembroke, later Endeavour, leaving Whitby Harbour in 1768*, c.1790. National Library of Australia nla.obj-134301494.
15. Isaac Sailmaker, *Two Views of an East Indiaman of the Time of William III*, c.1685. © National Maritime Museum, Greenwich, London.
16. Artist unknown, 'Wilkes's triumphal entry into the city', from *Cassell's Illustrated History of England*, W. Howitt, London, 1861, Vol. 5, p. 55.
17. Benjamin West, *Joseph Banks F.R.S., F.S.A.*, c.1771–73. The Collection: Art and Archaeology in Lincolnshire (Usher Gallery, Lincoln).
18. James Gillray, *A new Map of England & France. The French Invasion, or John Bull bombarding the Bum Boats*, London, Hannah Humphrey, 1793, © Trustees of the British Museum.
19. Photographer unknown, 'Aireyholme Farm, near Great Ayton', c.1970, © Middlesbrough Museums Service, Middlesbrough Council.
20. Joseph Mallord William Turner, *Whitby*, c.1824, Trustees of the Tate Gallery.
21. Joseph F.W. Des Barres, 'West shore of Richmond Isle', (Six views of Cape Breton Island), published in *The American Neptune*, 1774–84, © National Maritime Museum, Greenwich, London.
22. Dominic Serres, *The defeat of the French Fireships attacking the British Fleet at Anchor before Quebec 28 June 1759*, 1767, Library and Archives Canada, Dominic Serres Collection/c004291k.
23. William Henderson, *Mrs. Elizth Cook, Aged 81 years*, 1830, Collection of the Mitchell library, State Library of New South Wales.
24. J. Cook, 'A Sketch of the Island of Newfoundland: Done from the latest observations by James Cook, 1763', National Museum of the Royal Navy, Portsmouth, ADL MSS 368/21.
25. Francois Valentyn, 'Kaart der Reyse van Abel Tasman', in *Oud en Nieuw Oose-Indien*, Amsterdam, 1726, Vol. 3, Part 2, p. 47. National Library of Australia nla.obj-231300135.
26. Didier Robert de Vaugondy, 'Carte réduite de l'Australasie', in Charles de Brosses, *Histoire des navigations aux Terres*

Australes, Vol. 2, Paris, 1756, National Library of Australia nla.obj-41292347.
27. James Stephanoff, *Buckingham House: The Octagon Library*, 1818, Royal Collection Trust, © Her Majesty Queen Elizabeth II 2017.
28. Joan Blaeu, *Archipelagus Orientalis sive Asiaticus*, 1659, © Staatsbibliothek zu Berlin – Preussischer Kulturbesitz.
29. Nathaniel Dance, *Captain James Cook, 1728-79*, 1776, © National Maritime Museum, Greenwich, London.
30. Sketch map showing the track of HMB *Endeavour*, 25 August 1768 – 12 July 1771, orig. by author, graphic by D. Fraser @CartoDavid.
31. Sydney Parkinson (artist), Samuel Middiman (engraver), 'Venus Fort, Erected by the Endeavors people to secure themselves during the Observation of the transit of Venus at Otaheite', from Sydney Parkinson, *A journal of a voyage to the South Seas, in his Majesty's ship, the Endeavour*, London, Printed for Stanfield Parkinson, the editor, 1773, Plate 4, Collection of the State Library of New South Wales, Call no. Q78/10.
32. Sydney Parkinson (artist), R.B. Godfrey (engraver), 'A war canoe of New Zealand' from Sydney Parkinson, *A journal of a voyage to the South Seas, in his Majesty's ship, the Endeavour*, London, Printed for Stanfield Parkinson, the editor, 1773, Plate 18.
33. J. Cook, 'A Chart of Newzeland or the islands of Aeheinomouwe and Tovypoenammu lying in the South Sea. by Lieut. J. Cook. Commander of His Majestys Bark the Endeavour, circumnavigated by the said bark in the latter end of 1769 and beginning of 1770', British Library Add. Ms. 7085 f.16, in David, Charts & Coastal Views, Vol. 1, p. 160.
34. Unnumbered page, Cook, Holograph, 'Journal of H.M.S. Endeavour, 1768–1771' [manuscript online], MS 1, National Library of Australia https://nla.gov.au/nla.obj-229031188.
35. J. Cook, 'A Chart of Newzeland or the Islands of Aeheinomouwe and Tovypoenammu Lying in the South Sea', 1770, British Library Add. Ms. 7085 f.17, in Skelton, Chart XII, National Library of Australia https://nla.gov.au/nla.obj-588079294/view.
36. Giovanni Cassini, 'La Nuova Zelanda Delineata Sulle Osservazioni Del Capitan Cook', 1798, National Library of Australia nla.obj-232569565.
37. J. Cook, 'A chart of the Sea Coast of New South Wales or the East Coast of New Holland, by J. Cook, 1770'. British Library Add. Ms. 7085 f.34, Published in Skelton No. XX; David, Vol. 1, p. 260, National Library of Australia https://nla.gov.au/nla.obj-588080489/view.
38. Sketch map of Bass Strait and parallel 38 South, orig. by author, graphic by D. Fraser @CartoDavid.
39. J. Russell (engraver), 'Sketch of Van Diemen Land explored by Capt. Furneaux in March 1773', in Cook, *A Voyage towards the South Pole*, Vol. 1, 1777, Plate VIII, National Library of Australia nla.obj-230618345.
40. J. Cook, 'A sketch of Botany Bay in New South Wales: latitude 34°00' S, 1770', British Library Add. Ms. 7085 f.40, published in Skelton, Charts, No. XXIIa. https://nla.gov.au/nla.obj-588080804/view.
41. Joseph Lycett, 'View of the heads at the entrance to Port Jackson', 1818, from *Views in Australia*, London, Souter, 1824, National Library of Australia nla.obj-135701554.
42. Nicolas-Martin Petit, 'Norou-gal-derri, guerrier des environs du port Jackson, s'avancant pour combattre, 1802', from F. Peron, *A Voyage of Discovery the the Southern Hemisphere*, 1807, Atlas, Plate XX, State Library of New South Wales, Call no. MRB/F18 Atlas.
43. Sketch map of the region between Botany Bay and Sydney Harbour, orig. by author, graphic by D. Fraser @CartoDavid.
44. Augustus Earle, *Sydney Heads*, c.1825, National Library of Australia nla.obj-135318052.
45. Sketch map Cape York and nearby islands, orig. by the author, graphic by D. Fraser @CartoDavid.
46. Jan van Ryne (artist), Robert Sayer (publisher), 'The city of Batavia in the Island of Java and Capital of all the Dutch Factories & Settlements in the East Indies', London, c.1754, Kerry Stokes Collection, Perth.
47. John Gilfillan (artist), Samuel Calvert (engraver), "Captain Cook taking possession of the Australian continent on behalf of the British Crown AD 1770', c.1857, National Library of Australia nla.obj-135699884.
48. Unknown artist, *Return fleet from Batavia*, c.1674, Collection of Stedelijk Museum Alkmaar, Netherlands.
49. Hawkesworth's *Voyages*, first edition, Image source: www.donaldheald.com
50. Louis Freycinet, *Carte générale de la Nouvelle Hollande*, Paris, 1811, National Library of Australia nla.obj-230971556.
51. James Cook's election certificate, Royal Society Archives, EC/1775/27.

Endnotes

Chapter 1
1. Thomas Hornsby, 'On the Transit of Venus', *Philosophical Transactions of the Royal Society*, Vol. 55, 1765, pp. 326–344.
2. Hornsby, p. 343.
3. Hornsby, p. 336.
4. J.B. Harley, *The New Nature of Maps: Essays in the History of Cartography*, edited by Paul Laxton, Baltimore, Johns Hopkins University Press, 2001, p. 88.
5. Harley, *Essays*, p. 57.
6. Hornsby, p. 344.
7. Hornsby, p. 344.

Chapter 2
1. *Hollandia Nova detecta 1644, Terre Australe decouverte l'an 1644*, Melchisédech Thévenot, Paris, 1663. National Library of Australia nla.obj-334686747.
2. *A Complete map of the Southern Continent*, Emanuel Bowen, London, 1744, National Library of Australia nla.obj-163902730.
3. M. Cameron-Ash, 'French Mischief: A Foxy Map of New Holland', *The Globe*, 2011, No. 68, pp. 1–14.
4. J. Gordon Hayes, *Antarctica: A Treatise on the Southern Continent*, London, Richards Press, 1928, p. 4.
5. Susan Woodburn, 'John George Bartholomew and the Naming of Antarctica', *Cairt*, Vol. 13, 2008, pp. 4–6.
6. James Burney, *A chronological history of the discoveries in the South Sea or Pacific Ocean*, Part III, London, 1813, p. 59.
7. Abel Jansz Tasman, The Huydecoper Journal, 1642–1643, Mitchell Library, State Library of New South Wales, Sydney, Safe 1/72, p. 43.
8. Tasman, Huydecoper, p. 44.
9. Comte de Redern, 'Considérations sur le globe sur le continent antarctique', *Mémoires de l'Académie Royale de Berlin*, 1765. Vol. 21, pp. 3–13.

Chapter 3
1. Stephen White, 'Les Acadiens aux Îles Malouines en 1764', *Les Cahiers de la Société historique Acadienne*, Vol. 15, Nos 2 & 3, 1984, pp. 100–105.
2. J.C. Beaglehole, *The Life of Captain James Cook*, California, Stanford University Press, 1974, at p. 46
3. John Dunmore, *Storms and Dreams: The Life of Louis de Bougainville*, University of Alaska Press, Fairbanks, 2007. p. 49.
4. Jean-Etienne Martin-Allanic, *Bougainville navigateur et les découvertes de son temps*, Vol. 1, Paris, Presses Universitaires de France, 1964, pp. 263–264, trans. by John Murray.
5. Étienne Taillemite, ed., *Bougainville et ses compagnons autour du monde, 1766–1769: Journaux de navigation*, Vol. 1, Paris, Imprimerie nationale, 1977, p. 13.
6. Bougainville, Taillemite. p. 14
7. Dunmore, *Storms*, p. 110.
8. John Milton, *A manifesto of the Lord Protector of the Commonwealth of England, Scotland, Ireland, &c.*, London, Millar, 1738, p. 25.

Chapter 4
1. N.A.M. Rodger, *The Insatiable Earl: A Life of John Montagu, Fourth Earl of Sandwich, 1718–1792*, London, HarperCollins, 1993, p. 209.
2. Nicholas Tracy, 'The Gunboat Diplomacy of the Government of George Grenville, 1764–1765: The Honduras, Turks Island and Gambian Incidents', *The Historical Journal*, Vol. 17, 1974, p. 711.
3. George Anson. *A Voyage round the World in the Years 1740–1744. Compiled by Richard Walter, Chaplain to his Majesty's Ship the 'Centurion'*, London, John and Paul Knapton, 1748.
4. Keene to Bedford, 21 May 1749, PRO, SP 94/135, f. 265–9. Published in A. Frost and G. Williams, 'The Beginnings of Britain's Exploration of the Pacific Ocean in the Eighteenth Century', *Mariner's Mirror*, Vol. 83, 1997, pp. 410–418, at p. 413.
5. John Byron, *Byron's Journal of his Circumnavigation 1764–1766*, ed. by Robert E. Gallagher, Cambridge, Hakluyt, 1964, p. xxvii.
6. Washington to Col. Elias Dayton, 26 July 1777, Founders Online, U.S. Archives (accessed 10 September 2017).
7. Lewis Namier and John Brooke, *The History of Parliament: The House of Commons 1754–1790*, Vol. 1, London, HMSO, 1964, p. 121.
8. F.B. Wickwire, 'Admiralty Secretaries and the British Civil Service', *Huntington Library Quarterly*, Vol. 28, No. 3, 1965, pp. 235–254, at p. 241.
9. Francis P. Renaut, *Le secret service de l'Amirauté britannique au temps de la guerre d'Amérique: 1776–1783, d'après des documents retrouvés dans les archives britanniques*, Paris, Éditions du Graouli, 1936, pp. 29–33, trans. John Murray.
10. Rodondo, 'Observations on some political characters', *The Oxford magazine: or, Universal museum*, Vol. 5, Supplement, 1770, pp. 270–271.
11. James Colnett, R.N., *A voyage to the South Atlantic and round Cape Horn into the Pacific Ocean, for the purpose of extending the spermaceti whale fisheries, and other*

objects of commerce, by ascertaining the ports, bays, harbours, and anchoring births [sic], in certain islands and coasts on those seas at which the ships of the British merchants might be refitted, London, Bennett, 1798, pp. iii–vi.
12 Memoir from the King to serve as instructions to Mr de Bougainville, Versailles, 26 October 1766, in L.-A. de Bougainville, *The Pacific Journal of Louis-Antoine de Bougainville, 1767–1768*, trans. and ed. by John Dunmore, London, Hakluyt Society, 2002, p. xlv.
13 Charles de Brosses, *Histoire des navigations aux Terres Australes*, 3 vols, Paris, Durand, 1756, Vol. 1, p. iv.
14 B.G. Corney, ed., *The Quest and Occupation of Tahiti by Emissaries of Spain During the Years 1772–1776*, Vol. 1, London, Hakluyt Society, 1913, p. 45.
15 Phillip's Instructions (issued when the French expedition of Lapérouse was known to be in the Pacific) to colonize Norfolk Island 'as soon as circumstances may admit of it … to prevent its being occupied by the Subjects of any other European Power', Georgius Rex, 25 April 1787, in *HRNSW*, Vol. 1, Pt 2, pp. 85–91, at p. 89.
16 E.g., Governor King to the Duke of Portland, 21 May 1802, in *HRA*, Series I, Vol. 3, pp. 488–491, at p. 490, requesting permission to establish a base to forestall 'the probability of the French having it in contemplation to make a settlement [on the coast of Bass Strait], which I cannot help thinking is a principal object of their researches'.
17 Governor Macquarie to Undersecretary Henry Goulburn, 24 September 1817, in *HRA*, Series I, Vol. 9, p. 488.

Chapter 5
1 Alan Frost, 'Shaking off the Spanish Yoke: British Schemes to Revolutionize Spanish America, 1739–1807', in M. Lincoln, ed., *Science and Exploration in the Pacific*, Woodbridge, Boydell Press in association with the National Maritime Museum, 1998, p. 24.
2 Byron, *Journal*, p. 162.
3 Byron, *Journal*, p. xl, f.1.
4 Byron, *Journal*, p. xxi.
5 Byron, *Journal*, p. xxii.
6 Byron, *Journal*, pp. xxiv–xxvii.
7 Richard Grenville-Temple, Earl, *The Grenville Papers*, ed. by W.J. Smith, 4 vols, London, John Murray, 1852, Vol. 2, p. 445.
8 J. Byron, *The narrative of the Honourable John Byron … on the coast of Patagonia 1740–1746*, London, S. Baker and G. Leigh, 1768, p. 127.
9 Sealed orders and instructions, 17 June 1764, in Corney, *Tahiti*, Vol. 2, pp. 432–437 at 437.
10 Corney, *Tahiti*, Vol. 2, at p. 434.
11 *St. James's Chronicle*, London, 1764, issue 525, 14–17 July.
12 Byron, *Journal*, p. 26.
13 Byron, *Journal*, p. 60.
14 Dunmore, *Storms*, p. 125.
15 Byron, *Journal*, p. 159.
16 Byron, *Journal*, p. lv.
17 Byron, *Journal*, p. 105.
18 *The Gentleman's Magazine*, Vol. 36, 1766, p. 291.
19 Corney, *Tahiti*, Vol. 1. p. 29.
20 Dunmore, *Storms*, p. 135.
21 Byron, *Journal*, p. lxiii, f. 3.
22 *A Voyage round the world, in His Majesty's ship the Dolphin, commanded by the Honourable Commodore … by an officer on board*, London, Newbery, 1767, p. 123.

Chapter 6
1 Helen Wallis, Correspondence, *The Geographical Journal*, Vol. 149, No. 2, 1983, pp. 276–277.
2 George Robertson, *The discovery of Tahiti: a journal of the second voyage of H.M.S. Dolphin … under the command of Captain Wallis, 1766–1768*, ed. by Hugh Carrington, London, Hakluyt Society, 1948, p. xxvii.
3 Helen Wallis, ed., *Carteret's Voyage Round the World 1766–1769*, 2 vols, Cambridge, Hakluyt Society, 1965, Vol. 1, p. 8, n. 3.
4 Byron, *Journal*, p. lxiii, n. 3.
5 Randolph Cock, 'Precursors of Cook: The Voyages of the Dolphin, 1764–8', *The Mariner's Mirror*, Vol. 85, No.1, 1999, pp. 30–52, at pp. 34, 40.
6 Cock, 'Precursors', p. 31.
7 Robertson, *Discovery*, p. 130.
8 Beaglehole, *Journals* I, p. xcv.
9 John Hawkesworth, ed., *An account of the voyages undertaken by the order of His present Majesty for making discoveries in the southern hemisphere, and successively performed by Commodore Byron, Captain Wallis, Captain Carteret, and Captain Cook, in the Dolphin, the Swallow, and the Endeavour*, 3 vols, 1773, London, Vol. 1, p. 482.
10 Robertson, *Discovery*, p. 159.
11 D.J. Childs, 'Captain Samuel Wallis's Voyage Around the World', *The Naval Review*, Vol. 73, No. 3, 1985, pp. 227–233, at p. 231.
12 '[The shoplifter] from Mr. Ramsden's shop in Piccadilly was brought back and … when he was conducting before a Magistrate, he with every mark of joy in his countenance, and twirling his hat over his head, hollowed out "Botany Bay a hoy!"' *The Times*, Tuesday 10 October 1786, p. 3, issue 551; see also Babette Smith, *Australia's Birthstain: The Startling Legacy of the Convict Era*, Crows Nest, N.S.W., Allen & Unwin, 2008, at p. 102.
13 J. de Surville, *The Expedition of the St. Jean-Baptiste to the Pacific, 1769–1770*, trans. and ed. by John Dunmore, London, Hakluyt Society, 1981, p. 23.

Chapter 7

1. Bougainville, *Pacific Journal*, p. xlv.
2. L.-A. de Bougainville, *Voyage autour du monde, par la frégate du Roi La Boudeuse en 1766–1769*, Paris, Chez Saillant & Nyon, 1771, p. 53.
3. Bougainville, *Pacific Journal*, p. 60.
4. Bougainville, *Pacific Journal*, p. 63.
5. Bougainville, *Pacific Journal*, p. 70.
6. Bougainville, *Pacific Journal*. p. 66.
7. Louis Bougainville, *A voyage round the world 1766–1769*, trans. J.R. Forster, London, Norse, 1772, p. 305.
8. Bougainville, *Voyage*, p. 305.
9. Bougainville, *Voyage*, p. 304.
10. Bougainville, *Voyage*, p. 447.
11. Bougainville, *Pacific Journal*, p. lxv.

Chapter 8

1. Howard T. Fry, *Alexander Dalrymple (1737–1808) and the Expansion of British Trade*, Toronto, Royal Commonwealth Society, 1970, p. 115.
2. Fry, *Dalrymple and Trade*, p. 66.
3. Fry, *Dalrymple and Trade*, p. 75.
4. Fry, *Dalrymple and Trade*, p. 112.
5. A. Dalrymple, *An Account of the discoveries made in the South Pacifick Ocean*, 1767, reissued with an essay by Andrew Cook, Sydney, Australian National Maritime Museum, 1996, p. xxvii.
6. Dalrymple, *Account*, p. 2.
7. Dalrymple to Earl of Chatham, 24 November 1766, Chatham Papers, The National Archives, Kew. U.K., TNA 30/8/31, f.11, AJCP NLA Reel PRO 5992.
8. A. Dalrymple, 'Memoirs of Alexander Dalrymple Esq.', *European Magazine*, Vol. 42, 1802, pp. 323–327* and 421–424.
9. Adam Smith to Earl of Shelburne, 12 February 1767, in *The Correspondence of Adam Smith*, ed. by E. Mossner and I. Ross, Oxford, Clarendon Press, 1977, No. 101.
10. Dalrymple, *Account*, p. 73.
11. Dalrymple, *Account*, pp. xiii–xiv.
12. Andrew S. Cook, Alexander Dalrymple (1737–1808), Hydrographer to the East India Company and to the Admiralty, as Publisher: A Catalogue of Books and Charts, Vol. I, PhD thesis, St Andrews, 1993, p. 35, n. 43.
13. Andrew S. Cook, 'James Cook and the Royal Society', in G. Williams (ed,), *Captain Cook: Explorations and Reassessments*, London, Boydell Press, 2004, at p. 43.
14. Beaglehole, *Journals* I, pp. 604–605.
15. Cock, 'Precursors', p. 31.
16. Dalrymple, 'Memoirs', p. 325*
17. Howard Fry, 'Alexander Dalrymple and Captain Cook: The Creative Interplay of Two Careers', in Fisher and Johnston, eds, pp. 41–57, at p. 237, n. 18.

Chapter 9

1. Dalrymple, 'Memoirs', p. 325*
2. A. Dalrymple, *A Letter from Mr Dalrymple to Dr Hawkesworth occasioned by some groundless and Illiberal Imputations in his account of the late Voyages to the South*, London, Nourse, 1773, at pp. 2 and 32.
3. Dalrymple to de Brosses, in Fry, *Dalrymple and Trade*, p. 115, n. 23.
4. John Cary, *An essay on the state of England in relation to its trade, its poor, and its taxes, for carrying on the present war against France*, Bristol, Bonny, 1695, p. 85, in S A. Reinert, *Translating Empire: Emulation and the Origins of Political Economy*, Cambridge, Mass., Harvard University Press, 2011, p. 91.
5. John Campbell, *Navigantium atque itinerantium bibliotheca*, London, 1744–1748, Vol. 1, pp. 331–332.
6. Young to Alexander Davison, 3 February 1793, in *HRNSW*, Vol. 2, pp. 9–11.
7. A. Dalrymple, *An Historical collection of the several voyages and discoveries in the South Pacific Ocean*, 2 vols, London, Nourse, 1770–1771, Vol. I, p. xxvi.
8. Walpole to Mann, 19 March 1767, in *Letters of Horace Walpole to Horace Mann 1760 to 1785*, 4 vols, London, Bentley, 1843, Vol. 1, p. 335.
9. Benjamin Franklin to John Ross, 14 May 1768, Founders Online, U.S. Archives.
10. H.B. Carter, 'The Royal Society and the Voyage of H.M.S. *Endeavour* 1768–71', *Notes and Records of the Royal Society*, Vol. 49, No. 2, 1995, pp. 245–260, at p. 252.

Chapter 10

1. Newcastle to Yorke, 3 April 1759, cited in J.S. Corbett, *England in the Seven Years' War*, 2 vols, London, Longmans, Green, 1907, Vol. 2, p. 9.
2. Neil Chambers, 'Letters from the President: The Correspondence of Sir Joseph Banks', *Notes and Records of the Royal Society*, Vol. 53, 1999, pp. 27–57, at p. 40.
3. Banks to Buache de la Neuville, 30 November 1788, SLNSW, Banks Papers, Series 73.022.
4. Harold B. Carter, *Sir Joseph Banks, 1743–1820*, London, British Museum (Natural History), 1988, p. 38.
5. Averil M. Lysaght, 'Some early Letters from Joseph Banks (1743–1820) to William Phelp Perrin (1742–1820)', *Notes and Records of the Royal Society*, Vol. 29, No. 1, 1974, pp. 91–99, at p. 93.
6. A.M. Lysaght, *Joseph Banks in Newfoundland and Labrador, 1766: His Diary, Manuscripts and Collections*, Berkeley, University of California Press, 1971, p. 142.
7. Carter, *Banks*, p. 55.
8. *Lloyd's Evening Post*, London, 17–19 August 1768, Issue 1735.
9. Banks to Perrin, 16 August 1768, in Neil Chambers, ed.,

The Letters of Sir Joseph Banks: A Selection, 1768–1820, London, 2000, p. 2.

10 Banks to Perrin, 16 August 1768, in Chambers, *Selection*, p. 1.

Chapter 11

1 Dan O'Sullivan, *In Search of Captain Cook: Exploring the Man Through his own Words*, London, I.B. Tauris, 2008.

2 Rosalin Barker, 'Cook's Nursery: Whitby's Eighteenth-Century Merchant Fleet', in Williams, *Reassessments*, pp. 7–20.

Chapter 12

1 John Robson, *Captain Cook's War and Peace: The Royal Navy Years 1755–1768*, Sydney, UNSW Press, 2009, p. 194.

2 H.M. Scott, *The Birth of a Great Power System, 1740–1815*, Harlow, England, Pearson Longman, 2006, p. 108.

3 Anne Byrne McLeod, The Mid-Eighteenth Century Navy from the Perspective of Captain Thomas Burnett and his Peers, PhD thesis, University of Exeter, 2011, p. 232.

4 Beaglehole, *Life*, p. 46.

Chapter 13

1 Colville to Clevland, 30 December 1762, in Beaglehole, *Life*, p. 59.

2 Philip C. Yorke, *The Life and Correspondence of Philip Yorke, Earl of Hardwicke, Lord High Chancellor of Great Britain*, 3 vols, Cambridge, Cambridge University Press, 1913, Vol. 3, at p. 287.

3 Egremont to Lords of Trade, 5 May 1763, in *Documents Relating to the Constitutional History of Canada 1759–1791*, Ottawa, Dawson, 1907, at p. 95.

4 W.H. Whitely, 'James Cook and British Policy in the Newfoundland Fisheries, 1763–7', *Canadian Historical Review*, Vol. 54, No. 3, 1973, pp. 245–272, at p. 250.

5 Robson, *War*, p. 136.

6 Adams to *Boston Patriot* newspaper, May 1812, available at Founders Online, October 27, 1783, note 3.

7 Egmont to Grenville, 3 December 1763, in Grenville-Temple, Papers, p. 173.

8 Whitely, 'Fisheries', p. 255; Beaglehole, *Life*, p. 76.

9 Whitely, 'Fisheries', pp. 255–256.

10 James Cook, A sketch of the island of Newfoundland done from the latest observations by James Cook 1763, National Museum of the Royal Navy, ADL MSS 368/21.

11 O'Sullivan, *Search*, p. 82.

12 John Robson, 'James Cook's Contribution to the Mapping of Newfoundland and Newfoundland's Contribution to the Career of James Cook', *Association of Canadian Map Libraries and Archives Bulletin*, Vol. 124, 2005, pp. 3–13, at p. 12.

13 Beaglehole, *Life*, p. 80.

14 G. Huxtable and I. Jackson, 'Journey to Work: James Cook's Transatlantic Voyages in the Grenville 1764–1767', *The Journal of Navigation*, Vol. 63, 2010, pp. 207–214.

15 Beaglehole, *Life*, pp. 86–86.

16 Lysaght, *Newfoundland*, p. 47.

17 J. Bevis, 'An observation of an Eclipse of the sun at the Island of New-found-land, August 5, 1776, by Mr. James Cook, with the Longitude of the Place of Observation deduced from it', *Philosophical Transactions of the Royal Society*, Vol. 57, 1767, pp. 215–216.

18 Whitely, 'Fisheries', p. 266.

19 Beaglehole, *Life*, p. 97; Carter, 'Royal Society', p. 253.

Chapter 14

1 Wickwire, 'Admiralty', p. 253.

2 R. Knight, (2004-09-23), 'Stephens, Sir Philip, baronet (1723–1809), Admiralty official', *Oxford Dictionary of National Biography*, available online at http://www.oxforddnb.com.

3 J.R. Forster, *History of the voyages and discoveries made in the North, translated from the German*, London, Robinson, 1786, pp. 297–298.

4 Frank McLynn, *Captain Cook: Master of the Seas*, New Haven, Yale University Press, 2011, p. 10; A. Kennerley, 'Writing the History of Merchant Seafarer Education, Training and Welfare: Retrospect and Prospect', *Northern Mariner*, Vol. 12, No. 2, 2002, pp. 1–21, at p. 4.

5 Beaglehole, *Journals* I, pp. cclxxix–cclxxxiv.

6 *Lloyd's Evening Post*, London, 1719 August 1768, Issue 1735.

7 G.B. Barton, *History of New South Wales from the Records*, Sydney, Charles Potter, Government Printer, 1889, Vol. 1, pp. 177–178.

8 E. Vattel, *Le droit des gens, ou, Principes de la loi naturelle, appliques a la conduite et aux affaires des nations et des souverains*, 1758, translated by C.G. Fenwick, 3 vols, Washington, D.C., Carnegie Institution of Washington, 1916, at I.XVIII, s. 207, p. 84, quoted in Beaglehole, *Journals* III, pp. 769–770, n. 2.

9 W.G. Grewe, *The Epochs of International Law*, trans. and revised by M. Byers, Berlin, De Gruyter. 2001, p. 398.

10 Beaglehole, *Journals* II, p. 112, n. 2; Beaglehole, *Life*, p. 225.

Chapter 15

1. *Lloyd's Evening Post*, London, 14–16 November 1757, Issue 51.

2. Harley, *Essays* p. 95.

3. Harley, *Essays* p. 160.

4. J.K. Wright, 'Map Makers are Human: Comments on the Subjective in Maps', *Geographical Review*, Vol. 32, 1942, pp. 527–544.

5. Roosevelt to Morgenthau, 14 May 1942, in J. Bratzel and L. Rout, 'FDR and the "Secret Map"', *Wilson Quarterly*, Vol. 9, No.1, 1985, pp. 167–173.

6. Harley, *Essays*, p. 91.

7. J.G. Kohl, *A Descriptive Catalogue of Those Maps, Charts, and Surveys Relating to America Which are Mentioned in Volume III of Hakluyt's Great Work*, Washington, Henry Polkinhorn, 1857, p. 80.

8. Adrian Webb, The Expansion of British Naval Hydrographic Administration, 1808–1829, PhD thesis, University of Exeter, 2010, pp. 289, 303.

9. W. Monson, *The Naval Tracts of Sir William Monson*, ed. by M. Oppenheim, 5 vols, London, Navy Records Society, 1902-1914, Vol. 4, pp. 387–388.

10. Byron, *Journal*, p. lxiii, n. 3.

11. Beaglehole, *Journals* I, p. cclxxxiv.

12. George Forster, *A Voyage Round the World*, ed. by Nicholas Thomas and Oliver Berghof, 2 vols, Honolulu, University of Hawai'i Press, 2000, Vol. 1, p. 292.

13. Beaglehole, *Journals* II, pp. 315–316, n. 3.

14. Royal Navy, *Regulations and Instructions Relating to His Majesty's Service at Sea*, London, Privy Council, 1808, pp. 2–3.

Chapter 16

1. Francois Valentyn, *Oud en nieuw Oost-Indien*, 5 vols, Dordrecht, J. van Braam, 1724–1726, Vol. 3, p. 47.

2. Günter Schilder, *Australia Unveiled: The Share of the Dutch Navigators in the Discovery of Australia*, trans. Olaf Richter, Amsterdam, Theatrum Orbis Terrarum, 1975, p. 170.

3. Tasman, Huydecoper, p. 33.

4. Valentyn, *Oud*, p. 49.

5. Schilder, *Australia*, p. 197.

Chapter 17

1. Admiralty to Cook, 22 July 1768, in Beaglehole, *Journals* I, p. 620.

2. Carter, *Banks*, at pp. 71–73.

3. Beaglehole, *Journals* I, p. cxxxv.

4. David Mackay, *In the Wake of Cook: Exploration, Science and Empire, 1780–1801*, Wellington, N.Z., Victoria University Press, 1985, at p. 21.

Chapter 18

1. Joseph Banks, *The Endeavour Journal of Joseph Banks: 1768–1771*, 2 vols, ed. by J.C. Beaglehole, Sydney, Angus & Robertson, 1962, Vol. 1, p. 176.

2. J.M. Matra, *A journal of a voyage round the world, in His Majesty's ship Endeavour, 1768–1771*, London, Becket, 1771, reproduced in Alan Frost, *The Precarious Life of James Mario Matra: Voyager with Cook, American Loyalist, Servant of Empire*, Melbourne, Miegunyah Press, 1995, at p. 14; see also Sydney Parkinson, *A journal of a voyage to the South Seas, in his Majesty's ship, the Endeavour*, London, Printed for Stanfield Parkinson, the editor, 1773, at p. 22.

3. Parkinson, *Journal*, p. 22.

4. Banks, *Journal*, Vol. 1, p. 207.

5. Christopher Hodson, *The Acadian Diaspora: An Eighteenth-Century History*, New York, Oxford University Press, 2012, p. 142.

6. Banks, *Journal*, Vol. 1, p. 212.

7. Beaglehole, *Life*, pp. 147–148.

8. Beaglehole, *Journals* I, p. cclxxx.

9. Beaglehole, *Journals* I, p. 62.

10. Banks, *Journal*, Vol. 1, p. 240.

11. Fry, *Dalrymple and Trade*, p. 273.

12. Banks, *Journal*, Vol. 1, p. 251.

13. Beaglehole, *Journals* I, p. 74.

14. Banks, *Journal*, Vol. 1, p. 247.

Chapter 19

1. Beaglehole, *Journals* I, p. 89, n. 2.

2. Banks, *Journal*, Vol. 1, p. 41.

3. Beaglehole, *Journals* I, p. 82.

4. Robertson, *Discovery*, p. xxxvii.

5. Charles Blagden diary in Carter, *Banks*, at p. 86.

6. Beaglehole, *Journals* I, p. 97.

7. Wayne Orchiston, 'James Cook's 1769 Transit of Venus Expedition to Tahiti', in D.W. Kurtz, ed., *Transits of Venus: New Views of the Solar System and Galaxy*, Proceedings IAU Colloquium No. 196, 2004, International Astronomical Union, pp. 52–66.

8. Banks, *Journal*, Vol. 1, p. 261

9 Beaglehole, *Journals* I, p. 100.
10 Banks, *Journal*, Vol. 1, p. 312.

Chapter 20

1 Beaglehole, *Life*, pp. 193–194.
2 Morton, James Douglas, Earl, Hints offered to the consideration of Captain Cooke, Mr Bankes, Dr Solander and the other gentlemen who go upon the expedition on board the *Endeavour* 10 August 1768, reproduced in *Journals* I, pp. 514–519.
3 Beaglehole, *Journals* III, p. 769.
4 Banks, *Journal*, Vol. 1. p. 318.
5 Parkinson, *Journal*, p. 99.
6 Beaglehole, Journals I, p. 151.
7 Banks, *Journal*, Vol. 1, p. 329.
8 Banks, *Journal*, Vol. 1, p. 387.
9 Banks, *Journal*, Vol. 1, p. 388.
10 Parkinson, *Journal*, p. 116.
11 Beaglehole, *Journals* I, p. 161.
12 Banks to the Comte de Lauraguais, 6 December 1771, in Chambers, *Selection*, p. 18.
13 Beaglehole, *Journals* I, pp. cclxxxii–cclxxxiii.
14 Parkinson, *Journal*. p. 118.
15 R.A. Skelton, 'Captain James Cook as a Hydrographer', *Mariner's Mirror*, Vol. 40, 1954, pp. 92–119, at p. 109.
16 Banks, *Journal*, Vol. 1, p. 397.
17 Bill Keir, 'Captain Cook's Longitude Determinations and the Transit of Mercury – Common Assumptions Questioned', *Journal of the Royal Society of New Zealand*, Vol. 40, 2010, pp. 27–38, at p. 34.
18 Campbell, *Navigantium*, Vol. 1, pp. 325–336.
19 Valentyn, *Oud*.

Chapter 21

1 Banks, *Journal*, Vol. 1, p. 399, n. 8.
2 J.B. Marshall, 'The Handwriting of Joseph Banks, his Scientific Staff and Amanuenses', *Bulletin of the British Museum (Natural History), Botany*, Vol. 6, No. 1.,1978, pp. 15–16.
3 Beaglehole, *Journals* I, p. 274.
4 Parkinson, *Journal*, p. 122.
5 Beaglehole, *Journals* I, p. 172, n. 3.
6 Brian Hooker, 'James Cook's Secret Search in 1769', *Mariner's Mirror*, Vol. 87, No. 3, 2001, pp. 297–302.
7 Beaglehole, *Journals* I, p. 173.

8 Beaglehole, *Journals* I, p. 204.
9 Beaglehole, *Journals* I, p. 278.
10 Surville, *Expedition*, p. 42.
11 Banks, *Journal*, Vol. 2, n. 1.
12 Banks, *Journal*, Vol. 1, p. 449.
13 Beaglehole, *Life*, p. 209.
14 Banks, *Journal*, Vol. 1, p. 447.

Chapter 22

1 Beaglehole, *Journals* I, p. 238.
2 Dalrymple, *Account*, p. 64n.
3 Banks, *Journal*, Vol. 1, p. 457.
4 Banks, *Journal*, Vol. 1, p. 461.
5 Beaglehole, *Journals* I, p. 243.
6 Beaglehole, *Life*, p. 215.
7 Beaglehole, *Journals* I, p. 243, n. 2; Banks, *Journal*, Vol. 1, p. 462; and Robert McNab, *From Tasman to Marsden: A History of Northern New Zealand from 1642 to 1818*, Dunedin, 1914, facsim. reprint, Christchurch, N.Z., Cadsonbury Publications, 1996, p. 53.

Chapter 23

1 Beaglehole, *Journals* I, p. 250.
2 Banks, *Journal*, Vol. 2, p. 468.
3 Beaglehole, *Journals* I, p. 252, n. 4.
4 Beaglehole, *Journals* I, pp. 253–254.
5 Beaglehole, *Journals* I, p. 253, n. 1.
6 Banks, *Journal*, Vol. 1, p. 470.
7 Skelton, 'Hydrographer', p. 115.
8 Beaglehole, *Journals* I, p. 263, n. 2.
9 M. Cameron-Ash, 'Political Captain Cook', *The Globe*, No. 75, 2014, pp. 1–10; and M. Cameron-Ash, 'Whitehall's Secrets and Captain Cook', *Cook's Log*, Vol. 38, No. 2, 2015, pp. 4–8.
10 Beaglehole, *Journals* II, p. 131.
11 Beaglehole, *Journals* I, p. 263.
12 Beaglehole, *Journals* I, p. 263, n. 2.
13 Robert McNab, *Murihiku: A History of the South Island of New Zealand and the Islands Adjacent and Lying to the South, from 1642 to 1835*, Wellington, N.Z., Whitcombe & Tombs, 1909, p. 24.
14 J. Cook, 'Chart of New-Zealand, explored in 1769 and 1770 by Lieut. I: Cook, Commander of His Majesty's Bark Endeavour, 1773, engraved by J. Bayly', published in Hawkesworth, *Voyages*, Vol. 2, facing p. 281, available online at National Library of Australia nla.obj-230689929.

Chapter 24

1. Banks, *Journal*, Vol. 1, p. 472.
2. Beaglehole, *Life*, p. 225.
3. Beaglehole, *Journals* I, pp. 272–273.
4. Banks, *Journal*, Vol. 2, p. 38.

Chapter 25

1. Captain Vancouver to Lord Grenville, 9 August 1791, *Historical Records of New Zealand*, Vol. 1, p. 132, available online: http://nzetc.victoria.ac.nz/tm/scholarly/tei-McN01Hist-t1-b4-d13.html.
2. Beaglehole, *Journals* I, p. 273.
3. Banks, *Journal*, Vol. 2, p. 42.
4. Parkinson, *Journal*, p. 117.
5. Beaglehole, *Journals* I, p. 298.
6. Beaglehole, *Journals* I, p. 299, n. 1.
7. Beaglehole, *Journals* I, p. 299. Cook is probably jesting here, as 'Dirk Rembrantz' is too brief. However, the *Endeavour* library also held the more illuminating Valentyn. See Chapter 16 above.
8. Ernest Scott, 'English and French Navigators on the Victorian Coast', *Victorian Historical Magazine*, Vol. 2, No. 4, 1912, pp. 145–176, at p. 151.
9. Available online at https://nla.gov.au/nla.obj-588080489/view. BL.Add.MS 7085.34, reproduced in R.A. Skelton, ed., *Charts and Views Drawn by Cook and his Officers and Reproduced from the Original Manuscripts*, Cambridge, Hakluyt Society, 1955, Plate XX; and Andrew David, *Charts and Coastal Views of Captain Cook's Voyages*, 3 vols, London, Hakluyt Society, 1988–1997, Vol. 1, p. 260.
10. Beaglehole, *Journals* I, pp. 298–299.
11. George Bass, 'Journal of a Whaleboat Voyage', printed in *HRNSW*, Vol. 3, pp. 312–333, at p. 321.
12. Trevor Lipscombe, 'Cook's Point Hicks: Error that Just Won't go Away', *Cook's Log*, Vol. 38, No. 2, 2015, pp. 26–32.
13. Scott, 'English', at p. 149.
14. Banks, *Journal*, Vol. 2, p. 49.
15. A Chart of New South Wales, or the East Coast of New Holland. Discover'd and Explored by Lieutenant J: Cook, Commander of his Majesty's Bark Endeavour, 1770, engraved by William Whitchurch, published in Hawkesworth, 1773, Vol. 3, p. 480; and David, *Charts*, Vol. 1, p. 262, available at nla.obj.232572777.

Chapter 26

1. Beaglehole, *Journals* II, p. 735.
2. Beaglehole, *Journals* II, p. 152.
3. R. Brookes, ed., *The general gazetteer or, Compendious geographical dictionary*, 8th. ed., London, 1794, p. 222.
4. 'Furneaux's Journal' is printed in Beaglehole, *Journals* II, pp. 143–161; 'Furneaux's Narrative' is printed in Beaglehole, *Journals* II, pp. 729–745.
5. Beaglehole, *Journals* II, p. 153, n. 4.
6. Bass, Journal, pp. 326–327.
7. Beaglehole, *Journals* II, pp. 152–153.
8. David, *Charts*, Vol. 2, pp. 90–91.
9. Beaglehole, *Journals* II, p. 143.
10. Beaglehole, *Journals* II, pp. 164–165.
11. Beaglehole, *Journals* II, p. 165, n. 1.
12. Beaglehole, *Journals* II, p. 736.
13. Beaglehole, *Journals* II, p. xxxv.
14. Beaglehole, *Journals* II, p. 165.
15. Cook, James, *A voyage to the Pacific Ocean ... for making discoveries in the northern hemisphere, in His Majesty's ships the Resolution and Discovery, 1776–1780*, 3 vols, London, Printed by W. and A. Strahan, 1784, Vol. I, at p. xv.
16. Beaglehole, *Journals* II, p. 700.
17. Beaglehole, *Journals* II, p. 656, n. 2.
18. Beaglehole, *Journals* III, p. 25, n. 4. Robert de Vaugondy, Hemisphere Austral ou Antarctique, Paris, 1773, available at http://nla.gov.au/nla.obj-232630517.
19. Beaglehole, *Journals* III, p. 1524.
20. Beaglehole, *Journals* III, p. 787.
21. Beaglehole, *Journals* III, p. ccxxi.
22. Beaglehole, *Journals* III, p. 56.
23. Beaglehole, *Journals* III, pp. xcvi–xcvii.
24. William Bradley, journal titled 'A Voyage to New South Wales', December 1786 – May 1792, p. 56, 15 January 1788, State Library of New South Wales, Safe 1/14.
25. Matthew Flinders, *A voyage to Terra Australis, 1801–1803, in His Majesty's ship the Investigator*, 2 vols, London, G. and W. Nicol, 1814. Vol. 1, 'Introduction, Prior Discoveries', at p. cxxxviii.
26. N. Baudin, *The journal of post Captain Nicolas Baudin, Commander-in-Chief of the corvettes Géographe and Naturaliste*, trans. Christine Cornell, Adelaide, Libraries Board of South Australia, 1974, pp. 2–3.
27. Governor King to Lord Hobart, 9 November 1802, in *HRA* Series I, Vol. 3, p. 697, at p. 698.

Chapter 27

1. Beaglehole, *Journals* I, p. 304.
2. P.S. Roy and E.A. Crawford, *Holocene Geological Evolution of the Southern Botany Bay – Kurnel Region, Central New South Wales Coast*, reprinted from the Records of the Geological Survey of New South Wales, Vol. 20, Pt 2, pp. 159–250, Sydney, Department of Mineral Resources, 1979, at p. 166.
3. Banks, *Journal*, Vol. 2, p. 53.
4. Beaglehole, *Journals* I, p. 305, n. 3.
5. Andrew Stevenson, *Sydney Morning Herald*, 18 April 2005; Cliff Thornton, 'The *Endeavour* Replica – Return to Australia', *Log*, Vol. 28, No. 3, 2005, p. 12.
6. Roy, *Holocene*, pp. 210, 225.
7. Beaglehole, *Journals* I, p. 310, n. 4; the successive changes of name can be seen in the manuscript online at the Nation Library of Australia, nla.obj-229042401.
8. Hawkesworth, Vol. 3, p. 501.

Chapter 28

1. Beaglehole, *Journals* I, pp. 312–313.
2. Phillip, Comments on a draft of his instructions, c.11 April 1787, Colonial Office Records, The National Archives, Kew, U.K., TNA CO 201/2, f.128–131; reprinted in Barton, *History*, p. 46.
3. Barton, *History*, p. 46, n.
4. Alan Frost, *Arthur Phillip, 1738–1814: His Voyaging*, Melbourne, Oxford University Press, 1987, p. 296, n. 3.
5. Arthur Phillip, *The voyage of Governor Phillip to Botany Bay*, London, John Stockdale, 1789, p. 47.
6. P.R. Stephensen, *The History and Description of Sydney Harbour*, Adelaide, Rigby, 1966, at p. 5.
7. La Pérouse, Jean-François de Galaup, comte de, *The journal of Jean-François de Galaup de la Pérouse, 1785–1788*, trans. and ed. by John Dunmore, 2 vols, London, Hakluyt Society, 1994–1995, Vol. 2, pp. 446, n. 2.
8. Bertie, C.H., 'Captain Cook and Botany Bay', *JRAHS*, Vol. 10, No. 5, pp. 233–278, at p. 251.
9. Maria Nugent, *Captain Cook Was Here*, Melbourne, Cambridge University Press, 2009, p. 67.
10. James Boswell. *Boswell's Life of Johnson*, ed. by G.B. Hill, rev. by L.F. Powell, 6 vols, Oxford, Clarendon Press, 1934, Vol. 2, p. 248.
11. Beaglehole, *Journals* I, p. 306, 310.
12. Beaglehole, *Journals* II, p. 161.
13. Garry Wotherspoon, 'The Road East', *Dictionary of Sydney*, 2011, available at http://dictionaryofsydney.org.
14. Alec Protos, *The Road to Botany Bay: The Story of Frenchmans Road Randwick Through the Journals of Lapérouse and the First Fleet Writers*, rev. ed., Sydney, Randwick and District Historical Society, 2000.
15. John White, *Journal of a Voyage to New South Wales*, London, J. Debrett, 1790, entry for 26 January 1788.

Chapter 29

1. Beaglehole, *Journals* I, p. 312.
2. Banks, *Journal*, Vol. 2, p. 67.
3. Banks, *Journal*, Vol. 2, p. 66.
4. Beaglehole, *Journals* I, p. 323.
5. Beaglehole, *Journals* I, p. 337.
6. Banks, *Journal*, Vol. 2, p. 79.
7. Beaglehole, *Journals* I, p. 376.
8. Banks, *Journal*, Vol. 2, pp. 104–105.
9. Beaglehole, *Journals* I, p. 385.

Chapter 30

1. Cook's ship time has been converted to civil time, then adjusted for the day lost in crossing the 180th Meridian. See R.B. Joyce, 'Time and Captain Cook', *Queensland Heritage*, Vol. 2, No. 2, 1970, pp. 8–12; and G.K. Mc Callum, 'A Date with Cook', *JRAHS*, Vol. 57, No. 1, 1971, pp. 1–9.
2. W.G. Grewe, *The Epochs of International Law*, translated and revised by M. Byers, Berlin, De Gruyter, 2001, at p. 396.
3. Beaglehole, *Journals* I, p. cciii; see also J.C. Beaglehole, 'Some Problems of Editing Cook's Journals', *Historical Studies Australia and New Zealand*, Vol. 8, No. 29, 1957, pp. 20–31, available online at http://nzetc.victoria.ac.nz/tm/scholarly/tei-BeaSome-t1-body1.html.
4. Beaglehole, *Journals* I, p. 310, n. 4; the successive changes of name can be seen in the manuscript online at the Nation Library of Australia, nla.obj-229042401.
5. Beaglehole, *Journals* I, p. ccx.
6. Beaglehole, *Journals* I, p. cxciv.
7. See chapter 35.
8. Chapters 32 and 35.
9. Beaglehole, *Journals* I, p. cclxxxiii.
10. Schilder, Australia, p. 47.
11. G.C. Ingleton, 'A Brief History of Marine Surveying in Australia', *JRAHS*, Vol. 30, No. 1, 1944, pp. 1–44, at p. 15.
12. Banks, *Journal*, Vol. 2, p. 110, n. 1.
13. Beaglehole, *Journals* I, p. 387, n.4.
14. Parkinson, *Journal*, p. 198.
15. Banks, *Journal*, Vol. 2, p. 110.

16 GMS, manuscript abstract by Banks from Cook's journal, in Sir George Grey Special Collections, Auckland Libraries, New Zealand.
17 Beaglehole, *Journals* I, p. ccxl.
18 GMS 51, p. 136.
19 Beaglehole, *Journals* I, pp. 388–389.

Chapter 31

1 Beaglehole, *Journals* I, p. 417.
2 William Dampier, *A voyage to New Holland*, ed. by J. A. Williamson, 1939, p. 137.
3 Banks, *Journal*, Vol. 2, p. 152.
4 Banks, *Journal*, Vol. 2, p. 184.
5 Parkinson, *Journal*, p. 214.
6 Beaglehole, *Journals* I, pp. 429–430.
7 J.S. Stavorinus, *Voyages to the East-Indies*, translated from the Dutch by S.H. Wilcocke, 3 vols, London, Robinson, 1798, Vol. 1, p. 176.
8 Stavorinus, *Voyages*, p. 175.
9 Beaglehole, *Journals* I, p. 433.
10 Byron, *Journal*, p. 157.
11 Beaglehole, *Journals* I, p. cclxxxiii.
12 Cook to Stephens, 14 October 1770, in Beaglehole, *Journals* I, p. 499.
13 Beaglehole, *Journals* I, p. 627, n. 1.

Chapter 32

1 Banks, *Journal*, Vol. 2, pp. 188–189.
2 Beaglehole explains the process of throwing away pages when the original was redrafted: Beaglehole, *Journals* I, p. ccx.
3 Beaglehole, *Journals* I, pp. 387–388. The two pages of the digitized Holograph are available online at nla.obj-229062345 and nla.obj-229062649.
4 Elizabeth Evatt, 'The Acquisition of Territory in Australia and New Zealand', in *Grotian Society Papers 1968: Studies in the History of the Law of Nations*, ed. by C.H. Alexandrowicz, The Hague, Martinus Nijhoff, 1970, pp. 16–45, at p. 21, n. 23.
5 Beaglehole, *Journals* I, p. ccxxvii
6 Lieutenant Cook's Official Log, 22 August 1770, *HRNSW*, Vol. 1, Pt 1, p. 157.
7 Beaglehole, *Journals* I, p. ccxxviii.
8 Beaglehole, *Journals* I, p. 426.
9 Beaglehole, *Journals* I, p. ccxxix.
10 *HRNSW*, Vol. 1, Pt 1, p. 190.
11 Matra, *Journal*, at p. 65.
12 Grey Manuscript 51, pp. 136–137.
13 R.L. Jack, *Northmost Australia: Three Centuries of Exploration, Discovery, and Adventure in and around the Cape York Peninsula*, 2 vols, London, Simpkin, etc., 1921, Vol. 1, at p. 88.
14 Banks, *Journal*, Vol. 2, p. 110, n. 2.
15 Anon. (William Eden), *The history of New Holland, from its first discovery in 1616 to the present time*, London, Stockdale, 1787.
16 A New Chart of New Holland on which are delineated New South Wales, and a plan of Botany Bay, by John Andrews, 1787, available online at State Library of New South Wales IE3779206.
17 Barton, *History*, pp. 262–265.
18 Beaglehole, *Journals* I, pp. 499–501.
19 Beaglehole, *Journals* I, p. 502.

Chapter 33

1 P.H. van der Brug, 'Malaria in Batavia in the 18th Century', *Tropical Medicine & International Health*, Vol. 2, No. 9, pp. 892–902.
2 Bougainville, Forster, pp. 446–447.
3 Bougainville, Forster, p. 469; Bougainville, *Pacific Journal*, pp. 183–193.
4 James Lind, *An essay, on the most effectual means, of preserving the health of seamen, in the Royal Navy: Containing, cautions necessary for those who reside in, or visit, unhealthy situations ... And an appendix of observations, on the treatment of diseases in hot climates*, London, Millar, 1757, pp. 48–49.
5 Carter, *Banks*, p. 34.
6 Banks, *Journal*, Vol. 2, p. 82; J. Robson, 'William Perry in the *Gentleman's Magazine*', *Cook's Log*, Vol. 39, No. 4, 2016, pp. 7–14, at p. 8.
7 Banks, *Journal*, Vol. 2, p. 192; Beaglehole, *Journals* I, p. 441, n. 3.

Chapter 34

1 Banks, *Journal*, Vol. 2, p. 270.
2 Dalrymple, *Account*, p. xiv.
3 Banks, *Journal*, Vol. 2, p. 248.
4 Banks, *Journal*, Vol. 2, p. 249.
5 Beaglehole, *Journals* I, p. 479.
6 Banks, *Journal*, Vol. 2, p. 270.
7 Cook to Stephens, 23 October 1770, in Beaglehole, *Journals* I, pp. 499–501, at p. 501.
8 Bougainville, Forster.
9 Beaglehole, *Journals* II, p. xxv.
10 Banks to the Comte de Lauraguais, 6 December 1771 in Banks, *Journals*, Vol. 2, at p. 329.
11 Beaglehole, *Life*, p. 295.
12 Beaglehole, *Life*, p. 304.
13 Beaglehole, *Journals* II, p. clxviii.

Chapter 35

1 Bougainville, *Pacific Journal*, p. ix; Beaglehole, *Journals* I, pp. cxciv–cciv.

2 Dunmore, *Storms*, p. 217.

3 Fry, Creative, at p. 47; Sir Archibald Geikie, *Annals of the Royal Society Club: The Record of a London Dining-club in the Eighteenth & Nineteenth Centuries*, London, Macmillan, 1917, p. 110.

4 Serge Tcherkezoff, *First Contacts in Polynesia: The Samoan Case (1722–1848): Western Misunderstanding about Sexuality and Divinity*, Canberra, 2004, p. 32, n. 7.

5 L.-A. Bougainville, *Voyage autour du monde, par la frégate du Roi La Boudeuse en 1766–1769*, Paris, Chez Saillant & Nyon, 1771; Dunmore, *Storms*, p. 220.

6 Bougainville, Forster.

7 Beaglehole, *Journals* I, p. cxciv.

8 James Cook, Journal of H.M.S. *Endeavour*, 1768–1771, MS 1, Holograph manuscript, available online at http://nla.gov.au/nla.obj-228958440.

9 Voyaging Accounts, available at http://southseas.nla.gov.au.

10 Beaglehole, *Journals* I, p. ccliii.

11 Benjamin Franklin, Introduction to a Plan for Benefiting the New Zealanders, 29 August 1771, Founders Online, U.S. Archives.

12 J.M. Matra, *A journal of a voyage round the world, in His Majesty's ship Endeavour, 1768–1771*, London, Becket, 1771.

13 Frost, *Life of James Matra*, at p. 6.

14 J.M. Matra, *Supplément au voyage de M. de Bougainville, ou, Journal d'un voyage autour du monde, fait par MM. Banks & Solander, Anglois, en 1768–1771 traduit de l'anglois, par M. de Freville*, Paris, 1772.

15 *Daily Advertiser*, Thursday 16 April 1772, Issue 12890.

16 Banks to the Comte de Lauraguais, 6 December 1771, in Banks, *Journal*, Vol 2, pp. 323–329.

17 Matthew Fishburn, 'The Book that Joseph Banks Burned', *SL Magazine*, Vol. 10, No. 4, Summer 2017–2018, pp. 26–29.

18 John Hawkesworth, ed., *An account of the voyages undertaken by the order of His present Majesty for making discoveries in the southern hemisphere, and successively performed by Commodore Byron, Captain Wallis, Captain Carteret, and Captain Cook, in the Dolphin, the Swallow, and the Endeavour*, 3 vols, 1773, London.

19 Beaglehole, *Journals* II, pp. 661–662.

20 Beaglehole, *Journals* I, p. ccxx; W.J.L. Wharton, ed., *Captain Cook's journal during his first voyage round the world made in H.M. Bark 'Endeavour', 1768–71*, London, Elliot Stock, 1893.

21 Hawkesworth, Vol 3, p. 615.

22 Beaglehole, *Journals* I, p. 387.

23 John Barrow to Robert Wilmot-Horton, undersecretary at the War and Colonial Office, 22 January 1824, in *HRA*, Series III, Vol. 5, pp. 751–753, at p. 752.

24 National Library of Australia, *Mapping our World: Terra Incognita to Australia*, Canberra, National Library of Australia, 2013, p. 198.

25 R.A. Skelton, ed., *Charts and Views Drawn by Cook and his Officers and Reproduced from the Original Manuscripts*, Hakluyt Society, 1955.

26 Andrew David, *Charts and Coastal Views of Captain Cook's Voyages*, 3 vols, London, Hakluyt Society; 1988–1997.

27 A Chart of New South Wales, or the East Coast of New Holland. Discover'd and Explored by Lieutenant J: Cook, Commander of his Majesty's Bark Endeavour, 1770, engraved by William Whitchurch, published in Hawkesworth, 1773, Vol. 3, p. 480; and David, *Charts*, Vol. 1, p. 262.

28 Victor-Donatien Musset-Pathay, *Souvenirs historiques, ou Coup d'oeil sur les monarchies de l'Europe et sur les causes de leur grandeur ou de leur décadence*, Paris, D. Colas, 1810, pp. 111–112, extract translated and reproduced in *The Anti-jacobin Review*, May 1810, No. 36, pp. 496–506.

29 Bonaparte to Augereau, 12 November 1803, in *A Selection from the Letters and Despatches of the First Napoleon*, ed. by D.A. Bingham, London, Chapman and Hall, 1884, 3 vols, Vol. 2, p. 37.

30 François Péron, *Voyage de decouvertes aux terres australes: execute par ordre de sa Majeste, l'Empereur et Roi,1801–1804*, Vol. 1, Paris, De l'Imprimerie Imperiale, 1807.

31 Anon. (Barrow), 'Review of Voyage de decouvertes aux terres australes par F. Peron', *Quarterly Review*, Vol. IV, No. viii, 1810, pp. 42–60.

32 Matthew Flinders, *General chart of Terra Australis or Australia: showing the parts explored between 1798 and 1803 by M. Flinders Commr. of H.M.S. Investigator*, London, 1814, available at nla.obj-232588549.

33 Stephens to Cook, 10 February 1776, in Beaglehole, *Journals* III, p. 1486.

34 Stephens to Cook, 6 July 1776, in Beaglehole, *Journals* III, p. 1510.

35 Background note, Sir Joseph Banks Papers, State Library of NSW, available online at http://www.sl.nsw.gov.au/banks/ section-04/series-09; and see Helen Wallis, 'Publication of Cook's Journals: Some New Sources and Assessments', *Pacific Studies*, Vol. 1, No. 2, 1978, at. 177.

36 Beaglehole, *Journals* I, p. ccxviii.

37 Certificate of Election EC/1775/27, The Royal Society.

38 Beaglehole, *Life*, p. 450.

Index

Aberdeen, 66
Acadia, Nova Scotia, Canada, 24, 28
Adams, John, 88
Adams, Thomas, 73
Admiral Pocock, 201
Admiralty Bay, 146
Adventure, 155–159, 204
Adventure Bay, Tasmania, 155, 160, 161
Aeheinomouwe, North Island, 129
Africa, 18–20, 116, 201
Agincourt, 211
Ahutoru, 53, 55, 124, 190
Aireyholme Farm, Yorkshire, 76, 78
Alaska, 102
American colonies, 10, 60, 147, 187
Amsterdam, Netherlands, 104, 105
Anderson, William, 125
Angeac, François-Gabriel d', 87
Anson, George, 27, 29–35, 36–39, 103, 104
Antarctica, 16, 18–23, 44 *see also* Southern Continent
Apollo 11, 100
Arafura Sea, 181
Arapawa Island, (Arapaoa Island) N.Z., 136–138
Arias, Juan Luis, 58
Armstrong, Neil, 100
Arnhem Land, Australia, 181
Ascension Island, 202
Augereau, Charles, 211
Austral Islands, 126
Australia, name re-allocation, 18–23, 130
　Australia (meaning modern Australia or the fifth continent) *see* New Holland
Australia (meaning Great South Land, Terra Australis Incognita, Antarctica or the sixth continent) *see* Southern Continent
Australia del Espiritu Santo *see* Quiros's Land
Australische Compagnie, 98
Azambuja, Count de, 114

Babel Island, 156
Baie Accaron, 28, 41
Baie de Prise de Possession (Turtle Bay), 204
Balambangan Island, Malaysia, 57, 67

Ball, Henry Lidgbird, 168
Balmoral, Sydney, 167
Banks, Joseph, 17, 20, 43, 69–75, 93, 104, 110–112, 113–140 passim, 146–149, 154, 164–178, 182–186, 190–195, 199 204, 206–208
Banks, Sarah Sophia, 199
Banks Island, 140
Banks Peninsula, 140–141
Banks Strait, Australia, 105, 156
Banks's Continentmongers *see* Continentalists
Banks's dogs, 74, 110, 114, 121, 185, 203
Bare Island, 168
Baret, Jeanne, 51, 52, 115, 124, 190
Barrow, John, 209, 211
Barton, George Burnett, 96, 168
Bass, George, 153, 162
Bass Strait, 8–10, 105, 148–162, 203, 210
Batavia, Java, 21, 42, 55, 115, 129, 134, 152, 185–200 *passim*, 203, 205, 213
Batemans Bay, 163
Bathurst, Lord, 35
Batts, Elizabeth *see* Cook, Elizabeth
Baudin, Nicolas, 162, 170, 210, 211, 212
Bay of Biscay, 80
Bay of Fires, 156
Bay of Islands, N.Z., 133
Bayly, William, 157, 161
Beaglehole, John Cawte, 8, 9, 110, 144–161 *passim*, 181, 184, 194, 206, 208, 210, 213
Beersheba, 165
Belle Isle, Strait of, Labrador, 88
Bellevue Hill, Sydney, 8, 172, 174
Bellin, Jacques, 98, 106
Bellona, 121
Bengal, 37, 67, 202
Bennelong Point, 175
Benoit, François, 24
Bering Strait, 159, 161
Berkeley, Frances, 38
Berkeley Sound, East Falkland, 24, 28, 41
Bevis, John, 93
Billings, Joseph, 161
Bird, John, 92
Blaeu, Joan, 107–109

Blaeu, Willem, 98
Blagden, Charles, 227 n. 5
Bligh, William, 11, 161
Bloomsbury, 72
Blue Mountains, 174
Bonaparte, Napoleon, 211
Bondi, 163, 169, 174
Bora Bora, Society Islands, 126
Borneo, 57
Boston, Massachusetts, 147
Boswell, James, 171
Botany Bay (previously Stingray Bay), 8, 24, 163–175, 195
Boudeuse, 51, 52
Bougainville, Louis Antoine de, 10, 22, 23, 24–28, 29, 34, 35, 39–41, 50–55, 97, 113, 123, 124, 190–193, 198, 202–203, 205
Bougainville Reef, 54
Bourbon family, 28, 115
Bouvet de Lozier, Jean Baptiste Charles, 155, 204
Bouvet Island *see* Cape Circumcision
Bowen, Emanuel, 19
Bradley, William, 161
Brest, France, 39, 51, 71
Brisbane, 176
Briscoe, Peter, 73, 118
Bristol, 66
Brittany, 28
Broken Bay, 170
Brosses, Charles de, 34, 64, 113
Buache, Philippe, 106
Buchan, Alexander, 110
Buckingham House, London, 44, 88, 107, 108
Buenos Aires, 51, 52, 99, 115
Bulanaming Road, 172–174
Burgeo Islands, 92
Burin Peninsula, 92
Burney, James, 21, 157, 161
Bustard Bay, 176, 180
Byron, John, 11, 23, 36–43, 44–46, 73, 95, 121, 188, 207

Calais, 144
Calcutta, 38
California, 27, 28, 38, 39, 41
Callao, Peru, 22
Camp Cove, 169
Campbell, John, 66, 97, 129
Canada, 24–26, 28, 88, 93, 123, 142
Canton, 57

Cap des Adieux, 211
Cape Banks, 166, 173, 174
Cape Breton Island, 82
Cape Circumcision (Bouvet Island), 27, 115, 155, 204
Cape Farewell, 149
Cape Flyaway, 104, 117, 128
Cape Horn, 27, 28, 30, 37–39, 45, 50, 52, 56, 66, 96, 98, 102, 103
Cape Howe, 153, 154, 163
Cape Keerweer, 181
Cape Leeuwin, 204
Cape Maria van Diemen, 21, 128, 133–135, 150
Cape of Good Hope, 38, 39, 49, 66, 75, 96, 108, 147, 154, 208
Cape Race, Newfoundland, 91
Cape Ray, Newfoundland, 89
Cape Town, 42, 113, 155, 159, 199, 201, 202
Cape Turnagain, 132, 139
Cape York, 152, 154, 179, 180–183, 195, 210
Capricorn *see* Tropic of Capricorn
Carpentaria, Gulf of, 152, 154, 191, 192, 195, 210
Carpentaria, Queensland, 50, 106, 181, 210
Carteret, Philip, 37, 45, 46, 207
Castries, Maréchal de, 169
Catherine the Great, 187
Centennial Park, 8
Chateau Bay, Labrador, 73, 88, 89
Chatham, Lord *see* William Pitt the Elder
Chesapeake Bay, 121
Chile, 38, 58, 59, 61, 104, 111, 116, 142
China, 39, 50, 51, 57, 201
Choiseul, Duc de, 26–28, 34, 35, 42, 45, 71, 86, 87
Ciliwung River, 186
Clarence River, 171
Clerke, Charles, 43, 73, 113, 121, 159, 160, 191
Clevland, John, 29, 32, 86
Clive, Lord, 37, 38, 67
Coffs Harbour, 171
Colnett, James, 33
Columbus, Christopher, 22, 58
Colville, Lord, 83, 84, 86, 95
Commerson, Philibert, 51, 52, 115
Constantia, 201
Constantinople, 187
Continentalists, 116, 117, 121, 122, 126, 127, 130, 131, 139, 140, 146
Coogee, 174
Cook, Elizabeth, 78, 85, 87, 88, 110, 164, 203, 206
Cook, James:
 birth, 77

childhood, 76–78
marriage, 85
children, 85, 88, 91, 110, 203
death, 11, 91, 121, 161, 196, 213
career in merchant navy, 78–79
joins King's navy, 80
under enemy fire, 26, 80, 82, 83
surveyor, 82, 84, 87
master and commander, 89–90
application for transit voyage, 17, 86, 89, 92, 93
probable first meeting with Banks, 73, 93
appointment to *Endeavour*, 76, 93
rank, courtesy title, 93
climbs a hill, 76, 137, 138, 172–174, 178, 182–183
second voyage, 11, 33, 96, 97, 101, 142, 148, 155–159, 172, 204, 208
third voyage, 96, 112, 121, 148, 159–161, 208, 213
Cook, James, senior, 76, 77, 203
Cook Strait, 22, 132, 137, 138, 139, 172
Cook's Harbour, Newfoundland, 90
Cooks River, 165, 173, 174
Cooktown, 54, 178
Coral Sea, 22, 54, 134, 178
Cornwall, 32, 45, 203
Coromandel Peninsula, 133
Courageux, 121
Cromwell, Oliver, 28
Croque Harbour, 88
Crozet, Julien, 159, 160, 161
Crozet Islands, 204

Dalrymple, Alexander, 17, 56–62, 63–68, 74, 75, 93, 94, 111, 113, 119, 137, 182, 201, 206
Dampier, William, 54, 59, 63, 97, 102, 108, 185
Dance, Nathaniel, 112
Davis, Edward, 39
Deal, Kent, 110, 203
Deptford, London, 45, 62, 91, 94
Derwent River, 162
Diane Reef, 54
Dirk Hartog Island, 204
Discovery, 159, 160
Dixon, George, 161
Dolphin, 36–43, 45–49, 51, 58, 74, 93, 101, 120, 121, 191
Doubtful Sound, 146
Doubtless Bay, (Lauriston Bay) N.Z., 134
Douglas, Charles, 87, 88
Douglas, John, 208
Dover, 144, 203

Downs, The, 110, 203
Drake, Francis, 15, 39, 99, 100, 101, 104
Dublin, 66
Duc d'Aquitaine, 80
Duke of Gloucester, 201
Durand, François Michel, 42, 45
Dusky Sound, 10, 142, 158
Dutch Cape Colony *see* Cape Town
Dutch East Indies, 23, 55, 96, 104, 108, 147, 181, 186, 200

Eagle, 80
Earl of Pembroke (renamed *Endeavour*), 62
East India House, Leadenhall Street, London, 57, 60
Easter Island, 117
Eddystone Point, Tasmania, 105, 148, 149, 156, 161
Eddystone Rocks, English Channel, 156
Eden, William, 231 n. 15
Edinburgh, 10, 56
Egmont, Lord, 36, 41, 44, 89
Egmont, Port *see* Port Egmont
Egremont, Lord, 87
Elliot, John, captain, 203
Elliott, John, midshipman, 101
Endeavour, 17, 20, 49, 62, 63, 63, 74, 75, 93, 94, 100, 101, 103, 113–154 passim, 163–193 passim, 199, 201–208 passim
Endeavour Bay, 132
Endeavour River, 178, 180
English Channel, 15, 31, 71, 79, 144, 156
Etoile, 51, 52
Europa, 201
Evatt, Elizabeth, 192
Exeter, 66

Falkland Islands, 10,11, 24–28, 29, 30, 35, 37–44, 50, 51, 52, 113, 115, 142, 202
Fannin, Peter, 157
Ferdinand VI of Spain, 30
Fernandez, Juan, 58, 116, 117
Ferolle Point, Newfoundland, 91
Fiji, 21, 22
First Fleet, 161, 168, 174, 195
Flinders, Matthew, 150, 153, 157, 162, 211, 212
Forster, Georg Adam, 101
Forster, Johann Reinhold, 205
Foveaux Strait, 10, 140–145, 148, 149, 210, 213
Frankfurt, 18
Franklin, Benjamin, 68, 72, 206
Frenchmans Road, 172, 173

Freycinet, Louis, 211, 212
Frost, Alan, 168
Fulham, London, 94
Furneaux, Tobias, 45–48, 119, 155–161, 172, 204
Furneaux's Land, 157

Gagarin, Yuri, 11
Garden Island, 174
George III of England, 16, 37, 40, 41, 44, 48, 61, 68, 85, 88, 107, 108, 130, 132, 142, 192, 196, 204, 209, 215
George IV of England, 182
Georges River, 165
Gilfillan, John, 195
Gillray, James, 71
Glasgow, 66
goat, 45, 110, 200
Goat Island, 174
Golfe Bonaparte, 211
Golfe Josephine, 211
Gonzal, Jean, 183
Good Success Bay, Tierra del Fuego, 116
Gore, John, 45, 46, 48, 74, 113, 120–122, 133, 139, 140, 166, 204
Grand Banks, Newfoundland, 86, 91
Graves, Thomas, 84, 87–89, 95
Graves's Island, (now Nobles Island, Quirpon), 89
Great Australian Bight, 211
Great Ayton, Yorkshire, 76–78
Great Barrier Reef, 54, 78, 124, 177, 193
Great South Land *see* Southern Continent
Green, Charles, 116, 118, 120, 122, 133, 197
Greenwich, London, 10, 153, 212
Grenville, George, 37, 69, 86
Grenville, 88–93
Grenville family, 69, 89
Grenville Harbour, Labrador, 89
Grey, George, 184, 231 n. 16
Groote Eylandt, 181
Grotto Point, 167
Guerchy, Comte de, 101
Gulf of Carpentaria *see* Carpentaria, Gulf of

Halifax, Nova Scotia, 82, 83
Halley, Edmond, 14, 16, 59, 63
Harley, J. B., 15, 99
Harrison, John, 37, 155
Hawaii, 11, 91, 161, 213
Hawke, Edward, 63, 64, 71, 74, 94, 98
Hawkesbury River, 171
Hawkesworth, John, 64, 145, 154, 166, 171, 181, 206– 213, 215
Hawkins, Richard, 39, 41
Hergest, Richard, 157
Hermitage Bay, Newfoundland, 92
Hicks, Zachary, 114, 122, 150, 153, 165, 187, 194, 202
  see also Point Hicks
Hirst, William, 57, 58
Hobart, Lord, 162
Hobart, 8, 35, 162, 204
Holland *see* Netherlands
Holland, Samuel Johannes, 82
Honter, Johannes, 18, 19, 23
Hornsby, Thomas, 14–17, 49, 56, 72, 123
Houghton, 201
Huahine, Society Islands, 125, 126
Huis ter Meijen, 189
Hull, 66
Humber River, Newfoundland, 93
Hunter, John, 162
Hunter River, 171
Huydecoper (Huijdecoper), 223 n. 7
Hyde Park, Sydney, 174

Iceland, 204
Île de France *see* Mauritius
Indonesia, 102, 186
Invercargill, 144
Ireland, 78

Jamaica, 72
Java, 21, 108, 185, 186
Jervis Bay, 163
Johnson, Samuel, 171

Kaikoura Peninsula, 140
Kaitapeha Ridge, N.Z., 137
Kamchatka, 169
Kealakekua Bay, Hawaii, 213
Keene, Benjamin, 30
Kelger, Frederick, 196, 197
Kempe, Arthur, 157
Kent Group, 156
Kerguelen Island, 155, 204
Kerguelen-Trémarec, Yves-Joseph de, 204, 210
King, James, 112, 159
King, Philip Gidley, 162
King George's Island *see* Tahiti
King George's Islands *see* Tuamotu Archipelago
Krakatoa, 186
Kronenburg, 196, 197

Kupang (Concordia), 185
Kurnell, 164, 165
Kuypers Island, 186, 199

Labrador, Canada, 73, 88, 89
Ladrones Islands (now Mariana Islands), 75
Land's End, Cornwall, 91
Lapérouse, Jean-François de Galaup, 34, 102, 169, 170, 172, 195, 210
Latouche-Tréville, Louis-René Levassor, 159
Lauraguais, Louis-Léon-Féliciaté, Comte de, 127, 207
Le Maire, Jacob, 20, 98
Le Maire Strait, Tierra del Fuego, 98
Leadbetter, Charles, 92
Ledyard, John, 161
Lincolnshire, 69, 71, 72
Lind, James, 198
Linnaeus, Carl, 130
Lisbon, 73
Liverpool, 66
Lizard Island, 178
Lookers On Island, 140
Louis XV of France, 26, 28, 34, 35, 50, 52, 54, 191, 205
Louis XVI of France, 169
Louisburg, Nova Scotia, Canada, 82, 86
Louisiana, North America, 27

Macquarie, Lachlan, 35
Madagascar, 66
Madame, Isle (Richmond Isle), Nova Scotia, 81
Madeira, 40, 113
Madras, 56, 57
Madrid, 26, 30, 42, 58
Magallon, Fernando de, 26
Magellan, Ferdinand, 18, 20, 58
Magellan, Strait of, 10, 24, 27, 39–41, 44–46, 52, 61, 98, 115
Malacca, Strait of, 57
Malay Archipelago, East Indies, 20, 57
Malouine Islands (Malvinas) *see* Falkland Islands
Manly, 167, 168
Mariana Islands, 42
Marion Dufresne, Marc-Joseph, 159, 204, 210
Marlborough Sounds, 136
Marlo, 152, 154
Maroo Track, Sydney, 172, 173, 174
Maroubra, 173, 174
Maskelyne, Nevil, 61
Masserano, Prince Fieschi de, 42
Matavai Bay, Tahiti, 47, 49, 53, 119, 120, 123

Matra, James Mario, 114, 191, 194, 206, 207
Mauritius (Île de France), 21, 49, 80, 104, 105, 159, 201, 202, 211
McNab, Robert, 9, 144, 145, 150
Melanesia, 18, 182, 183
Mercury Bay, N.Z., 133, 176, 180, 196
Michell, Keith, 171
Micronesia, 18
Middle Harbour, 167
Mile End Road, London, 103, 203, 206
Milner, Thomas, 62
Milton, John, 28
Miquelon Island *see* St Pierre and Miquelon
Molyneux, Robert, 45, 120, 122, 163, 164
Monkhouse, William, 138, 199
Monmouth, 71
Monson, William, 100
Montcalm, Marquis de, 25
Montevideo, Uruguay, 28, 40
Montreal, Canada, 26
Moorea Island, Tahiti, 122
Morton, Lord, 61, 63, 72, 74
Motuara Island, N.Z., 136, 138
Mouat, Patrick, 37
Mount Egmont, 136
Musset-Pathay, Victor-Donatien de, 210

Narrabeen, 170
Negev Desert, 165
Nelson, Horatio, 62, 164
Netherlands, 18, 82, 188, 189, 197
New Albion, California, 39, 160
New Britain, 193
New Guinea, 50, 55, 58, 59, 75, 104–106, 113, 152, 178, 182, 185, 193
New Hebrides, 54
New Holland (modern Australia – mainland), 10, 18–23, 50, 51, 54, 58, 66, 96, 97, 102, 106–109, 146, 148–163, 170, 175, 176–183, 185, 191–194, 209–213, 215
New Ireland, 193
New Wales, 192, 193
New York, 83, 99
Newcastle, Australia, 168, 171
Newcastle, Duke of, 71
Nierop, Dirck Rembrantsz Van, 9, 104, 129, 150, 229 n. 7
Niger, 73, 92
Noddy Harbour, 88, 91
Norfolk, 162

Norfolk Island, 35, 224 n. 15
North Cape, N.Z., 135
North Head, Sydney, 169
North Island, N.Z., 21, 133, 136, 139
Northumberland, 83, 84, 86
Northwest Passage, 26, 27, 39, 43, 51, 102, 159
Norway, 78, 123
Nouvelle-Cythère (Tahiti), 48, 53

Omai, 159
Onrust Island, 186, 188, 197, 199
Orinoco River, 38
Orton, Richard, 181, 188, 191, 196, 201, 203, 205, 207–209, 213
Otaheiti *see* Tahiti
Outer Sister Island, 156
Oxford Street, Sydney, 8, 172
Oxford University, 14, 16, 69, 72, 11, 204

Palliser, Hugh, 80, 84, 89, 91–93, 95, 111
Panama Canal, 27, 100
Paramour, 16
Paris, 11, 14, 26, 34, 42, 50, 51, 54, 55, 73, 86, 89, 113, 169, 205, 207
Parkinson, Stanfield, 207
Parkinson, Sydney, 110, 114, 115, 126, 127, 132, 133, 149, 183, 187, 194, 207
Passage Isle, 184, 191, 192, 194
Pearl Harbor, Hawaii, 99
Pembroke, 25, 45, 82, 83, 91
Penguin Island, 160
Pennsylvania, 68
Pepys Island, 39, 40
Peron, François, 211
Perrin, William Phelp, 72–75
Peru, 22, 58, 61, 134, 142
Petropavlovsk, 169
Philip III of Spain, 22
Philippines, 30, 42, 57
Phillip, Arthur, 167–170, 195, 213
Phipps, Constantine John, 69, 71, 72
Pickersgill, Richard, 45, 130, 138
Pinchgut Island, 174
Pitt, William, the Elder (Lord Chatham), 69, 81, 86, 87, 92, 108
Pitt, William, the Younger, 69
Pitts Harbour, Labrador, 89
Pittwater, 171
Plains of Abraham, 25
Plymouth, England, 40, 45, 73, 80, 110, 114

Point Hicks, 153, 154, 158
Point Levis, Quebec, 25, 83
Point Riche, 89
Point Venus, Tahiti, 120, 122
Polynesia, 18, 47, 48, 53, 55, 121, 124, 126, 138
Pondicherry, 49, 134, 159
Port de la Croisade, 28 *see also* Port Egmont
Port Egmont, Saunders Island, West Falkland, 28, 41, 44
Port Famine, 4
Port Jackson (Sydney Harbour), 8, 134, 167–175, 195, 203, 213
Port Macquarie, 171
Port St Louis, 24, 28, 50, 51, 115
Port Stephens, 168, 171
Portland, 202
Portlock, Nathaniel, 161
Portsmouth, 198
Portugal, 27, 97, 121
Possession Island, Queensland, 180, 184, 192, 193, 195
Poverty Bay, 132, 183, 196
Prince Frederick, 46
Prince of Orange, 45
Prince of Wales (later George IV), 182
Prince of Wales Island, Torres Strait, 182, 193
Princes Highway, Sydney, 172
Providence Island, Unalaska, 78
Providential Channel, Queensland, 78, 178
Pyrmont Peninsula, 174

Quebec, 25, 26, 45, 83
Queen Charlotte of England, 138
Queen Charlotte Sound, 136, 138, 146, 158, 172, 196
Queen Isabella of Spain, 98
Queen Oberea (Purea), 47, 120
Quiberon Bay, 63, 98
Quiros, Pedro Fernandez de, 22, 54, 59
Quiros's Land (also Espiritu Santo, Land of the Holy Spirit, Grandes Cyclades, New Hebrides, Vanuatu), 22, 50, 54, 104, 106, 178
Quirpon Harbour, Newfoundland, 88, 89

Raiatea, Society Islands, 125, 196
Ram Head, Australia, 152, 153
Ramsden, Jesse, 224 n. 12
Randwick, 173, 174
Ranelagh, Lord, 213
Redern, Sigismund, Count von, 20, 22, 23, 45, 58, 104
Rembrantz *see* Nierop
Resolution, 122, 125, 155, 158, 159, 204
Revesby Abbey, Lincolnshire, 69, 71

Richmond River, 171
Rijders Eylandt, 183
Ringmann, Matthias, 18
Rio de Janeiro, 37, 40, 48, 52, 55, 113, 114, 115, 187
Riou, Edward, 161
Robertson, George, 46, 48
Rochford, Lord, 51
Rodondo, 33, 223 n.10
Roebuck, 185
Roosevelt, Franklin, 99
Roseberry Topping, Yorkshire, 76, 137, 172
Royal George, 33
Ruapuke Island, 141
Russia, 11, 169, 187

Sahara Desert, 165
Saint-Germain, Louis, 55
Samoan Group, 54
Sanderson, Thomas, 78
Sandwich, Lord, 66, 69, 73, 86, 89, 111, 207, 213
Sandwich, Port, Labrador, 89
Saunders, Charles, 95
Saunders, Thomas, 60
Saunders Island, West Falkland, 41
Savu, 185
Schilder, Günter, 105
Schouten, Willem, 98
Scott, Ernest, 150, 154
Seville, 98
Shark Island, 174
Shelburne, Lord, 51, 59, 60, 61
Ship Cove, 136, 138
Siberia, 14, 169
Sirius, 162
Skelton, R.A., 140, 210
Skottowe, Thomas, 76–78
Slade, Thomas, 62
Slade Point, Queensland, 62
Smith, Adam, 59, 60
Smith, Isaac, 164
Snowy River, 154
Society Islands (Leeward Islands), 125, 160
Soho Square, London, 112, 121
Solander, Daniel Carl, 19, 20, 72, 110, 111, 121, 122, 126, 130–132, 137, 138, 146, 182, 183, 190, 192, 199, 203, 204, 213
Solander, Point, 166, 173
Solomon Islands, 15, 42, 43, 55, 134
South Head, Sydney, 167–169
South Island, N.Z., 9, 21, 136, 139–142, 146

South Pole, 16, 18–20, 23, 204
South Sea House, Threadneedle Street, London, 38
Southern Continent (now Antarctica), 18–23, 27, 34, 39, 44–46, 58, 59, 74, 75, 103, 111, 116, 117, 125–128, 130, 137, 147, 155, 204
Spain, 15, 22, 27, 28, 33, 44, 50–52, 97, 98
St Aloüarn, Louis Aleno de, 204
St Helena, 113, 201, 202, 211
St Jean Baptiste, 49, 134
St John's, Newfoundland, 73, 83, 84, 88, 91–93
St Lawrence River and Gulf, 25, 83, 86
St Malo, 27, 55
St Petersburg, 14, 169
St Pierre and Miquelon, 87, 88, 91, 108, 142, 162
Staithes, 78
Stavorinus, Johan, 187
Stephens, Philip, 11, 29–35, 36, 39, 61, 62, 63, 72, 74, 86, 87, 92, 94–96, 103–108, 170, 188, 196, 203, 205, 208, 212, 213
Stewart Island, 9, 140–145, 210
Stingray Bay (now Botany Bay), 166, 175, 181
Suez Canal, 27, 100
Sulu, Philippines, 57
Sumatra, 186
Sunda Strait, 186
Surville, Jean François Marie de, 49, 134, 210
Sutherland, Forby, 164
Swallow, 45, 46
Sydney Airport, 8, 165
Sydney Cove, 169, 173, 175
Sydney Harbour *see* Port Jackson
Sydney Heads, 8, 168, 170, 177

Table Bay, 201
Tahiti, 15, 44–46, 53, 55, 93, 95, 101, 103, 116–119, 120–124, 125, 134, 159, 187
Taiata, 124, 199
Tamar, 36, 37
Tank Stream, 174
Tararua Range, 132
Tasman, Abel, 21, 22, 45, 54, 97, 103–109, 127–129, 130–135, 136, 137, 148–150, 183
Tasman Sea, 137, 146, 148, 149, 174
Tasmania *see* Van Diemen's Land
Tempe, 174
Temple Bay, Labrador, 89
Terra Australis Incognita *see* Southern Continent
Terre Napoleon, Southern Australia, 162, 211
Texel, Netherlands, 188
Thames, Firth of, N.Z., 133

Thames, River, London, 62, 78
Thévenot, Melchisédech, 19
Thirsty Sound, 180
Three Kings Island, 135
Tierra del Fuego, 22, 38, 98, 103, 113, 116
Timor, 152, 185
Tinian, Mariana Islands, 42, 49
Tonga Islands, 21
Topaa, 136, 138, 141
Tordesillas, 97
Torres, Luis Vaez de, 58, 177, 178, 182, 183
Torres Strait, 59, 75, 152, 154, 178, 182, 184, 210, 213
Tovypoenammu, South Island, 129
Trafalgar, 62
Treaty Shore, Newfoundland, 87–89
Trincomalee, 203
Tropic of Capricorn, 46, 53, 54, 117, 126, 170, 176, 178
Troy, 175
Tuamotu Archipelago, 42, 43, 44, 118
Tulbagh, Rijk, 201
Tupaia, 124–126, 131, 132, 138, 164, 190, 196, 199
Turner, J.M.W., 77
Tweed, 87, 88
Twofold Bay, 163

Unfortunate Cove, Newfoundland, 91
Uppsala, Sweden, 19

Vahitahi, Tuamotu Archipelago, 118
Valentine, 62
Valentyn, Francois, 104, 106, 129
Valparaiso, 39
Van Delft, Maarten, 185
Van der Parra, Petrus Albertus, 188
Van Diemen, Anthony, 134
Van Diemen's Land (now Tasmania), 21, 35, 54, 96, 104–108, 135, 142, 148–154 155–162, 193, 204, 209, 210
Vancouver, George, 11, 33, 148, 161
Vanuatu *see* Quiros's Land
Vattel, Emmerich, 96, 97

Vaugondy, Didier Robert de, 22, 106, 160
Venus, Fort, Tahiti, 120, 122, 123
Versailles, 27, 29, 39, 50, 55
Vespucci, Amerigo, 18
Victory, 62, 164
Visscher, Franz, 132
Vrouwe Kornelia Hillegonda, 188

Wager, 38
Waldseemüller, Martin, 18
Wales, Prince of, *see* Prince of Wales
Walker, John, 78, 79, 82, 85, 94
Wallis, Helen, 44, 45
Wallis, Samuel, 11, 23, 34, 44–49, 51, 53, 61, 74, 93, 95, 101, 104, 115, 119, 120, 121, 134, 203, 207
Walpole, Horace, 67
Wapping, 78, 85
Washington, George, 31
Waterloo, 211
Western Port, 153
Weyland, Jacob, 185
Wharton, W.J.L., 208
Whitby, 61, 62, 77, 78, 82, 204
White, John, 174
Whitsunday Passage, 177
Wilkes, John, 67, 68
Wilkinson, Francis, 120
William III of England, 108
Wilson's Promontory, 156, 157, 211
Wolfe, James, 25, 82
Woolwich, 37
Wright, J.K., 99

York Harbour, *see* Chateau Bay
York, Duke of, 179
Young, George, 66
Young, Nicholas, 128
Young Nick's Head, 128

Zeehaen's Bight, 22, 128, 132, 133, 136, 146

Margaret Sanger

"Every Child a Wanted Child"

Margaret Sanger

"Every Child a Wanted Child"

by Nancy Whitelaw

A People in Focus Book

DILLON PRESS
New York

Maxwell Macmillan Canada
Toronto

Maxwell Macmillan International
New York   Oxford   Singapore   Sydney

To Eva Whitelaw Barrett, my granddaughter—with love

Acknowledgments

The author is grateful to Peter C. Engelman, assistant editor, Sophia Smith Collection, who read the manuscript, offered many valuable suggestions, and helped collect and label the photos. She thanks him also for his strong support and encouragement.

Funding for this book was made available in part by the Fund for the Arts in Chautauqua County, which is managed by the Arts Council for Chautauqua County.

Library of Congress Cataloging-in-Publication Data

Whitelaw, Nancy.
    Margaret Sanger : "every child a wanted child" / by Nancy Whitelaw. — 1st ed.
      p. cm. — (People in focus)
    Includes bibliographical references (p. 157) and index.
    Summary: A biography of Margaret Sanger, the indomitable fighter for birth control and a feminist who asked women to take responsibility for their freedom.
    ISBN 0-87518-581-9
    1. Sanger, Margaret, 1879-1966—Juvenile literature. 2. Feminists—United States—Biography—Juvenile literature. 3. Birth control—United States—History—Juvenile literature. [1. Sanger, Margaret, 1879-1966. 2. Feminists. 3. Birth control—History.] I. Title. II. Series.
HQ764.S3.W6   1994
305.42'092—dc20
[B]   93-13635

Copyright © 1994 by Nancy Whitelaw

All rights reserved. No part of this book may be reproduced or transmitted in any form or by any means, electronic or mechanical, including photocopying, recording, or by any information storage and retrieval system, without permission in writing from the Publisher.

Dillon Press   Maxwell Macmillan Canada, Inc.
Macmillan Publishing Company   1200 Eglinton Avenue East
866 Third Avenue   Suite 200
New York, NY 10022   Don Mills, Ontario M3C 3N1

Macmillan Publishing Company is part of the Maxwell Communication Group of Companies.

First edition

Printed in the United States of America

10 9 8 7 6 5 4 3 2 1